GERTRUDE JEKYLL
ON GARDENING

GERTRUDE JEKYLL ON GARDENING

Edited with a commentary by

PENELOPE HOBHOUSE

VINTAGE BOOKS
A DIVISION OF RANDOM HOUSE
NEW YORK

First Vintage Books Edition, April 1985

Introduction, editorial matter and this arrangement
copyright © 1983 by Penelope Hobhouse

Library of Congress Cataloging in Publication Data

Jekyll, Gertrude, 1843-1932.
Gertrude Jekyll on gardening.

Reprint. Originally published: London : National Trust :
W. Collins, 1983.

Bibliography: p.
Includes index.
1. Landscape gardening. 2. Flower gardening.
3. Landscape gardening—England. 4. Flower gardening—
England. I. Hobhouse, Penelope. II. Title.
SB473.J34   1985   716   84-40530
ISBN 0-394-72924-2

Manufactured in the United States of America

Cover photograph of background by Susan Woods
Cover photograph of garden by Kenneth Scowen
Cover design by Paul Gamarello/Eyetooth Design

To John

From An Appreciation of Gertrude Jekyll in *Country Life*
written by Avray Tipping after her death:

Who of us as gardeners today have not profited by the
experience and teaching of this entirely capable
woman, easily efficient in all she set out to know and
do? . . . She opened our eyes to the possibilities of the
herbaceous border, of the woodland garden, of the
bulb-set glade. She was no mere theorist, but a practical worker who practised much and well first and
then taught and wrought. Thus her books are the
fruits of long experience critically treated and plainly
set forth.

CONTENTS

	page
Preface	11
Introduction	13
Introductory to *Wood and Garden*	23
January	27
February	41
March	61
April	83
May	103
June	127
July	153
August	171
September	193
October	213
November	231
December	245
Colour	257
Water, Natural and Formal	299
The Pergola	309
Bibliography	322
Books and articles by Gertrude Jekyll	323
Appendix on Colour Theories	325
Acknowledgements	326
Index	327

COLOUR PLATES

*facing
page*

Hollyhocks, Blyborough (*painting by G. Elgood*)   192

Phlox and daisy (*painting by G. Elgood*)   193

Michaelmas daisies, Munstead Wood (*painting by H. Allingham;
The Leger Galleries Ltd*)   224

Orange lilies and larkspur (*painting by G. Elgood*)   225

BLACK AND WHITE ILLUSTRATIONS

page

Frontispiece: Gertrude Jekyll (*Country Life*)

Quercus ilex at The Salutation (*John Malins*) 55

Helleborus orientalis (*Pat Brindley*) 66

Viburnum opulus (*Pat Brindley*) 66

Myrrhis odorata (*Pat Brindley*) 89

Polygonatum multiflorum giganteum (*Pat Brindley*) 89

The North Garden court, Munstead Wood (*Richard Bryant*) 90

Approach to the porch, Munstead Wood (*Richard Bryant*) 92

Asplenium trichomanes (*Pat Brindley*) 92

Omphalodes linifolia (*Iris Hardwick Library*) 116

Athyrium felix-feminia (*Pat Brindley*) 116

The Dutch Garden at Hestercombe (*Country Life*) 147

The east rill at Hestercombe (*Country Life*) 147

The hanging terrace at Hestercombe (*Country Life*) 148–9

Across the Plat to Lutyens's orangery at Hestercombe
(*Country Life*) 150

The pergola, Hestercombe (*Country Life*) 150

Eryngium giganteum (*Pat Brindley*) 162

Lathyrus latifolius (*Pat Brindley*) 162

Miscanthus sinensis (*Pat Brindley*) 185

Aruncus dioicus (*Pat Brindley*) 185

Choisya ternata (*Pat Brindley*) 185

Silver birch and Aesculus parviflora at Munstead Wood
(*Richard Bryant*) 199

The broad steps at Hestercombe (*Country Life*) 237

One of Graham Thomas's borders at Cliveden (*John Malins*) 277

PLANS

	page
Munstead Wood, from lawn to copse	94
Rose Garden with Lily Pool	134
The Grey Border at Hestercombe	144–5
The Border, Munstead Wood	260–1
The Spring Garden	268–9
The Hidden Garden	272–3
The June Garden	274–5
The West Border, Cliveden	278–9
The East Border, Cliveden	280–1
The Gold Border	286–7
The Blue Garden	288–9
Reconstruction of Banks around a Pool	305–6

PREFACE

Throughout I have selected passages of Miss Jekyll's writings which appear to me to be most relevant for today's gardeners. The grand schemes for some of Lutyens's large country houses, plans for steps, terraces and water canals entailing lavish expenditure have been omitted, but details from some of these can be re-interpreted for modern gardens of modest scale. I have quoted her writings on plants and planting rather than discussing her role as a designer. My own comments appear in brackets.

The book has been arranged to follow the pattern of Miss Jekyll's first complete work *Wood and Garden*, which was compiled mainly from previously written articles and which describes the months of the year in chronological order. Further chapters deal with her philosophy of colour, the water garden and the pergola. Material has been used from all her writings including her other books and many articles in gardening journals, covering a period from the mid-1890s almost to her death in 1932. In a sense, therefore, the book covers her development as a gardener, giving a complete picture of how she valued and used plants over a period of nearly forty years.

A complete bibliography is included but I have depended greatly on a select list of books which have proved invaluable in bringing botanical nomenclature up to date.

W. J. Bean   *Trees and Shrubs Hardy in the British Isles*
  8th ed.   John Murray, 1970–6
Ingwersen's Manual of Alpine Plants   Will Ingwersen and
  Dunnsprint Ltd, 1978
The Reader's Digest *Encyclopaedia of Garden Plants and
  Flowers*   2nd ed., 1978
Graham Stuart Thomas   *Perennial Garden Plants*
  Dent, 1976
Graham Stuart Thomas   *Plants for Groundcover*   Dent, 1970

P.H.

INTRODUCTION

THIS BOOK IS an anthology of Gertrude Jekyll's writing on gardens and gardening. It is not a book on the theory of garden design, but a practical guide in the use of her ideas on planting and on colour associations between plants. Although the writing is taken mainly from her first complete book, *Wood and Garden* (1899), from articles on The Pergola and on Water Gardens, and from her introduction to *Colour Planning of the Garden* by Tinley, Humphreys and Irving (Jack, 1924), I have also quoted freely from her other works.

Her thoughts and experience of gardening and her very down-to-earth approach to running a garden throughout the seasons give us commonsense teaching of garden lore combined with out-of-the-common sensitive descriptions of woodland and her beloved Surrey countryside. She never described a plant or a method of gardening without having had personal experience of it, as her description of the day-to-day management of her own garden makes quite clear.

The book is not biographical except insofar as it is necessary to place her in her own time, and into the gardening context of that period. Nor is it about her plans for individual gardens, very few of which survive in a form which can show us how they were realized. Instead, emphasis is placed on her philosophy of gardening and on her favourite plants and their place in bed or border. Her basic wisdom and her knowledge of the management of plants can be aptly translated into terms relevant to modern small gardens, particularly if the detail of planting and planting association is looked for, rather than the grand schemes for a complete garden. (Her own famous colour border was two hundred feet by eighteen, protected by a sandstone wall, with good shrubs and climbers which served as a backdrop to the mainly herbaceous planting.) The Latin names of plants, correct for her period, have been brought up to date, and occasionally plants more recently introduced or new hybrids and cultivars have been suggested as improvements. Bearing in mind the cost and rarity of labour, I have occasionally interrupted her to suggest the use of modern techniques of grass management, weedkillers etc. She would readily have adapted to present-day gardening, making use of practical aids and the best plants, but it is interesting to note how many of her preferred and much-loved plants are still considered first-class.

Her methods were the antithesis of modern instant gardening, made so easy and impulsive by the neighbouring garden centre. She liked to study a plant, relating it to its natural habitat, and then using it appropriately, placing it comfortably next to plants with similar environmental needs. As a modern example of the rightness of this approach we can mention the garden stands that Beth Chatto puts up at the Horticultural Shows, where the design carefully places plants from hot dry areas together, or plants loving moisture in one place only, quite different from the arrangement practised by most nurserymen, where attractive flower and foliage association rather than suitability are considered. What seems so obvious now was revolutionary a few years ago, and will have helped the amateur to learn about plant requirements in quite a practical and 'Jekyllian' way. During her long life (she was almost ninety when she died in 1932) her popularity made her famous colour borders a 'smart' garden fashion, but they have seldom endured, partly because they are relatively labour intensive, but also because her essential aesthetic sense, combined with practicality, is now absent. For correct interpretation her plans required a complete understanding of plant needs and behaviour, as well as a grasp of the composition of the picture she was painting with living and constantly growing plants.

Today we can extract from her writings the essence of her art and, forgetting the scale on which she and her contemporaries (and clients) gardened, make use of certain elements in her plant pictures that will fit smoothly into corners of the small garden, or form the basis of a whole garden scheme. Two plants placed together, or two groups of plants in drifts beside each other, can convey much of her spirit if the choice is good. She always advocated simplicity of plant or colour scheme rather than a multiplicity and jumble, which result from the mistaken desire to use many different genera just because they are available.

In her writing she constantly evokes the whole spirit of a garden. The simple gravity of her descriptions gives evidence of a remarkable feeling for atmosphere, her own life being carefully balanced between house and garden and the Surrey landscape. Her philosophy combines the qualities of her painter's training with a genuine and simple love of flowers and woodland, and a deep respect for the traditional methods that she had learned from acute observation of humble cottage life around her.

Gertrude Jekyll (1843–1932) is considered one of the most important and influential garden designers and writers of the early twentieth century. She had originally trained as a painter, long before women had established their right to self-expression and independence, but failing eyesight in her fifties led to her abandoning this career in favour of an increasing interest in gardening and garden design. She was fifty-six before her first book, *Wood and Garden*, was published, but by this time she was by no means an amateur in the horticultural world. For some years she had been a regular contributor to William Robinson's publications and much of her first book had already appeared in instalments in the *Manchester Guardian* during the 1890s.

In 1891 she met Edwin Lutyens, then an unknown young architect employed on building his first country house. This meeting was to mark the beginning of a brilliant partnership. Lutyens provided the framework of stone and brick while she completed the garden picture by imaginative and sensitive planting, which depended not only on her sense of form and colour but also on her exceptional knowledge of plants and their requirements. Later, in collaboration with Lutyens, at The Deanery Garden (from 1901), Marsh Court (from 1905), Folly Farm (from 1906) and Hestercombe (1908), she continued to use her essentially cottage style, softening the grand geometric stonework by her informal planting. There was nothing haphazard in her use of plants, but by sheer artistry she translated many of her most successful planting ideas from her own garden at Munstead Wood into these firm and formal settings.

Altogether she undertook over fifty garden designs working with Lutyens, and when nearly ninety years old helped to plan borders of hardy plants at one of his great palaces, Gledstone

Hall in West Yorkshire, with a formal water garden, rather similar to that of Marsh Court but in a very different climate. She worked, too, with other architects, such as Lorimer and George, and was frequently called in on her own, sometimes for a part only of a garden. Fortunately for posterity many of these plans can be studied on paper, and at Hestercombe in Somerset the garden has been completely and faithfully reconstructed, using almost entirely the original planting plans. From them it is possible to grasp the essence of her schemes; she was painting a picture, arranging her plants just as an artist arranges his paints.

It is, however, to her writing that we must turn to understand how to make these living pictures, and her teaching is as fresh today as when she wrote it. Her first two books – *Wood and Garden* quickly followed by *Home and Garden* in 1900 – contain all the essential ingredients of her later works, although as the years passed she became more assured and perhaps less of a romantic. These books, written in her elegant and rich descriptive prose, stretch beyond the practical, and give the reader an insight into her deep love, not only for flowers and the garden, but for woodland and her native countryside. As an article in *Country Life* pointed out, her books are marked by 'intimate knowledge of nature, by great fascination of style and by a certain quality of sagacity and shrewdness in which is to be found . . . their principal charm'.

From her childhood years at Bramley, near Godalming, the area to which she and her family later returned, she was intensely interested in traditional and vernacular buildings as well as in the country life and beauty around her, deriving pleasure and stimulus from hedgerow and cottage-garden plants. Among her best and most evocative chapters are those describing the low tones of winter colouring among the trees, the colour and texture of bark, and the faded brown of bracken as it withers.

To many she is remembered only in the context of the flowery garden, where she excelled in careful and harmonious blending of the colour and texture of flower and leaf. Some of this she learned in her training as a painter (in 1839 Chevreul had produced his *Circle chromatique* to demonstrate the relationships between the colours of the spectrum), but much was inspired by her instinctive appreciation of nature and her ability to utilize what she observed so closely. Perhaps her poor eyesight made her more sharply and acutely aware of the subtle differences in shades of green and brown, so often missed in the casual glance.

Few artists – Leonardo being a notable exception – have described so accurately the patterns of colour in leaf and bark, which change subtly in sun or shadow, and at dawn or in evening light, in wind or in still weather. Like Leonardo, she observed the difference between the depth of colour of the bark of a tree on its south-facing side and that on its northern aspect, when it lies between the observer and the sun. Like him she would have been aware of the effects of wind: 'But if you are on the side whence the wind is blowing you will see the trees looking much lighter than you would see them on the other sides; and this is due to the fact that the wind turns up the reverse side of the leaves which in all trees is much whiter than the upper side; and, more especially, they will be very light if the wind blows from the quarter where the sun is, and if you have your back turned to it.' (*Notebooks of Leonardo da Vinci*, World's Classics, Oxford 1952, pp. 140–2.)

In *Home and Garden* she describes the trees on an April day, 'where the sun catches the edges of the nearer trunks it lights them in a sharp line, leaving the rest warmly dark; but where the trees stand in shade the trunks are of a cool grey . . . the trunks seen quite against the sunlight look a pale greenish-brown, lighter than the shadow they cast, and somewhat warmed by the sunlit dead bracken at their feet. As I move forwards into the shade . . . I only see their true colour of warm purplish-grey, clouded with paler grey lichen . . . I wish I had with me some young student of painting . . .'

She was equally trained and observant in her garden planning. At Munstead Wood she planned her garden planting to melt into the surrounding woodland. There was no abrupt transition, rather a gradual drift from colourful planting to more muted shades beyond. A contemporary describes it: 'Every glade and clearing has become a lovely picture, a gratifying surprise. Here a narrow mown way winds between aboriginal fern and grass and colonized shrub and plant: there rhododendron and azalea, with just such shade and shelter as they desire, cover their wide stretching boughs with bloom. And everywhere there is composition. The wood approaches the border area or billows on to the lawn without intrusion or abruptness. All is suave and engaging, all is friendly and beautiful. It is a home of undisputed peace.'

These first books so finely revealing her love of the country-side also defined her standpoint as garden artist and contained the quintessence of her style as gardener. *Wall and Water Garden* (1901) not only gives some very practical ideas for building and planting dry walls but contains some fine writing on informal water-gardening, where she pleads for natural and not exotic planting round the fringes of a pond or lake. In *Colour Schemes for the Flower Garden* (1908) she expanded her philosophy of colour associations. She gardened to create a picture with living plants, translating into terms of the colour and texture of flower and leaf all the vision and technique of a painter. She abhorred inappropriate planting and pretentious showmanship, and encouraged others to design gardens not as museums for a collection of plants but so that each good plant or group of plants should depend on another to produce a cohesive whole.

Her early friendship and association with William Robinson, the great advocate of natural and wild gardening, led her to use many hardy perennials in her planting schemes. Even before meeting him she had come to appreciate these hardy survivors in local vicarage or cottage gardens. She can be considered the originator of what has become the traditional herbaceous border, which depends for its effect on massing wide borders with blending colours and with heights and depths for extra visual interest. In fact, she also used annuals in season, and sunk pots of flowering plants to extend the periods of colour. She lived long enough to see the end of the fashion for carpet bedding designed purely for the sake of ostentatious display.

Writing in 1928 on the 'Changing Fashions of Gardening in the Nineteenth Century' she says of the fashion for ribbon borders of blue, yellow and scarlet and the taste for mosaiculture with circular beds planted in rings of succulents: 'One cannot but deplore the amount of misdirected labour in the preparation, planting and maintenance that the wretched thing entailed . . . It was not the fault of the plants themselves that they were unfairly used, and if the scarlet geranium reigned supreme it was not the geranium's fault that it was made to sit upon the throne.'

Her garden of fifteen acres seems large to us, but it was not thought grand or extensive in her own day, although at one time she employed nine gardeners. She studied the use of separate garden areas, in each of which were created seasonal effects by designing for winter, spring, early summer, and for autumn a garden full of mellow colours. She varied this by using distinct areas for one type of plant or plantings. She had a rose garden, a paeony garden, a primrose garden (Munstead Primroses are still famous today), a Michaelmas daisy border and she cut glades in the woods for shade-loving plants. She preferred to group together plants which were in flower at the same time, leaving long stretches of green in between these groups, green which itself had differing depths of colour and texture. She recommended this in preference to flowering plants spotted through her borders, which never give a satisfying picture. She designed golden borders, dependent on evergreen golden foliage for winter interest and yellow flowers for summer pleasure. She planned grey and silver borders with pink or blue drifts, allowing her colours and textures to melt into each other, and to be continued, confirmed and extended into planting in background walls. In her great borders she graded colours, starting at one end with flowers of pale and cool colouring, followed by yellow and then stronger yellow, passing to deep orange and stronger scarlet banked with rich but softer red. The progression then should recede in the same general order till it comes again at the furthest end 'to a quiet harmony of lavender and purple and tender pink, with a whole setting of grey and silver foliage'.

Her soil was thin, quickly draining sand 'of the poorest possible soil, sloping a little down towards the north . . . a thin skin of peaty earth on the upper part, with a natural growth of heath, whortleberry and bracken, where a wood of Scotch fir had been cut some twelve years before; the middle part a chestnut plantation, the lower, a poor sandy field with a hard plough bed about eight inches down.' After many years of double trenching and copious manuring she had a right to feel a twinge of resentment when a casual visitor might remark, 'With your soil you can grow anything.' The preparation of the soil and the care of her plants was done as carefully as the detailed planting schemes.

She understood and studied the importance of aspect as well as soil and individual plant needs, and was often asked to help design gardens in parts of the country and abroad with situations very different from her own poor Surrey sand. She seemed to develop an almost uncanny feeling for appropriateness of planting on sites ranging from the suburban gardens of her own county to wild, almost moorland planting. At Castle Drogo, on the edge of Dartmoor, the planting on the drive had to fit in with the desolate moor beyond, without offence or disharmony. She used Scots pine, birch and holly, giving a hint at domesticity by great groups of ilex (*see* p. 55). In the most bleak situations some of her plants failed to survive: at Lambay, an island off Dublin swept by salt winds; at Lindisfarne, where she planned a rectangular cottage-type garden; and at Gledstone, where the winter was very severe. But considering that after 1904 she was unable to travel beyond her native county (except for a railway journey to Lindisfarne in 1906 and a summer holiday at Folly Farm in 1916) it is still astonishing how sure her touch was, especially when her plans were carried out in their entirety.

In 1904 Miss Jekyll and Lutyens embarked on a plan for Millmead, close to her old home at Bramley, where some old cottages had been demolished. The garden was only half an acre, and on a steeply sloping site, but it gave an opportunity for planning and planting nearer to the dimensions of a garden today. As usual she made use of the old fruit trees and natural features, including the view towards her previous home. The garden ground was a long narrow strip which she divided into rectangles on different levels, each with its own identity and yet a comfortable sense of general cohesion (*see* Jekyll-Weaver *Gardens for Small Country Houses*).

Not content with visual effects, she studied the pleasure of scent in the garden and in her surrounding woodland. In the former she recommended bushes of bay, rosemary, santolina and thyme, placed where they would be brushed against in passing. In the woodland she could recognize the individual scent of heather, buttercups, birch leaves and lime flowers. As her sight deteriorated, so her sense of smell and touch developed. She framed doorways with architectural shrubs and used ever-green leaves to soften the lines of masonry. At Munstead Wood

her two choisyas framing a doorway on the sunny side of a wall
still remain, and at the back, in the shade, is one of the pair of
guelder roses she describes in her books. She encouraged simplicity of design for garden statuary, seats and pergolas, feeling
that ornamentation was only necessary when it had a useful
function. She had an absolute contempt for any slipshod work
and always maintained the highest standard in execution. The
preface to *Old West Surrey* (1904) shows that she was distressed
by the disappearance from cottage and farmhouse of 'articles of
furniture and ordinary household gear . . . of pure material and
excellent design', which were being sold as curiosities and
antiquities and replaced by 'pretentious articles got up with
veneer and shoddy material'. Whenever she could she bought
old cottage furniture and tools so that they should not be forgotten. In this she was a pioneer at a time when others were only
just becoming aware of the extent to which old ways were
threatened with extinction. (Already, before it was too late,
Cecil Sharp was making his collection of folk songs handed down
by oral tradition.)

    She believed firmly in the unity of house and garden, which
together should fit into the natural landscape beyond. As
garden merged into countryside she used the indigenous trees
and underplanting as a good designer of the 1980s would
recommend. If she were alive today she would be in the van of
those preserving the countryside, fighting for appropriate
woodland planting and the rescue of threatened wild flora. It
seems a sad commentary on her work in rescuing hardy cottage
plants from oblivion or obscurity that we are again faced with
the loss of many of the original plants, leaving us only new and
so-called improved garden cultivars, sometimes lacking the
charm of simplicity and often scentless. Shortage of labour has
led to a new emphasis on mixed planting with permanent plants,
and relatively few gardens have their seasons extended by the
use of annuals. The few large gardens which attempt to follow
her patterns of colour are owned by the National Trust, and it is
interesting to compare an herbaceous border designed recently
for Cliveden by Graham Stuart Thomas with one of hers because
here her formative influence becomes clear. For the average and
much smaller garden ingenious ways can be found to adapt the

more lavish Jekyll schemes without losing the essence of her design and colour sense. It is easy enough to pick planting associations, what we may call 'plant pictures', straight from Munstead Wood or from plans for other gardens, but it is more difficult to achieve the cohesion of the whole. It is not enough to study her methods of using plants to complement each other; we need to understand her thoughts and her philosophy.

As we read her books, or the following extracts from them, we get to know the plants and schemes she especially favoured: the leathery-leaved bergenia which she used for edging, *Clematis flammula* and the white everlasting pea for trailing over delphinium stalks for late summer flowering, free-growing roses cascading out of holly trees, and the primrose wood in spring. But to do these things successfully we must also extract something of her spirit. Her plans are only a guide to planting harmony and restraint, one needs also to absorb her sense of rhythm and proportion which unites the whole of a garden. Gertrude Jekyll, though acutely sensitive to colour and form in nature, saw it whole and identified herself with it. Her love of it was not that of the observer and collector, and plants would not have pleased her by their rarity. She might have found it hard to understand the modern naturalist who seems always to need some focus – of birds, butterflies or wild flowers – for his explorations. Similarly, in the garden she loved to think of the whole picture she was creating, caring little for grand effects arrived at by using the new and exotic, striving rather for simplicity and plainness.

In *Colour Schemes* she says of her life's work: But good gardening means patience and dogged determination. There must be many failures and losses, but by always pushing on there will also be the reward of success. Those who do not know are apt to think that hardy flower gardening of the best kind is easy. It is not easy at all. It has taken me half a lifetime merely to find out what is best worth doing, and a good slice of another half to puzzle out the ways of doing it.

Introductory to *Wood and Garden*

THERE ARE already many and excellent books about gardening;
but the love of a garden, already so deeply implanted in the
English heart, is so rapidly growing that no excuse is needed for
putting forth another.

I lay no claim either to literary ability, or to botanical knowledge, or even to knowing the best practical methods of cultivation; but I have lived among outdoor flowers for many years,
and have not spared myself in the way of actual labour, and have
come to be on closely intimate and friendly terms with a great
many growing things, and have acquired certain instincts which,
though not clearly defined, are of the nature of useful knowledge.

But the lesson I have thoroughly learnt, and wish to pass on
to others, is to know the enduring happiness that the love of a
garden gives. I rejoice when I see anyone, and especially
children, inquiring about flowers, and wanting gardens of their
own, and carefully working in them. For the love of gardening
is a seed that once sown never dies, but always grows and grows
to an enduring and ever-increasing source of happiness.

If in the following chapters I have laid special stress upon
gardening for beautiful effect, it is because it is the way of
gardening that I love best, and understand most of, and that
seems to me capable of giving the greatest amount of pleasure.
I am strongly for treating garden and wooded ground in a
pictorial way, mainly with large effects, and in the second place
with lesser beautiful incidents, and for so arranging plants and
trees and grassy spaces that they look happy and at home, and
make no parade of conscious effort. I try for beauty and harmony
everywhere, and especially for harmony of colour. A garden so
treated gives the delightful feeling of repose, and refreshment,
and purest enjoyment of beauty, that seems to my understanding
to be the best fulfilment of its purpose; while to the diligent
worker its happiness is like the offering of a constant hymn of
praise. For I hold that the best purpose of a garden is to give
delight and to give refreshment of mind, to soothe, to refine, and
to lift-up the heart in a spirit of praise and thankfulness. It is

23

certain that those who practise gardening in the best ways find it to be so.

But the scope of practical gardening covers a range of horticultural practice wide enough to give play to every variety of human taste. Some find their greatest pleasure in collecting as large a number as possible of all sorts of plants from all sources, others in collecting them themselves in their foreign homes, others in making rock-gardens, or ferneries, or peat-gardens, or bog-gardens, or gardens for conifers or for flowering shrubs, or special gardens of plants and trees with variegated or coloured leaves, or in the cultivation of some particular race or family of plants. Others may best like wide lawns with large trees, or wild gardening, or a quite formal garden, with trim hedge and walk, and terrace, and brilliant parterre, or a combination of several ways of gardening. And all are right and reasonable and enjoyable to their owners, and in some way or degree helpful to others.

The way that seems to me most desirable is again different, and I have made an attempt to describe it in some of its aspects. But I have learned much, and am always learning, from other people's gardens, and the lesson I have learned most thoroughly is, never to say 'I know' – there is so infinitely much to learn, and the conditions of different gardens vary so greatly, even when soil and situation appear to be alike and they are in the same district. Nature is such a subtle chemist that one never knows what she is about, or what surprises she may have in store for us.

Often one sees in the gardening papers discussions about the treatment of some particular plant. One man writes to say it can only be done one way, another to say it can only be done quite some other way, and the discussion waxes hot and almost angry, and the puzzled reader, perhaps as yet young in gardening, cannot tell what to make of it. And yet the two writers are both able gardeners, and both absolutely trustworthy, only they should have said, 'In my experience *in this place* such a plant can be done in such a way.' Even plants of the same family will not do equally well in the same garden. Every practical gardener knows this in the case of strawberries and potatoes; he has to find out which kinds will do in his garden; the experience of his friend in the next county is probably of no use whatever.

I have learnt much from the little cottage gardens that help to make our English waysides the prettiest in the temperate world. One can hardly go into the smallest cottage garden without learning or observing something new. It may be some two plants growing beautifully together by some happy chance, or a pretty mixed tangle of creepers, or something that one always thought must have a south wall doing better on an east one. But eye and brain must be alert to receive the impression and studious to store it, to add to the hoard of experience. And it is important to train oneself to have a good flower-eye; to be able to see at a glance what flowers are good and which are unworthy, and why, and to keep an open mind about it; not to be swayed by the petty tyrannies of the 'florist' or show judge; for, though some part of his judgment may be sound, he is himself a slave to rules, and must go by points which are defined arbitrarily and rigidly, and have reference mainly to the show-table, leaving out of account, as if unworthy of consideration, such matters as gardens and garden beauty, and human delight, and sunshine, and varying lights of morning and evening and noonday.

But many, both nurserymen and private people, devote themselves to growing and improving the best classes of hardy flowers, and we can hardly offer them too much grateful praise, or do them too much honour. For what would our gardens be without the roses, paeonies, and gladiolus of France, and the tulips and hyacinths of Holland, to say nothing of the hosts of good things raised by our home growers, and of the enterprise of the great firms whose agents are always searching the world for garden treasures?

Let no one be discouraged by the thought of how much there is to learn. Looking back upon nearly thirty years of gardening (the earlier part of it in groping ignorance with scant means of help) I can remember no part of it that was not full of pleasure and encouragement. For the first steps are steps into a delightful Unknown, the first successes are victories all the happier for being scarcely expected, and with the growing knowledge comes the widening outlook, and the comforting sense of an ever-increasing gain of critical appreciation. Each new step becomes a little surer, and each new grasp a little firmer, till, little by little, comes the power of intelligent combination, the nearest thing we can know to the mighty force of creation.

And a garden is a grand teacher. It teaches patience and careful watchfulness; it teaches industry and thrift; above all, it teaches entire trust. 'Paul planteth and Apollos watereth, but God giveth the increase.' The good gardener knows with absolute certainty that if he does his part, if he gives the labour, the love, and every aid that his knowledge of his craft, experience of the conditions of his place, and exercise of his personal wit can work together to suggest, that so surely as he does this diligently and faithfully, so surely will God give the increase. Then with the honestly-earned success comes the consciousness of encouragement to renewed effort, and, as it were, an echo of the gracious words, 'Well done, good and faithful servant.'

JANUARY

Beauty of woodland in winter — [Garden and wood — Hollies and birches] — The nut-walk — Thinning the overgrowth — A nut nursery — *Iris stylosa* — Its culture — Its home in Algeria — Discovery of the white variety — Flowers and branches for indoor decoration — [January scents].

A HARD FROST is upon us. The thermometer registered eighteen degrees last night, and though there was only one frosty night next before it, the ground is hard frozen. Till now a press of other work has stood in the way of preparing protecting stuff for tender shrubs, but now I go up into the copse with a man and chopping tools to cut out some of the Scotch fir [*Pinus sylvestris*] that are beginning to crowd each other.

How endlessly beautiful is woodland in winter! Today there is a thin mist; just enough to make a background of tender blue mystery three hundred yards away, and to show any defect in the grouping of near trees. No day could be better for deciding which trees are to come down; there is not too much at a time within sight; just one good picture-full and no more. On a clear day the eye and mind are distracted by seeing away into too many planes, and it is much more difficult to decide what is desirable in the way of broad treatment of nearer objects.

The ground has a warm carpet of pale rusty fern [*Pteris aquilina*]; tree-stem and branch and twig show tender colour-harmonies of grey bark and silvery-green lichen, only varied by the warm feathery masses of birch spray. Now the splendid richness of the common holly [*Ilex aquifolium*] is more than ever impressive, with its solid masses of full deep colour and its wholesome look of perfect health and vigour. Sombrely cheerful, if one may use such a mixture of terms; sombre by reason of the extreme depth of tone, and yet cheerful from the look of glad life, and from the assurance of warm shelter and protecting comfort to bird and beast and neighbouring vegetation. The picture is made complete by the slender shafts of the silver-barked birches [*Betula pendula*], with their half-weeping heads of delicate warm-coloured spray. Has any tree so graceful a way of throwing up its stems as the birch? They seem to leap and spring into the air, often leaning and curving upward from the very root, sometimes in forms that would be almost grotesque were it not for the never-failing rightness of free-swinging poise and perfect balance. The tints of the stem give a precious lesson in colour. The white of the bark is here silvery-white and there milk-white, and sometimes shows the faintest tinge of rosy flush. Where the bark has not yet peeled, the stem is clouded and banded with delicate grey, and with the silver-green of lichen. For about two feet upward from the ground, in the case of young trees of about seven to nine inches diameter, the bark is dark in colour, and lies in thick and extremely rugged upright ridges, contrasting strongly with the smooth white skin above. Where the two join, the smooth bark is parted in upright slashes, through which the dark rough bark seems to swell up, reminding one forcibly of some of the old fifteenth-century German costumes, where a dark velvet is arranged to rise in crumpled folds through slashings in white satin. In the stems of older birches the rough bark rises much higher up the trunk and becomes clothed with delicate grey-green lichen.

[In 1900 a contemporary of Miss Jekyll described the relationship between her house and the garden and wood-land: 'The house takes advantage of every view of wood and garden, and the wood and garden miss no view of the house. All is the result of careful thought and in the wood the marks of interference with nature have been . . . artist-ically concealed.' Today the visitor to Munstead Wood can see a change. The trees and undergrowth have been pushed back from the house and a harsher line is evident between the true wildness of nature and the lawn areas flowing down towards garden beds and borders.

Miss Jekyll carefully planned glades and vistas to match the views from doors and windows, stretching up into the darker more thickly treed areas beyond. Birch, holly and chestnut predominated and she planted at their edges, making a soft and gentle transition from the formality of garden bed to planting mixtures of wild flowers and hardy ferns, intermixed with suitable drifts of bulbs and garden plants. In shade, shrubs such as *Gaultheria shallon, Leucothoe fontanesiana*, pieris and juniper were planted with hellebores, corydalis and dentaria. There were thickets of pernettya, *Rhododendron praecox* and *R. ferrugineum*. In sun, cistus and wild heaths and brooms predominated, interrupted by block-plantings of wild daffodils (*see* plan on p. 94).

Today, with little gardening labour, efforts are concentrated on beds and flowers near to the house, and mown lawn stretches to the edge of the woodland, where it is not possible to maintain this natural transition from garden to copse. In the wood itself chestnut, birch, holly and bracken are undercarpeted with the foreign gaultheria, which spreads in a thick green mass to control bramble and elder.

In the modest gardens of today there may be space under the canopy of birch and holly for small woodland plants and bulbs. Instead of the spiny-leaved common holly, a specimen of the almost smooth-leaved *Ilex aquifolium* 'J. C. Van Thol' or the elegant pyramid-shaped *I.* × *altaclarensis* 'Camelliifolia' would be attractive and easier of management, and there is a wide choice of Asian and American birches, as beautiful as the native *Betula pendula* but with more exotic and startling barks. *Betula jacquemontii* has an almost white peeling stem, and in *B. albosinensis* 'Septentrionalis' it is pink and white and sometimes orange. Both of these are from western China; *B. papyrifera*, with the whitest bark, is from North America.]

The nut-walk was planted twelve years ago. There are two rows each side, one row four feet behind the other, and the nuts are ten feet apart in the rows. They are planted zigzag, those in the back rows showing between the front ones. As the two inner rows are thirteen feet apart measuring across the path, it leaves a shady border on each side, with deeper bays between the nearer trees. Lent hellebores [*Helleborus orientalis*] fill one border from end to end; the other is planted with the Corsican [*Helleborus corsicus*, an evergreen almost shrub-like plant with elegant and firm greyish-green leaves and stems bearing clusters of pale green cups in early spring] and the native kinds [*H. foetidus* and *H. viridis*] so that throughout February and March there is a complete bit of garden of one kind of plant in full beauty of flower and foliage.

[*Helleborus foetidus* has deeply divided dark evergreen leaves and flowers are clustered, each one a small bell of pale green edged with maroon and borne from February on into spring. Elsewhere Miss Jekyll recommends planting it to contrast with the shining leaves of bergenia and the large grey corrugated foliage of *Hosta sieboldiana*, or in association with silver-foliage plants. *Helleborus viridis* is from the green-flowered group with deciduous leaves and rather small flowers. *H. cyclophyllus* and *H. bocconei* from southern Europe have rather larger flowers. *H. orientalis* hybrids usually have colours varying from blush-white to plum colour, and variously spotted inside with crimson and maroon. They make beautiful groundcover for deciduous shrubs and thrive in north-facing borders. Botanists separate certain forms but the ordinary gardener can be content with mixed seedlings. They flower from March to late April.]

The nut-trees [*Corylus avellana*, the hazel or Kent cob nut may have been planted with *C. maxima*, the filbert, with larger leaves and nuts; its purple form makes a rich splash of colour in spring] have grown into such thick clumps that now there must be a vigorous thinning. Each stool has from eight to twelve main stems, the largest of them nearly two inches thick. Some shoot almost upright, but two or three in each stool spread outward, with quite a different habit of growth, branching about in an angular fashion. These are the oldest and thickest. There are also a number of straight suckers one and two years old. Now when I look at some fine old nut alley, with the tops arching and meeting overhead, as I hope mine will do in a few years, I see that the trees have only a few stems, usually from three to five at the most, and I judge that now is the time to thin mine to about the right number, so that the strength and growing power may be thrown into these, and not allowed to dilute and waste itself in growing extra faggoting. The first to be cut away are the old crooked stems. They grow nearly horizontally and are all elbows, and often so tightly locked into the straighter rods that they have to be chopped to pieces before they can be pulled out. When these are gone it is easier to get at the other stems, though they are often so close together at the base that it is difficult to chop or saw them out without hurting the bark of the ones to be left. All the young suckers are cut away. They are of straight, clean growth, and we prize them as the best possible sticks for chrysanthemums and potted lilies.

After this bold thinning, instead of dense thickety bushes we have a few strong, well-branched rods to each stool. At first the nut-walk looks woefully naked, and for the time its pictorial value is certainly lessened; but it has to be done, and when summer side-twigs have grown and leafed, it will be fairly well clothed, and meanwhile the hellebores will be the better for the thinner shade.

The nut-catkins are already an inch long, but are tightly closed, and there is so sign as yet of the bright crimson little sea-anemones that will appear next month, whose bases will grow into nut-bearing twigs. Round the edges of the base of the stools are here and there little branching suckers. These are the ones to look out for, to pull off and grow into young trees. A firm grasp and a sharp tug brings them up with a fine supply of good fibrous root. After two years in the nursery they are just right to plant out.

The trees in the nut-walk were grown in this way fourteen years ago, from small suckers pulled off plants that came originally from the interesting cob-nut nursery at Calcot, near Reading.

I shall never forget a visit to that nursery some six-and-twenty years ago. It was walled all round, and a deep-sounding bell had to be rung many times before anyone came to open the gate; but at last it was opened by a fine, strongly-built, sunburnt woman of the type of the good working farmer's wife, that I remember as a child. She was the forewoman, who worked the nursery with surprisingly few hands – only three men, if I remember rightly – but she looked as if she could do the work of 'all two men' herself. One of the specialities of the place was a fine breed of mastiffs; another was an old *Black Hamburg vine*, that rambled and clambered in and out of some very old greenhouses, and was wonderfully productive. There were alleys of nuts in all directions, and large spreading patches of palest yellow daffodils – the double *Narcissus cernuus* [double-flowered *N.c. plenus* white], now so scarce and difficult to grow. Had I then known how precious a thing was there in fair abundance, I should not have been contented with the modest dozen that I asked for. It was a most pleasant garden to wander in, especially with the old Mr Webb who presently appeared. He was dressed in black clothes of an old-looking cut – a Quaker, I believe. Never shall I forget an apple-tart he invited me to try as a proof of the merit of the 'Wellington' apple [now superseded by 'Bramley seedling']. It was not only good, but beautiful; the cooked apple looking rosy and transparent, and most inviting. He told me he was an ardent preacher of total abstinence, and took me to a grassy, shady place among the nuts, where there was an upright stone slab, like a tomb-stone, with the inscription:

TO ALCOHOL

He had dug a grave, and poured into it a quantity of wine and beer and spirits, and placed the stone as a memorial of his abhorrence of drink. The whole thing remains in my mind like a picture – the shady groves of old nuts, in tenderest early leaf, the pale daffodils, the mighty chained mastiffs with bloodshot eyes and murderous fangs, the brawny, wholesome forewoman, and the trim old gentleman in black. It was the only nursery I ever saw where one would expect to see fairies on a summer's night.

I never tire of admiring and praising *Iris stylosa* [*I. unguicularis*, the Algerian iris], which has proved itself such a good plant for English gardens, at any rate for those in our southern counties. Lovely in form and colour, sweetly scented and with admirable foliage, it has in addition to these merits the unusual one of a blooming season of six months' duration. The first flowers come with the earliest days of November, and its season ends with a rush of bloom in the first half of April. Then is the time to take up old tufts and part them, and plant afresh; the old roots will have dried up into brown wires and the new will be pushing. It thrives in rather poor soil and seems to bloom all the better for having its root-run invaded by some stronger plant. When I first planted a quantity I had brought from its native place, I made the mistake of putting it in a well-prepared border. At first I was delighted to see how well it flourished, but as it gave me only thick masses of leaves a yard long and no flowers, it was clear that it wanted to be less well fed. After changing it to poor soil, at the foot of a sunny wall close to a strong clump of alstroemeria [*Alstroemeria aurantiaca*] I was rewarded with a good crop of flowers; and the more the alstroemeria grew into it on one side and *Plumbago larpentae* [*Ceratostigma plumbaginoides*] on the other, the more freely the brave little iris flowered. The flower has no true stem; what serves as a stem, sometimes a foot long, is the elongated tube, so that the seed-pod has to be looked for deep down at the base of the tufts of leaves, and almost underground. The specific name, *stylosa*, is so clearly descriptive that one regrets that the longer and certainly uglier *unguicularis* should be preferred by botanists.

[Miss Jekyll implies that the little iris may need dividing frequently; in fact this is not the case. It should be left undisturbed for as long as possible, the only annual treatment necessary is to cut down the straggly foliage to half its length as soon as flowering is over. This allows the sun to bake the roots in summer. Today, as well as the beautiful white variety, the discovery of which is now described by Miss Jekyll, a very good dark cultivar, *Iris unguicularis speciosa* 'Mary Barnard', is obtainable but rare, and 'Walter Butt' is a vigorous plant with flowers of palest lilac.]

[Elsewhere she describes the iris:] There is a clean smooth look about the flower, trim and fresh in its light blue-purple dress with the lower half of the falls neatly striped with purple on white, and a middle stripe of pure yellow.

'Early Irises', *Country Life*, 11 March 1916

What a delight it was to see it for the first time in its home in the hilly wastes a mile or two inland from the town of Algiers! Another lovely blue iris was there too, *Iris alata* or *scorpioides*

[*I. planifolia* with larger flowers] growing under exactly the same conditions; but this is a plant unwilling to be acclimatized in England. What a paradise it was for flower-rambles, among the giant fennels [*Ferula communis* and *F. cheliantha*] and the tiny orange marigolds [*Calendula arvensis*] and the immense bulbs of *Scilla maritima* [*Urginea maritima*] standing almost out of the ground, and the many lovely bee-orchises [*Orchis apifera*] and the fairy-like *Narcissus serotinus*, and the groves of prickly pear [*Opuntia ficus-indica*] wreathed and festooned with the graceful tufts of bell-shaped flower and polished leaves of *Clematis cirrhosa* [*C. c. balearica*].

It was in the days when there were only a few English residents, but among them was the Rev. Edwyn Arkwright, who by his happy discovery of a white-flowered *Iris stylosa* [*see* above], the only one that has been found wild, has enriched our gardens with a most lovely variety of this excellent plant. I am glad to be able to quote his own words: 'The finding of the white *Iris stylosa* belongs to the happy old times twenty-five years ago, when there were no social duties and no vineyards in Algiers. My two sisters and I bought three horses, and rode wild every day in the scrub of myrtle, cistus, dwarf oak (*Quercus coccifera*, the Kermes oak) etc. It was about five miles from the town, on what is called the "Sahel", that the one plant grew that I was told botanists knew ought to exist, but with all their searching had never found. I am thankful that I dug it up instead of picking it, only knowing that it was a pretty flower. Then after a year or so Durando saw it, and took off his hat to it, and told me what a treasure it was, and proceeded to send off little bits to his friends; and among them all, Ware of Tottenham managed to be beforehand, and took a first-class certificate for it. It is odd that there should never have been another plant found, for there never was such a free-growing and multiplying plant. My sister in Herefordshire has had over fifty blooms this winter; but we count it in thousands, and it is the feature in all decorations in every English house in Algiers.'

Throughout January, and indeed from the middle of December, is the time when outdoor flowers for cutting and house decoration are most scarce; and yet there are Christmas roses [*Helleborus niger*] and yellow jasmine [*Jasminum nudiflorum*] and laurustinus [*Viburnum tinus*], and in all open weather *Iris stylosa* [*see* above] and Czar violets [a large flowered scented violet cultivated in frames for winter flowering]. A very few flowers can be made to look well if cleverly arranged with plenty of good foliage; and even when a hard and long frost spoils the few blooms that would otherwise be available, leafy branches alone are beautiful in rooms. But, as in all matters that have to do with decoration, everything depends on a right choice of material and the exercise of taste in disposing it. Red-tinted berberis always looks well alone, if three or four branches are boldly cut from two to three feet long. [*Mahonia aquifolium*, the Oregon grape, is a small suckering evergreen mahonia with polished green pinnate leaves, turning red and bronze in winter. The rich yellow flowers are borne in terminal clusters in early spring, and followed by black berries.]

Branches of the spotted aucuba [*Aucuba japonica* 'Variegata'] do very well by themselves, and are specially beautiful in blue china; the larger the leaves and the bolder the markings the better. [There are several new cultivars available, with even better marking contrasts.]

Where there is an old Exmouth magnolia [*M. grandiflora* 'Exmouth'] that can spare some small branches, nothing makes a nobler room-ornament. [Mrs Earle adds: 'Peel the stalks to make branches last one month.'] The long arching sprays of Alexandrian laurel [*Danaë racemosa*, a charming small evergreen with glossy leaves, now unfortunately difficult to get] do well with green or variegated box [*Buxus sempervirens* and cultivars], and will live in a room for several weeks. Among useful winter leaves of smaller growth, those of *Epimedium pinnatum* [*E. pinnatum colchicum*] have a fine red colour and delicate veining, and I find them very useful for grouping with greenhouse flowers of delicate texture. *Gaultheria shallon* is at its best in winter and gives valuable branches and twigs for cutting; and much to be prized are sprays of Japan privet [*Ligustrum japonicum*], with its tough, highly-polished leaves, so much like those of the orange. There is a variegated eurya [*Cleyera fortunei*], small branches of which are excellent; and always useful are the gold and silver hollies.

There is a little plant, *Ophiopogon spicatum* [*Liriope spicatum*], that I grow in rather large quantity for winter-cutting, the leaves being at their best in the winter months. They are sword-shaped and of a lively green colour, and are arranged in flat sheaves after the manner of a flag-iris. I pull up a whole plant at a time – a two-year-old plant is a spreading tuft of the little sheaves – and wash it and cut away the groups of leaves just at the root, so that they are held together by the root-stock. They last long in water, and are beautiful with Roman hyacinths or freesias or *Iris stylosa* and many other flowers. The leaves of the megaseas [bergenias], especially those of the *cordifolia* section, colour grandly in winter, and look fine in a large bowl with the largest bloom of Christmas roses [*Helleborus niger*] or with forced hyacinths. Much useful material can be found among ivies, both of the wild and garden kinds. When they are well established they generally throw out rather woody front shoots; these are the ones to look out for, as they stand out with a certain degree of stiffness that makes them easier to arrange than weaker trailing pieces.

[When this was written (probably 1899, or it may have been part of an earlier newspaper article) the little sarcococca, Christmas Box, was unknown to her. Most species, and in particular *Sarcococca hookerana*, *S. humilis* and *S. ruscifolia*, the best for beauty of leaf and berry, were not introduced from China until the early 1900s. With a sweet-smelling flower from Christmas until late in spring, this little evergreen shrub makes an invaluable contribution both to the winter garden and to decoration in the house. Fortunately it thrives on chalk soils, preferring a spot in shade either of a north wall or on the edge of woodland. Berries of black or dark red are carried throughout the summer.

The magnificent winter-flowering mahonias also provide both flower and foliage for winter. The best known is *Mahonia japonica*, but hybrids of this with the more tender *M. lomariifolia* such as *M.* × *media* 'Charity' and 'Buckland', are even better with stiffly-held sweetly-scented pale yellow lily of the valley flowers. I find that once these shrubs are well established, branches bearing these floriferous racemes can be brought into the house when the flowers are still at bud stage, and leaves and opening flowers last many weeks in water. In Miss Jekyll's time mahonias were still classified as berberis; she mentions their tinted leaves (*see* p. 45) probably referring to *M. aquifolium* or *M. pinnata*, both of which flower in early spring although without the delicious scent of those just mentioned.

The winter-flowering honeysuckles, *Lonicera fragrantissima* and *L. standishii*, start to flower in January. The flowers are cream and have a sweet fragrance, an elusive scent which comes and goes as you pass near.

Of course many other spring-flowering shrubs may be pot-grown and overwintered under glass to produce early spring and even January flowering. They give little work but need space in a cold greenhouse. Rhododendrons and azaleas, spring-flowering deutzias, particularly *D. gracilis*, and even small specimens of a splendid evergreen such as *Choisya ternata*, can be successfully handled in this way.]

I do not much care for dried flowers – the bulrush and pampas-grass decoration has been so much overdone that it has become wearisome – but I make an exception in favour of the flower of *Eulalia zebrina* [*Miscanthus sinensis* 'Zebrinus'] and always give it a place. It does not come to its full beauty out of doors; it only finishes its growth late in October, and therefore does not have time to dry and expand.

I grew it for many years before finding out that the closed and rather draggled-looking heads would open perfectly in a warm room. The uppermost leaf often confines the flower, and should be taken off to release it; the flower does not seem to mature quite enough to come free of itself. [This is the tiger grass, with leaves of similar size to *M. sinensis*, with wiry graceful clump-forming stems, thriving in sun or shade, in moist or dry soil, and an excellent architectural foil to more solid leaf textures and colours. Growing to six feet it can dominate an autumn border; this cultivar 'Zebrinus' has leaves with lateral yellow bands.]

Bold masses of helichrysum [the everlasting flower, *Helichrysum bracteatum*, is an annual grown only for drying and

GERTRUDE JEKYLL ON GARDENING

winter flower arranging] certainly give some brightness to a room during the darkest weeks of winter, though the brightest yellow is the only one I much care to have; there is a look of faded tinsel about the other colourings. I much prize large bunches of the native iris [*Iris foetidissima*] berries and grow it largely for winter room-ornament.

Among the many valuable suggestions in Mrs Earle's delightful book *Pot-pourri from a Surrey Garden* is the use indoors of the smaller coloured gourds. As used by her they give a bright and cheerful look to a room that even flowers cannot surpass.

Wood and Garden [In a later chapter Miss Jekyll writes:] The sweet scents of a garden are by no means the least of its many delights. Even January brings *Chimonanthus fragrans* [*C. praecox*, winter sweet, an easily grown shrub only requiring a warm wall for real success], one of the sweetest and strongest scented of the year's blooms – little half-transparent yellowish bells on an otherwise naked-looking wall shrub. They have no stalks, but if they are floated in a shallow dish of water, they last well for several days, and give off a powerful fragrance in a room. During some of the warm days that nearly always come towards the end of February, if one knows where to look in some sunny, sheltered corner of a hazel copse there will be sure to be some primroses, and the first scent of the year's first primrose is no small pleasure . . . in all open winter weather there have been . . . *Iris stylosa* [*I. unguicularis*], with its delicate scent, faintly violet-like, but with a dash of tulip. *Iris reticulata* is also sweet . . . but of all irises I know, the sweetest to smell is a later blooming one, *I. graminea*. Its small purple flowers are almost hidden among a thick mass of grassy foliage which rises high above the bloom; but they are worth looking for, for the sake of the sweet and rather penetrating scent, which is exactly like that of a perfectly ripened plum . . .

FEBRUARY

'Wild gardening in any stretches of rough ground, or in wood- 'Changes of Fashion in Gardening', land that may adjoin the garden, when practised with restraint and the most careful consideration, is, for true pleasure in *The Nineteenth Century*, 1928 beautiful effects, abundantly repaying. It should show the use of a restricted choice of plants that are proper to the nature of the ground. If the place is open and has a light peaty soil it will be well to plant it with heaths and some other of the ericaceous plants, in such groups as shall look as if they grew naturally in the place. If there is an existing growth of whortleberry and a background of bracken, so much the better, in order to be able to distribute the heaths in stretches cut out of the native plants. Such a place comes well after passing through a plantation of azaleas and rhododendrons, shrubs of kindred character.

When woodland is to be planted the opportunities are many, but should be severely restricted. It is enough to have one picture at a time, such as a group of white foxglove rising behind a mass of the common male fern, with the taller bracken at the back and with a more distant setting of silvery stemmed birches and a dark background of the common holly. Daffodils may run through the woodland in March and April and lily of the valley in May. This restricted treatment of the woodland fosters the sense of restfulness and does nothing to destroy the charm and mystery of beautiful woody places.'

Distant promise of summer — Ivy berries — Coloured leaves — Berberis aquifolium [*Mahonia aquifolium*] — Its many merits — Thinning and pruning shrubs — Lilacs — Removing suckers — Training *Clematis flammula* — [Pruning Clematis] — Forms of trees — Juniper, a neglected native evergreen — Effect of snow — Power of recovery — Beauty of colour — Moss-grown stems — [Spring flowers and bulbs — Evergreens in winter gardens — Calcareous soils — Silver-leaved shrubs — Ferns — Wall shrubs].

THERE IS ALWAYS in February some one day, at least, when one smells the yet distant but surely coming summer. Perhaps it is a warm •mossy scent that greets one when passing along the southern side of a hedge bank; or it may be in some woodland opening, where the sun has coaxed out the pungent smell of the trailing ground-ivy [*Nepeta glechoma*], whose blue flowers will soon appear; but the day always comes, and with it the glad certainty that summer is nearing, and that the good things promised will never fail.

How strangely little of positive green colour is to be seen in copse and woodland. Only the moss is really green. The next greenest thing is the northern sides of beech and oak. Walking southward they are all green, but looking back they are silver-grey. The undergrowth is of brambles and sparse fronds of withered bracken; the bracken less beaten down than usual, for the winter has been without snow; only where the soil is deeper and the fern has grown more tall and rank, it has fallen into thick almost felted masses, and the stalks all lying one way making the heaps look like lumps of fallen thatch. The bramble leaves – last year's leaves, which are held all the winter – are of a dark blackish-bronze colour, or nearly red where they have seen the sun. Age seems to give them a sort of hard surface

43

and enough of a polish to reflect the sky; the young leaves that will come next month are almost woolly at first.

[Elsewhere Miss Jekyll recommends *Rubus deliciosus* (now largely superseded in flowering merit by the hybrid *R. × tridel* 'Benenden'), but she probably would not have known *R. thibetanus* (1907) which, with attractive grey pinnate leaves and arching purple stems covered in white bloom, makes a lovely woodland plant. A woodland area of the smaller garden today can hardly spare space for the common bramble, *Rubus ulmifolius*.]

Grassy tufts show only bleached bents, so tightly matted that one wonders how the delicate young blades will be able to spear through. Ivy-berries hanging in thick clusters are still in beauty; they are so heavy that they weigh down the branches. There is a peculiar beauty in the form and veining of the plain-shaped leaves belonging to the mature or flowering state that the plant reaches when it can no longer climb, whether on a wall six feet high or on the battlements of a castle. Cuttings grown from such portions retain their habit, and form densely-flowering bushes of compact shape [often used by G.J. in her designs for gardens; after being overlooked for an era the so-called arborescent ivies (*Hedera arborescens*) are again much sought after for garden schemes, proving hardy, floriferous and shapely].

Beautiful colouring is now to be seen in many of the plants whose leaves do not die down in winter. Foremost among these is the foam-flower, *Tiarella cordifolia*. Its leaves, now lying on the ground, show bright colouring, inclining to scarlet, crimson and orange. Tellima, its near relation, is also well coloured. [This is the larger *Tellima grandiflora*; its form 'Purpurea' is even better but does not come true from seed and should be split up to increase. The modern hybrid between *Tiarella cordifolia* and *Heuchera × brizoides*, *Heucherella × tiarelloides* is worthy of a place in shade and has the pink erect sprays of the latter parent.] *Galax aphylla*, with its polished leaves of hard texture, and stalks almost as stiff as wire, is nearly as bright; and many of the megaseas [bergenias] are of a fine bronze red, the ones that colour best being the varieties of the well-known *M. crassifolia* and *M. cordifolia* [*Bergenia crassifolia* and *B. cordifolia*].

[Elsewhere she writes of these plants:] I am never tired of admiring the fine solid foliage of this family of plants, remaining, as it does, in beauty both winter and summer, and taking on a splendid winter colouring of warm red bronze. It is true that the flowers of *M. cordifolia* [*Bergenia cordifolia*] and *M. crassifolia* [*B. crassifolia*] are coarse-looking blooms of a strong and rank quality of pink colour, but the persistent beauty of the leaves more than compensates; and in the rather tenderer kind *M. ligulata* [*Bergenia ciliata ligulata*], and its varieties, the colour of the flower is delightful, of a delicate good pink, with almost scarlet stalks. There is nothing flimsy or temporary looking about the megaseas, but rather a sort of grave and monumental look that specially fits them for association with masonry, or for any place where a solid-looking edging or full-stop is wanted.

Wood and Garden

[Miss Jekyll loved other bergenias. The hybrid *Bergenia × schmidtii* has rich green toothed leaves and dense short heads of pink flowers early in the year, sometimes even in February, and *B. cordifolia* 'Purpurea', vivid pink flowers and handsome leaves colour bronze in winter. One of the most attractive modern cultivars is *B.* 'Silberlicht', which has white flowers tinged with pink, in April, when some of the earlier bergenias have finished flowering. The 'Ballawley' hybrids have crimson flowers borne on tall two-foot stems above round green leaves which colour purple-brown in winter, and prefer a sheltered woodland site.]

Among shrubs, some of the nearly allied genera, popularly classed under the name andromeda, are beautiful in reddish colour passing into green, in some of the leaves by tender gradation, and in others by bold splashing. [Andromedas are now generally classified as other genera including cassiope, leucothoe, and pieris; all are shrubs needing a very acid damp soil.] *Berberis aquifolium* [*Mahonia aquifolium*] begins to colour after the first frosts; though some plants remain green, the greatest number take on some rich tinting of red or purple, and occasionally in poor soil and in full sun a bright red that may almost be called scarlet.

What a precious thing this fine old berberis [mahonia] is. What should we do in winter without its vigorous masses of grand foliage in garden and shrubbery, to say nothing of its use indoors? Frequent as it is in gardens, it is seldom used as well or thoughtfully as it deserves. There are many places where, between wood and garden, a well-considered planting of berberis, combined with two or three other things of larger stature, such as the fruiting barberry [berberis] and whitethorn [*Crataegus monogyna* or *C. oxyacantha*] and holly [forms of *Ilex aquifolium*], would make a very enjoyable piece of shrub wild-gardening. When one reflects that *Berberis aquifolium* [*Mahonia aquifolium*] is individually one of the handsomest of small shrubs, that it is at its best in mid-winter, that every leaf is a marvel of beautiful drawing and construction, and that its ruddy winter colouring is a joy to see, enhanced as it is by the glistening brightness of the leaf-surface; and further, when one remembers that in spring the whole picture changes – that the polished leaves are green again, and the bushes are full of tufted masses of brightest yellow bloom, and fuller of bee-music than any other plant then in flower; and that even then it has another season of beauty yet to come, when in the days of middle summer it is heavily loaded with the thick clustered masses of berries, covered with a brighter and bluer bloom than almost any other fruit can show – when one thinks of all this brought together in one plant, it seems but right that we should spare no pains to use it well. It is the only hardy shrub I can think of that is in one or other of its varied forms of beauty throughout the year. It is never leafless or untidy; it never looks mangy like an ilex [*Quercus ilex*] in April, or moulting like a holly in May, or patchy and unfinished like a yew and box and many other evergreens when their young leafy shoots are sprouting.

We have been thinning the shrubs in one of the rather large clumps next to the lawn, taking the older wood in each clump right out from the bottom and letting more light and air into the middle. Weigelas grow fast and very thick. Quite two-thirds have been cut out of each bush of weigela, philadelphus and ribes, and a good bit out of *Ceanothus* 'Gloire de Versailles', my favourite of its kind, and all the oldest wood from *Viburnum plicatum*. The stuff cut out makes quite a respectable lot of faggoting. How extremely dense and hard is the wood of philadelphus, as close-grained as box, and almost as hard as the bright yellow wood of berberis [berberis and mahonia].

Some of the lilacs [syringa] have a good many suckers from the root, as well as on the lower part of the stem. These must all come away, and then the trees will have a good dressing of manure. They are greedy feeders and want it badly in our light soil, and surely no flowering shrub more truly deserves it. The lilacs I have are some of the beautiful kinds raised in France, for which we can never be grateful enough to our good neighbours across the Channel. The white variety (cultivar) 'Marie Legraye' [*Syringa vulgaris* 'Marie Legraye'] always remains my favourite. Some are larger and whiter, and have the trusses more evenly and closely filled, but this beautiful Marie fills one with a satisfying conviction as of something that is just right, that has arrived at the point of just the best and most lovable kind of beauty, and has been wisely content to stay there, not attempting to pass beyond and excel itself.

Its beauty is modest and reserved, and temperate and full of refinement. The colour has a deliciously-tender warmth of white, and as the truss is not over-full, there is room for a delicate play of warm half-light within its recesses. Among the many beautiful coloured lilacs, I am fond of Lucie Baltet and Princess Marie. There may be better flowers from the ordinary florist's point of view, but these have the charm that is a good garden flower's most precious quality. I do not like the cold heavy-coloured ones of the bluish-slaty kinds. No shrub is hardier than the lilac; I believe they flourish even within the Arctic circle. It is very nearly allied to privet; so nearly, that the oval-leafed privet [*Ligustrum ovalifolium*] is commonly used as a stock. Standard trees flower much better than bushes; in this form all the strength seems to go directly to the flowering boughs. No shrub is more persistent in throwing up suckers from the root and from the lower part of the stem, but in bush trees as well as in standards they should be carefully removed each year. In the case of bushes, three or four main stems will be enough to leave.

When taking away suckers of any kind whatever, it is much

better to tear them out than to cut them off. A cut, however close, leaves a base from which they may always spring again, but if pulled or wrenched out they will bring away with them the swollen base, that, if left in, would be a likely source of future trouble.

[If lilac is grafted on privet deep planting is essential, for unless scion-rooting occurs the plant will die in a few years. For the smaller garden the charming *Syringa microphylla* (introduced 1910) and its cultivar 'Superba' would be an excellent choice. The flowers are rosy-lilac and rosy-pink respectively and are borne intermittently after the first June flush until October. The fragrant flowers are carried in small panicles suitably sized to associate with the neat tidy leaves. The Canadian 'Preston' hybrids are very vigorous, hardy, long-living plants bearing flowers predominantly reddish-purple, with less coarse leaves than the ordinary *Syringa vulgaris* and its numerous cultivars. The individual flower of each panicle of these hybrids is longer and more slender. The Persian lilac, *S. × persica*, makes a rounded bush hardly more than six to eight feet high; it is May-flowering, lilac-coloured and heavily fragrant.]

Before the end of February we must be sure to prune and train any plants there may be of *Clematis flammula*. Its growth is so rapid when once it begins, that if it is overlooked it soon grows into a tangled mass of succulent weak young stuff, quite unmanageable two months hence, when it will be hanging about in helpless masses, dead and living together. If it is left till then, one can only engirdle the whole thing with a soft tarred rope and sling it up somehow or anyhow. But if taken now, when the young growths are just showing at the joints, the last year's mass can be untangled, the dead and the over-much cut out, and the best pieces trained in. In gardening the interests of the moment are so engrossing that one is often tempted to forget the future; but it is well to remember that this lovely and tenderly scented clematis will be one of the chief beauties of September, and well deserves a little timely care. [In fact many of the late-flowering clematis require the same treatment. It is possible to be quite ruthless, cutting away dead growth and pruning back all shoots to three feet or less above ground. Obviously some long growth can be left and flowers on these shoots will be borne correspondingly earlier. Examples from this group not all known to Miss Jekyll, but including her favourite *C. flammula*, are *C. viticella*, *C. rehderiana*, *C. tangutica*, *C. orientalis* and *C.* × *jackmanii*, *C. tangutica* and *C. orientalis*. They can, if only lightly pruned, start flowering in June. Hybrids with blood of one or more of these species usually require the same treatment, and all the June-flowering large-flowered hybrids need cutting back to the first pair of strong buds. Times of flowering can be made to vary according to the degree of fierceness, and those ignored for a year or so will still flower but with less vigour and high above your head. The spring-flowering species, hybrids and cultivars should have their flowering shoots cut out immediately after flowering, and any other tidying necessary done then too.]

In summer time one never really knows how beautiful are the forms of the deciduous trees. It is only in winter, when they are bare of leaves, that one can fully enjoy their splendid structure and design, their admirable qualities of duly apportioned strength and grace of poise, and the way the spread of the many-branched head has its equivalent in the wide-reaching ground-grasp of the root. And it is interesting to see how, in many different kinds of tree, the same laws are always in force, and the same results occur, and yet by the employment of what varied means. For nothing in the growth of trees can be much more unlike than the habit of the oak and that of the weeping willow, though the unlikeness only comes from the different adjustment of the same sources of power and the same weights, just as in the movement of wind-blown leaves some flutter and some undulate, while others turn over and back again. Old apple trees are specially noticeable for their beauty in winter, when their extremely graceful shape, less visible when in loveliness of spring bloom or in rich bounty of autumn fruit, is seen to fullest advantage.

Few in number are native evergreens, and for that reason all the more precious. One of them, the common juniper [*Juniperus communis*], is one of the best of shrubs either for garden or wild ground, and yet, strangely enough, it is so little appreciated that it is scarcely to be had in nurseries. Chinese junipers, junipers from Spain and Greece, from Nepal and Siberia, may be had, but the best juniper of all is very rarely grown. Were it a common tree one could see a sort of reason (to some minds) for overlooking it, but though it is fairly abundant on a few hill-sides in the southern counties, it is by no means widely distributed throughout the country. Even this reason would not be consistent with common practice, for the holly (*Ilex aquifolium*) is abundant throughout England and yet is to be had by the thousand in every nursery. Be the reason what it may, the common juniper is one of the most desirable of evergreens and is most undeservedly neglected. Even our botanists fail to do it justice, for Bentham describes it as a low shrub growing two feet, three feet or four feet high. I quote from memory only; these may not be the words, but this is the sense of his description. He had evidently seen it on the chalk downs only, where such a portrait of it is exactly right. But in our sheltered uplands, in sandy soil, it is a small tree of noble aspect, twelve to twenty-eight feet high. In form it is extremely variable, for sometimes it shoots up on a single stem and looks like an Italian cypress [*Cupressus sempervirens*] or like the upright Chinese juniper [*Juniperus chinensis*], while at other times it will have two or more tall spires and a dense surrounding mass of lower growth, while in other cases it will be like a quantity of young trees growing close together, and yet all the trees in all these varied forms may be nearly of an age.

[The so-called Irish juniper, *Juniperus communis* 'Hibernica', is a very compact form of the common native and makes a splendid column, slender and dense. It is most suitable for use where the formal vertical accent is sought, but tends to have leaves rather more grey-blue than the type. The dwarf creeping forms make excellent weed-suppressing ground cover and look attractive grown over paving and steps on the edge of flowerbeds. Hillier's *Manual of Trees and Shrubs* still lists fourteen varieties and cultivars of the common juniper, all useful in a garden of rather limited area.]

The action of snow is the reason for this unlikeness of habit. If, when young, the tree happens to have one main stem strong enough to shoot up alone, and if at the same time there come a sequence of winters without much snow, there will be the tall, straight cypress-like tree. But if, as is more commonly the case, the growth is divided into a number of stems of nearly equal size sooner or later they are sure to be laid down by snow. Such a winter storm as that of the end of December 1886 was especially disastrous to junipers. Snow came on early in the evening in this district, when the thermometer was barely at freezing point and there was no wind. It hung on the trees in clogging masses, with a lowering temperature that was soon below freezing. The snow still falling loaded them more and more; then came the fatal wind, and all through the night we heard the breaking trees. When morning came there were eighteen inches of snow on the ground, and all the trees that could be seen, mostly Scotch fir [*Pinus sylvestris*], seemed to be completely wrecked. Some were entirely stripped of branches and stood up bare, like scaffold poles. Until the snow was gone or half gone, no idea could be formed of the amount of damage done to shrubs; all were borne down and buried under the white rounded masses. A great holly on the edge of the lawn, nearly thirty feet high and as much in spread, whose head in summer is crowned with a great tangle of honeysuckle, had that crowned head lying on the ground weighted down by the frozen mass.

But when the snow was gone and all the damage could be seen, the junipers looked worse than anything. What had lately been shapely groups were lying perfectly flat, the bare-stemmed leafless portions of the inner part of the group showing, and looking like a faggot of dry brushwood, that, having been stood upright, had burst its band and fallen apart in all directions. Some, whose stems had weathered many snowy winters, now had them broken off half-way up, while others escaped with bare life, but with the thick strong stem broken down, the heavy head lying on the ground, and the stem wrenched open at the break, like a half-untwisted rope. The great wild junipers were the pride of our stretch of heathy waste just beyond the garden, and the scene of desolation was truly piteous, for though many of them already bore the marks of former accidents, never within our memory had there been such complete and comprehensive destruction.

But now ten years later so great is their power of recovery, that there are the same junipers, and, except in the case of those actually broken off, looking as well as ever. For those with many stems that were laid down flat have risen at the tips, and each tip looks like a vigorous young ten-year-old tree. What was formerly a massive bushy-shaped juniper, some twelve feet to fifteen feet high, now covers a space thirty feet across, and looks like a thick group of closely-planted healthy young ones . . . Among the many merits of the juniper, its tenderly mysterious beauty of colouring is by no means the least; a colouring as delicately subtle in its own way as that of cloud or mist, or haze in warm wet woodland. It has very little of positive green; a suspicion of warm colour in the shadowy hollows, and a blue-grey bloom of the tenderest quality imaginable on the outer masses of foliage. Each tiny blade-like leaf has a band of dead palest bluish-green colour on the upper surface, edged with a narrow line of dark green slightly polished; the back of the leaf is of the same full rather dark green with slight polish; it looks as if the green back had been brought up over the edge of the leaf to make the dark edging on the upper surface . . . This arrangement of mixed colouring and texture, and infinitely various position of the little spiny leaves, allows the eye to penetrate unconsciously a little way into the mass, so that one sees as much tender shadow as actual leaf surface, and this is probably the cause of the wonderfully delicate and, so to speak, intangible quality of colouring.

The merits of the juniper are not yet done with, for throughout the winter (the time of growth of moss and lichen) the rugged-barked old stems are clothed with loveliest pale-green growths of a silvery quality. Standing before it and trying to put the colour into words, one repeats, again and again, pale-green silver-palest silvery green! . . . Many another kind of tree stem is beautiful in its winter dress, but it is difficult to find any so full of varied beauty and interest as that of the juniper; it is one of the yearly feasts that never fails to delight and satisfy.

Gardeners Testament; 'Spring cyclamen and grape hyacinth', *Country Life*, 8 April 1916

[Elsewhere Miss Jekyll writes of spring flowers:] Some of the hardy cyclamen flower in late autumn, but there are two species that are essentially flowers of spring. *C. coum*, a native of Asia Minor and southern Europe, is in bloom in February and March.

It is a short-growing plant scarcely over three inches in height, and has dark crimson flowers and leathery roundish leaves, which, though they are faintly clouded with lighted colour, are wanting in the distinct whitish marbling that is so attractive in the foliage of some of the other species . . . In the open garden the plants should be in a sheltered nook in rockwork where there is thorough drainage, and it is all the better if they can have some kind of overhead protection . . . *C. repandum* is the pretty species that was commonly called *C. vernum* in gardens. The flowers of the type are pink or rosy, with bright purple at the base. There is a good white variety. It roots at the base of the tuber and should be planted three to four inches deep . . .

[In an article for *Country Life* she writes:] The race for preced-ence in time of flowering among the early anemones is between *A. blanda* and *A. hepatica* [*Hepatica nobilis*]; both may be looked for in February. *A. blanda* is a small Greek plant with much the same character as the larger, later and more free-growing *apennina*, but it keeps closer to the ground, the usual height being from three to four inches. The flowers are of deep blue colour [there are also pink and almost white forms in cultivation]. In our gardens it likes a warm bank or sheltered piece of rockwork, where it is an admirable companion to the various kinds of early iris and crocus . . . *A. hepatica* [*Hepatica nobilis*] . . . is a native of the Alps and southern Europe. It is a very old favourite in gardens. Parkinson, writing near 1629, describes ten varieties, of which two, a blue and a purple, are double. A double white has appeared from time to time; it is considered a great rarity and is always much prized . . . They all enjoy a rich loam or chalk, though they have been well grown at Wisley in light soil, planted with the roots tightly pressed between pieces of sand-stone. A stronger plant altogether is *Hepatica angulosa* [*H. transsilvanica*] . . . the flowers are of a fine light blue colour, as large again as those of the ordinary hepatica, and the leaves are better borne up by the stems.

Anemone fulgens, usually appearing before any of the *A. coronaria* varieties are in bloom, has the distinction of being the only true scarlet flower of its season. [Now thought to be a hybrid, the brilliant red flowers have narrow petals and a yellowish centre, doing well if given a comfortable site at the

'The early anemones', *Country Life*, March 1916

base of a warm wall.] *A. pulsatilla* [*Pulsatilla vulgaris*] is a beautiful low-growing species of our wind-swept chalk downs where the whole plant is only about three inches high. It gains much both in height and size in the shelter of our gardens, where the better development of the silky petals gives a softened quality to the rich but quiet purple of the blossom.

'Green things of the winter garden', *Country Life*, 29 January 1916

[In another article she writes about evergreens in winter gardens:] When the leaves are down and the flower borders are bare one turns with a feeling of grateful admiration to the evergreen trees, plants and bushes. They are still more to be appreciated because so many of them are now in their best and deepest coloured foliage. Holly, yew, bay [*Laurus nobilis*] and box are clothed in a kind of subdued splendour that is not only grateful to the eye but gladdening to the mind when one thinks of their shelter and comfort to the life of birds and other wild things. Then all the greys and faint browns and silvery greens of tree-bole and branch, and the thin mist so frequent during the days of early winter, form just the right setting for the deep rich colouring of the evergreens.

It sets one thinking how good it would be to have a good space set apart as a hardy winter garden; a space large enough to have a whole background of yew and holly, cypress and ilex ... such a place would be truly enjoyable from the middle of November and onward all through the winter, besides being a green garden of no little beauty. It would not be entirely without flowers for in a cool nook near the path there would be the giant Christmas rose [*Helleborus niger macranthus*] early in November, followed by the later-flowering kinds [*H. niger* and some of the modern garden forms, *see* p. 263]; and in another such place the Lent hellebores [*H. orientalis hybrids, see* p. 264 for full descriptions] blooming at a time when later winter joins hands with earliest spring. These might make a flowery undergrowth for quite a considerable space on the cooler side, while facing them on the sunny aspect there would be tufts of *Iris stylosa* [*I. unguicularis*] flowering in all open weather throughout the winter months ... the yellow Jasmine [*Jasminum nudiflorum*] would find a place, and could be so planted as to fall over the face of a scarp ... but there is no need to strain for more flowers, for just these few would give enough points of interest, and, with the

[Clipped cylinders of *Quercus ilex* at The Salutation.]
'When the site is a bare field, or any place without individuality, the designer has a free hand, but will be wise in choosing something that is definite, so as to give that previous quality of character. It can only be created by simplicity of aim; by doing one thing at a time as well and distinctly as possible and so avoiding complexity and confusion.' [Introduction to *Gardens for Small Country Houses*, Jekyll and Weaver, xxxviii.]

holly berries, enough of actual bright colouring. In fact, the winter garden is all the better for the fewness of its flowers. The summer garden is only too full of brilliant objects of beauty and interest, and the winter garden should have its own rather contrasting character as a place of comparative repose of mind and eye . . .

The winter garden on sandy or peaty soil would have many of the best sub-shrubs in quantity – *Gaultheria shallon*, the broad-leaved form of *Skimmia japonica* with its handsome red fruits and the still finer *S. j.* 'Foremanii' [which has distinctly broad obovate leaves and bears large bunches of brilliant red fruits; a female clone]; *Kalmia latifolia* and the flowering tree-ivies [arborescent ivies, see p. 44], beautiful for massing and growing into large, wide-spreading bushes. Then the dwarf rhododendrons and several of the andromedas, especially *Pieris floribunda* that grows into good-sized bushes, and the two species of Leucothoe, *L. catesbaei* [*L. fontanesiana*] and *L. axillaris* [a closely related species which is now correctly called *L. catesbaei*]. Another delight will be the Candleberry Gale, *Myrica cerifera*, whose leaves when crushed or bruised give off a delicious scent. [This American evergreen enjoys a damp site; the glaucous wax which covers the fruits can be made into fragrantly burning candles.] Then there will be tufts of that plant of rare beauty, the Alexandrian laurel, *Ruscus racemosus* [now *Danaë racemosa*], superb in strong yet delicate structural form, and the lower growing megaseas [bergenias] with large leathery leaves, and asarum, also with deep green, leathery leaves but the foliage small, much like that of cyclamen.

[For those of us gardening in calcareous soil there is also a large selection of low-growing shrubs and evergreen herbaceous plants which can make the garden interesting in winter. In the smaller garden of today a whole area or compartment can rarely be given up to winter foliage only. The plants we choose should also have summer flower or leaf value. If we follow Miss Jekyll's lead and search for those plants with leaves of different shades and textures of green, ignoring those with startling variegation, and for those with good grey and silver leaves (not all silver foliage plants look attractive in winter), it is possible to add to her list in a way which she might have approved. For acid soil only, the prostrate *Pachysandra terminalis* (it also has a variegated form) is attractive.

Shrubs that thrive in almost all soils and conditions and can survive considerable shade through the summer months are: *Viburnum davidii*, its excellent foliage enhanced by its turquoise berries; two medium-height berberis, *B. candidula* and *B. verruculosa*, glossy dark leaves with silvery-white undersides; *Mahonia aquifolium*; *Nandina domestica*, leaves with bronze tints; the hardier olearias and hebes; and *Vinca difformis*, which although reputedly a little tender has elegant evergreen leaves and bears gentle pale blue flowers from November throughout the winter months.

Among herbaceous plants with good evergreen foliage is *Chiastophyllum oppositifolium*, which has glossy rosettes all year with yellow spray flowers to eight inches in summer; epimediums, *Euphorbia robbiae*, *Lamium maculatum* 'Beacon Silver' (introducing a silvery note), *Tellima grandiflora*, *Saxifraga umbrosa* and *Tiarella cordifolia* are all fine plants. If some colour and interest is introduced by discreetly used coloured or variegated leaves, golden *Lysimachia nummularifolia*, pulmonarias, *Saxifraga stolonifera* all keep good winter colour even in the most extreme cold.

For the sunny side of a winter garden grey-leaved low-growing shrubs make an excellent foil to dark and glossy green. Those that keep a good silver tone even after frosts are *Atriplex halimus*, *Tanacetum densum*, *Euphorbia characias* hybrids with bluey-grey linear leaves, some helichrysums, *Othonnopsis cheirifolia*, *Senecio* 'Sunshine' and *S. monroi*, *Phlomis fruticosa*, *P. chrysophylla* and *P. italica*.]

[Continuing on winter Miss Jekyll writes:] Some of the native ferns are true winter plants. Polypody [*Polypodium vulgare*] is at its best in the earlier cold months; the prickly shield fern [*Polystichum setiferum* 'Acutilobum'] holds its dark green plumes the winter through, and male fern [*Dryopteris filix-mas*] is often in good order until after Christmas, and even for six weeks later unless there is snow – but snow makes an end of it. Hartstongue [*Asplenium scolopendrium*] is grand all the winter; it is a lime-loving plant and should be planted largely in calcareous soils. Another lime-loving plant good for the winter garden is *Iris foetidissima*, with its prosperous-looking sheaves of deep green, sword-like leaves, and, in November, its large seed pods, swinging heavily and opening to show the scarlet-coated, berry-like seeds.

'Evergreens on walls in winter', *Country Life*, 13 February 1915

[In another place she writes:] Shrubs with persistent foliage, that in summer pass almost without notice, acquire their full value in winter, and are then in their richest dress . . . In planting garden spaces against buildings the mistake is often made of having borders of temporary or summer plants only, especially in such places as narrow borders between house wall and terrace walk; but if these are filled with evergreens such as laurustinus [*Viburnum tinus*, to which we may add the excellent variegated form which has red stems and flowers very freely], rosemary, lavender and berberis, with, among them, a few points of interest as of China rose [probably the monthly rose, *R. chinensis* 'Old Blush', which flowers intermittently to Christmas] and lilies, there is a pleasant sense of permanence and a kind of dignity that is in harmony with the sentiment of a good building. When a garden is terraced, and there are retaining walls of solid masonry at the back of borders, the good use of evergreen shrubs is important, not only for their own display, but for winter clothing and as a background to the flowery masses of summer. There are many more shrubs suitable for such places than are generally thought of. Where walls are fairly high, there are such fine things as the evergreen magnolias [*Magnolia delavayi* and *M. grandiflora*, the former for mild counties only] and bay [*Laurus nobilis*] (no matter if they rise above the wall level), myrtle, azara and white jasmine, for though jasmine is not strictly evergreen not only does it hold its leaves till Christmas, but the mass of green stem shows with a general green effect. Some climbing roses have the same quality; . . . 'Reine Olga', that good red rose that makes yearly growths twelve to fifteen feet long, will be in fine foliage through February and even later . . . *Cistus cyprius* is a fine thing on a fairly high wall, its fragrant foliage turning strangely blue in winter. Shrubs with variegated leaves should be used with caution, to avoid the danger of a patchy effect; but where questions of colour are carefully considered and a harmonious background for flowers of bright yellow colouring is desired, it is well to train on the wall both the gold-splashed elaeagnus and the golden privet.

[Here she refers to the Mediterranean myrtle, *Myrtus communis*, and its narrow-leaved variety *M. c.* 'Tarentina', both of which need a warm wall in most districts. *Azara microphylla* has glossy small leaves and should be near a window or doorway as its early spring vanilla-scented flowers must be enjoyed. A variegated form is slow and perhaps more tender, but lights up a shady corner with its attractive leaves and graceful form. *A. serrata* is larger, with coarser leaves and darker yellow clusters of flowers in summer. Other species thrive in the warmer counties but are unreliable in the average garden. Miss Jekyll never mentions the evergreen silvery leaves of *Elaeagnus macrophylla* (or its hybrid, the stiffer *E.* × *ebbingei*) but this makes a first-class wall shrub, bearing small but very frequent flowers in autumn. There are several new cultivars of the gold-splashed elaeagnus, *E. pungens* 'Maculata', with different degrees of variegation, and the hybrid *E.* × *reflexa* has almost scandent branches, and with encouragement will clamber into an old tree, or it can be carefully tied back to cover a wall.]

Walls from five to seven feet high will take shrubs of medium height. One of the best is laurustinus, excellent for wall-training and yet but seldom used. All the three varieties well known in gardens are equally suitable, but of special beauty is the May-flowering *Viburnum* [*tinus*] *lucidum*. It is tenderer than the two other kinds, *V. tinus* and *V. hirtum* [*V. tinus hirtulum*] and is much benefited by being trained on a wall with a warm exposure . . . *Garrya elliptica*, with its pretty tassels of mid-winter bloom, is also suitable for . . . walls, and the handsome box, *Buxus balearica*, *Escallonia macrantha* and *E. philippiana* [*E. virgata*, only for acid soils, and tender] are both beautiful on walls, the latter flowering in late summer when shrub bloom is rare. [The tender grey-leaved *E. revoluta* is less particular about soil and flowers in August and September; the hybrid *E.* 'Iveyi' – named after the gardener at Caerhays – bears very large panicles of white flowers in autumn, and has strong healthy glossy leaves; it responds cheerfully to hard pruning.] *Choisya ternata* is one of the best of wall-shrubs, and rosemary, often seen on walls in Italy, should be so used at home. The grey sage-like foliage of *Phlomis fruticosa*, a shrub commonly grown as a bush in the open, is capital trained, and still better is the beautiful grey-leaved shrubby groundsel *Senecio greyii* [almost certainly *S.* 'Sunshine' and not the rarer and more tender *S. greyii*].

For lower walls there is still a good choice of evergreen covering, such as several of the lesser New Zealand veronicas [now all classified as hebes]. The taller *Veronica traversii* [*Hebe brachysiphon*] is of a size for a wall of medium height, but a dwarfer variety of this is well-suited for the lower terrace. Other New Zealanders, *Olearia hastii* [*O.* × *hastii*], *O. stellulata* [*O. phlogopappa*] and *O. macrodonta* [this, although one of the best and hardiest does, in fact, grow very large] will also be welcome, several kinds of cotoneaster, *Euonymus radicans* and *Daphne pontica*, the last filling the garden with its sweet scent in April and May. Aucubas can be used in shady places, and *Cassiaia fulvida* must not be overlooked, its tiny gold-backed leaves, set on long sprays that quickly grow, make it one of the prettiest things to cut and put with winter flowers in the house. Even *Berberis aquifolium* [*Mahonia aquifolium*], so useful and frequent a bush in every garden, can be trained on a low wall with singularly good effect.

MARCH

'I am strongly of an opinion that the possession of a quantity of *Colour Schemes*
plants, however good the plants may be themselves and however
ample their number, does not make a garden; it only makes a
collection. Having got the plants the great thing is to use them
with careful selection and definite intention. Merely having
them, or having them planted unassorted in garden spaces, is
only like having a box of paints from the best colourman, or, to
go a step further, it is like having portions of these paints set out
upon a palette. This does not constitute a picture; and it seems
to me that the duty we owe to our gardens and to our own better-
ing in our gardens is to use the plants that they shall form
beautiful pictures; and that, while delighting our eyes, they
should be always training those eyes to a more exalted criticism;
to a state of mind and artistic conscience that will not tolerate
bad or careless combination or any sort of misuse of plants, but
in which it becomes a point of honour to be always striving for
the best.'

Flowering bulbs — [Bulb and fern bank] — Dog-tooth violet — Rock garden — Variety of rhododendron foliage — A beautiful old kind — Suckers on grafted plants — Plants for filling up the beds — Heaths — Andromedas — Lady fern — *Lilium auratum* — [Other lilies] — Pruning roses — Training and tying climbing plants — Climbing and free-growing roses — The vine the best wall-covering — Other climbers — Wild clematis — Wild rose.

IN EARLY MARCH many and lovely are the flowering bulbs, and among them a wealth of blue, the more precious that it is the colour least frequent among flowers. The blue of *Scilla sibirica*, like all blues that have in them a suspicion of green, has a curiously penetrating quality; the blue of *S. bifolia* does not attack the eye so smartly. *Chionodoxa luciliae*, on the other hand, varies greatly; one may pick out light and dark blue, and light and dark of almost lilac colour. *C. gigantea* is a fine plant. There are some pretty kinds of *Scilla bifolia* that were raised by the Rev. J. G. Nelson of Aldborough, among them a tender flesh-colour and a good pink.

[If examined closely the basic difference between scilla and chionodoxa is that in the former the perianth segments are more or less free from each other, while in the chiono-doxa they are joined into a tube at the base. The chiono-doxa, or glory of the snow, to give it its popular name, occupies an alpine habitat near the snow line. In warmer countries the bulbs should be deeply planted in shade, and they will happily compete with lawn-grass and with plants in flowerbeds under deciduous trees. The later-flowering squills, which include our native wood hya-cinth, the bluebell now classified as *Endymion non-scriptus* and the Spanish squill, then *Scilla campanulata* but currently *Endymion hispanicus*, combine well for April flowering with the beautiful blue *Anemone nemorosa robinsoniana* and the slightly later-flowering *A. apennina*. Our white bluebell makes a good contrast with the blues.

In her book on colour schemes Miss Jekyll describes the border she designed for her early hard bulbs.]

Colour Schemes   On the further side of a path that bounds my June border is a border about seventy feet long and ten feet wide. At every ten feet along the back is a larch post planted with a free-growing rose. These are not only to clothe their posts, but to grow into garlands swinging on slack chains from post to post . . . The border slopes upward from the path, forming a bank of gentle ascent. It was first planted with hardy ferns in bold drifts; male fern [*Dryopteris filix-mas*] for the most part, because it is not only handsome but extremely persistent, the fronds remaining green into the winter. [There is a general edging of mossy saxifrage, *Saxifraga moschata*.] The colour scheme begins with the pink of *Megasea ligulata* [in this case probably *Bergenia* × *schmidtii*, one of Miss Jekyll's favourites and used extensively at Hestercombe] and with the lower toned pinks of *Fumaria bulbosa* [*Corydalis bulbosa*] and the dog-toothed violets (*Erythronium*).

At the back of these are Lent hellebores [*Helleborus orientalis*] of dull red colouring, agreeing charmingly with the colour of the bulbs. A few white Lent hellebores are at the end; they have turned to greenish white by the time the rather late *Scilla amoena* is in bloom. Then comes a brilliant patch of pure blue with white – *S. sibirica* and white hyacinths, followed by the also pure blues of *S. bifolia* and chionodoxa and later, the blue-white of puschkinia [*Puschkinia scilloides*, closely related to both scilla and chionodoxa and represented in gardens by this one species]; then again pure blues of *S. bifolia* and chionodoxa and the later more purple-blue of Grape Hyacinth [*Muscari neglectum* is the most commonly grown but there are many species and hybrids from which to choose today]. A long drift of white crocus comes next, in beauty in the border's earliest days; and later, the blue-white of puschkinia; then again pure blue and white of chionodoxa and white hyacinth.

Now the colours change to white and yellow and golden

foliage, with the bicolour trumpet daffodil 'Princeps' and beyond it the stronger yellow of two other small early kinds – *N. nanus* and the charming little *N. minor*, quite distinct though so often confounded with *nanus* in gardens.

[Both *N.* 'Princeps' and another, *N. horsfieldii*, are wild forms of *N. bicolor*. At the time she wrote they were classified as varieties of *N. pseudo-narcissus*. This embracing species then included practically all the wild daffodils with long trumpets, now given their own separate specific name. All are admirably suited to naturalizing in light woodland and rough grass; they vary from the robust Lent lily, *N. pseudo-narcissus* itself, to the smaller and choice *N. pallidiflorus* (the Pyrenean early daffodil, previously *N. pallida praecox*), *N. minor* and *N. nanus*. Even *N. cyclamineus* was once classified as *N. pseudo-narcissus*.]

With these, and in other strips and patches towards the end of the border, are plantings of the Golden valerian [*Valeriana Phu* 'Aurea'] so useful for its bright yellow foliage so early in the year. The leaves of the orange day-lily [*Hemerocallis fulva* 'Flore-Pleno'] are also of a pale yellowish-green colour when they first come up, and are used at the end of the border . . . Before the end of the bulb border is reached there is once more a drift of harmonized faint pink colouring of megasea [bergenia] and little fumaria (also known as *Corydalis bulbosa*) with the pale early Pyrenean daffodil, *N. pallidus praecox* . . . Through April and May the leaves of the bulbs are growing tall, and their seed-pods are carefully removed to prevent exhaustion. By the end of May the ferns are throwing up their leafy crooks; by June the feathery fronds are displayed in all their tender freshness; they spread over the whole bank and we forget that there are any bulbs between. By the time the June garden, whose western boundary it forms, has come into fullest bloom it has become a completely furnished bank of fern-beauty.

[Returning to March:] *Leucojum vernum*, with its clear white flowers and polished dark-green leaves, is one of the gems of early March; and flowering at the same time, no flower of the whole year can show a more splendid and sumptuous colour than the purple of *Iris reticulata*. Varieties have been raised,

some larger, some nearer blue, and some reddish purple, but the type remains the best garden flower. *I. stylosa* in sheltered nooks open to the sun, when well established, gives flower from November till April, the strongest rush of bloom being about the third week of March. It is a precious plant in our southern counties, delicately scented, of a tender and yet full lilac-blue. The long ribbon-like leaves make handsome tufts, and the sheltered place it needs in our climate saves the flowers from the injury they receive on their native windy Algerian hills, where they are nearly always torn into tatters.

What a charm there is about the common dog-tooth violet [*Erythronium dens-canis*]; it is pretty everywhere, in borders, in the rock garden, in all sorts of corners. But where it looks best with me is in a grassy place strewn with dead leaves, under young oaks, where the garden joins the copse. This is a part of the pleasure-ground that has been treated with some care, and has rewarded thought and labour with some success, so that it looks less as if it had been planted than as if it might have come naturally. At one point the lawn, trending gently upward, runs by grass paths into a rock garden, planted mainly with dwarf shrubs. Here are andromedas [now including other ericaceous

---

[*Viburnum opulus* 'Sterile' is the cultivated Guelder rose. The wholly sterile flowers are more showy than the type.]

'There are many places about the colder sides of houses, or where there are blank buildings or backs of sheds that would otherwise be unsightly, where a planting of Guelder rose would convert ugliness into beauty.' ['The Guelder rose', *Country Life*, 8 July 1916.]

[*Helleborus orientialis*, the Lent hellebore, has very variable flowers, from blush-white to plum and maroon. Some are exquisitely marked with crimson spots or green shading, the latter both within and without the flower petal.]

'The Lent hellebores are by no means so generally cultivated as their undoubted merit deserves, for at their time of blooming, from the end of February to nearly through March, they are the most important of the flowering plants of their season, both for size and general aspect. They are well suited to some place where wood and garden meet, and are also good at shrubbery edges, for they hold their foliage all the summer and are never unsightly.' ['Lent Hellebores', *Country Life*, 10 March 1923.]

genera such as pieris and leucothoe], pernettyas, gaultherias, and alpine rhododendron [*Rhododendron ferrugineum*], and with them three favourites whose crushed leaves give a grateful fragrance, Sweet gale [*Myrica gale*, the bog myrtle], *Ledum palustre* [wild rosemary or Labrador tea from northern moors] and *Rhododendron myrtifolium*. The rock part is unobtrusive; where the ground rises rather quickly are a couple of ridges made of large long lumps of sandstone half-buried, and so laid as to give a look of natural stratification. Hardy ferns are grateful for the coolness of their northern flanks, and cyclamens are happy on the ledges.

Beyond and above is the copse, or thin wood of young silver birch and holly, in summer below with bracken, but now bristling with the bluish spears of daffodils and the buds that will soon burst into bloom. The early Pyrenean daffodil [*Narcissus pallidus praecox*, later *N. pallidiflorus*] is already out, gleaming through the low-toned copse like lamps of pale yellow light. Where the rough path enters the birch copse is a cheerfully twinkling throng of the dwarf daffodil (*N. nanus*) looking quite at its best on its carpet of moss and fine grass and dead leaves. The light wind gives it a graceful dancing movement with an active spring about the upper part of the stalk. Some of the heavier trumpets not far off answer to the same wind with only a ponderous leaden sort of movement.

Further along, the garden joins the wood by a plantation of rhododendrons and broad grassy paths, and further still by a thicket of free-growing roses, some forming fountain-like clumps nine paces in diameter, and then again by masses of flowering shrubs, gradating by means of sweetbriar [*R. rubiginosa*], Water-elder [*Viburnum opulus*], dog-wood [*Cornus*], Medlar [*Mespilus germanica*] and thorn [*Crataegus monogyna* or *C. oxycantha*] from garden to wild wood.

[In an area with alkaline soil the planting might be rather different. Instead of andromedas, pernettyas, gaultherias, sweet gale etc., all of which require acid soil, it may be advisable to plant low-growing evergreen shrubs such as the leathery-leaved *Viburnum davidii*, variegated *Symphoricarpus*, *orbiculatus*, *Lonicera pileata*, *Buxus semper-*

virens and cultivars, *Rubus tridel,* all sorts of berberis and cotoneaster, sarcococcas and weigelas. All these shrubs thrive on the edge of woodland and welcome a degree of shade, giving a natural effect as planting areas shade gradually into woodland. Most viburnums thrive in all soils as do the wild roses, medlars and most dogwood. Probably Miss Jekyll refers above to the native *Cornus sanguinea (Thelycrania sanguinea).*]

[She expands on her wood:] When woodland joins garden *Colour Schemes* ground there is too often a sudden jolt; the wood ends with a hard line, sometimes with a path along it accentuating the defect . . . it would have been better if from the first the garden had not been brought quite so close to the wood, then the space between . . . might have been planted so as to bring them into unison . . . as to belong equally to garden and wood. The trees would take their place as the bounding and sheltering feature . . . the trees at the natural wood edge are better furnished with side branches. [For planting with young rhododendrons in her own garden Miss Jekyll recommends planting] 'hardy ferns . . . and groups of lilies . . .' Besides lilies, a few other flowering plants suitable for the rhododendron walk are: white foxgloves, white columbine, white *Epilobium angustifolium* [less invasive than the pink form of the type, the pretty French or rosebay willow-herb], trillium, *Epimedium pinnatum* [*E. p. colchicum*], *Uvularia grandiflora* [a relative of Solomon's Seal with hanging straw-yellow flowers in spring; not lime-tolerant], *Dentaria diphylla* and *Gentiana asclepiadea* . . .

Later it was found that these wood-path edges offered such suitable places for the late-blooming willow gentian (*G. asclepiadea*) that it was still more largely planted. It delights in a cool place in shade or half-shade, and when in mid-September so many flowers are over and garden plants in general are showing fatigue and exhaustion, it is a pleasure to come upon the grace-ful arching sprays, their upper portions set with pairs of long blue flowers, looking fresh and bright and full of vigour . . . When the garden comes on the sunny side of the wood the plant-ing would be quite different. Here is the place for cistuses; for the bolder groups the best are *C. laurifolius* and *C. cyprius,* backed by plantings of tamarisk, arbutus and white broom [*Cytisus multiflorus*] with here and there a free-growing rose of the wilder sort. If the fir-boughs [of the Scotch fir, *Pinus sylvestris*] come down within reach, the wild clematis (*C. vitalba*) can be led into them; it will soon ramble up a tree, filling it with its pretty foliage and abundance of August bloom.

[Miss Jekyll goes on to describe her larger rhododendrons in the wood at Munstead :] Now that the rhododendrons, planted nine years ago, have grown to a state and size of young maturity, it is interesting to observe how much they vary in foliage, and how clearly the leaves show the relative degree of relationship to their original parents, the wild mountain plants of Asia Minor and the United States. These, being two of the hardiest kinds, were the ones first chosen by hybridizers, and to these kinds we owe nearly all the large numbers of beautiful garden rhododendrons now in cultivation. The ones more nearly related to the wild *ponticum* have long narrow shining dark-green leaves, while the varieties that incline more to the American *R. catawbiense* have the leaves twice as broad, and almost rounded at the shoulder where they join the stalk; moreover, the surface of the leaf has a different texture, less polished and showing a grain like Morocco leather. The colour also is a lighter and more yellowish green, and the bush is not so densely branched. The leaves of all the kinds are inclined to hang down in cold weather, and this habit is more clearly marked in the *catawbiense* varieties . . .

Within March, and before the busier season comes upon us, it is well to look out for the suckers that are likely to come on grafted plants. They may generally be detected by the typical *ponticum* leaf, but if the foliage of a branch should be suspicious and yet doubtful, if on following the branch down it is seen to come straight from the root, and to have a redder bark than the rest, it may safely be taken for a robber. Of course the invading stock may be easily seen when in flower, but the good gardener takes it away before it has this chance of reproaching him. A lady visitor last year told me with some pride that she had a most wonderful rhododendron in bloom; all the flower in the middle was crimson, with a ring of purple-flowered branches outside. I am afraid she was disappointed when I offered condolence

instead of congratulation, and had to tell her that the phenome-
non was not uncommon among neglected bushes.

When my rhododendron beds were first planted, I followed
the usual practice of filling the outer empty spaces of the clumps
with hardy heaths. Perhaps it is still the best or one of the best
ways to begin when the bushes are quite young; for if planted
the right distance apart – seven to nine feet – there must be large
bare spaces between; but now that they have filled the greater
part of the beds, I find that the other plants I tried are more to
my liking. These are *Andromeda catesbaei* [*Leucothoe fontanesiana*], then lady fern [*Athyrium filix-femina*] and then the
dwarf *R. myrtifolium* [now correctly *R. kotschyi* (Bean, 8th
ed, 1976); it is very similar to *R. ferrugineum* and usually
replaces the latter as you travel east of the Alps and into the
mountains of Bulgaria and Yugoslavia. It is possible that Miss
Jekyll refers to the hybrid *R.* × 'Myrtifolium' which was the
result of a cross made in 1828 of *R. minus* and *R. hirsutum*, also
making a dense dwarf shrub to three or four feet, useful for its
late flowering.] The main spaces between the young bushes I
plant with *Cistus laurifolius*, a perfectly hardy kind; this grows
much faster than the rhododendrons, and soon fills the middle
spaces; by the time that the best of its life is over – for it is a
short-lived bush – the rhododendrons will be wanting all the
space. Here and there in the inner spaces I put *Lilium auratum*,
a lily that thrives in a peaty bed, and that looks its best when
growing through other plants; moreover, when the rhododendrons are out of flower, the lily, whose blooming season is
throughout the late summer and autumn, gives a new beauty
and interest to that part of the garden.

[*Lilium auratum* created a sensation when first exhibited
in 1862, after its introduction by John Gould Veitch. In
Lilies, Jan de Graaff and Edward Hyams write: 'Its hard tense
stems rise to a height of eight feet, its lustrous green leaves
are up to eight inches long and one foot wide; its flowers,
five or six to a stem in the wild but up to thirty or more in
good cultivation, are waxy white, rayed gold and spotted
crimson, very sweetly scented, and up to a foot across their
great open bowls.' As a species *L. auratum* cannot be

called easy to grow . . . it is excessively susceptible to virus-disease . . . These lilies are excessively fussy about soil drainage . . . they resent overfeeding' and are very intolerant of lime. At the same time when given the right conditions it can multiply itself generously, 'there can be no question of *L. auratum*'s title to the queenship of the genus'. Thus we must not all hope to emulate Miss Jekyll. At the same time we need not adopt the needlessly pessimistic advice of a prominent modern horticulturalist to treat lily bulbs as showy annuals, expensive but expendable.

In fact all lilies need perfect drainage and shelter from winds, a raised bed or gentle slope, grit for each crown to lie on, and a workable loamy soil. Those tolerant of lime are *L. martagon, L. henryi* (which positively dislikes peat), *L. regale, L. szovitzianum*, the old *L. bulbiferum croceum* (Miss Jekyll's 'Herring Lily'), many of the hybrids and the Madonna lily, *L. candidum*.]

Home and Garden

Croceum is the early blooming Orange lily that grows so well in London. It is the Herring Lily of the Dutch, blooming at the time when the great catches of herrings take place . . . Like other lilies long in cultivation, there are better and worse forms of it. The best one is a magnificent garden plant; in my borders, when full grown, the third year after planting, it is seven feet high; a sumptuous mass of the deepest orange colour . . . I grow behind it the white everlasting pea [*Lathyrus latifolius* 'Albus'], training the long flowering shoots over and among the lily stems, with what seems to me the happiest effect.

[All lilies except the Madonna need woodland conditions and plenty of leaf-mould. We all know and love the regal lily, *L. regale*, introduced by Wilson in 1903; it is robust and tolerant, an invaluable garden species, flowering in mid-summer in sun or shade. For late summer *L. henryi* and the martagons are easiest for lime, while an acid soil makes the choice far wider; so much hybridization has been done that lilies from many groups should be tried.

Miss Jekyll's sister, Lady Eden, grew Madonna lilies massed in half-shaded borders beneath a vine pergola in her famous 'Garden of Eden' on the Giudecca in Venice. This was copied by Lady Downe at Dingley Park, using espaliered and arching fruit trees as a framework. Today at Court Farm in Broadway, a similar effect has been created by using the lime-tolerant yellow June-flowering *L. szovitsianum* under a double walk of pleached limes.]

The time has come for pruning roses and for tying up and training the plants that clothe wall and fence and pergola. And this sets one thinking about climbing and rambling plants, and all their various ways and wants, and of how best to use them. One of my boundaries to a road is a fence about nine feet high, wall below and close oak paling above. It is planted with free-growing roses of several types – 'Aimée Vibert', 'Madame Alfred Carrière', 'Reine Olga de Württemberg' and 'Bouquet d'Or', the strongest of the Dijon teas. ['Aimée Vibert', a noisette climber, has rich green glossy leaves, flowers in clusters of pure white and almost double. It can be grown up a pillar of a pergola or allowed to grow freely into bushes or trees.]

For rambling through low tree growth and indeed any of the more free uses there are two roses, a red and a white, of extreme beauty, namely, 'Reine Olga de Württemberg' and 'Madame Alfred Carrière'. 'Reine Olga' will make shoots fifteen feet long in a season, and has the added merit of holding its admirable foliage in perfection for some weeks after Christmas. [Elsewhere she further describes 'Reine Olga'] 'whose half-double flowers of a fine crimson colour, of great beauty in the half-opened bud state, gladden us through the summer'. [An equivalent rose today might be the fragrant dark crimson Guinée.]

Gardeners' Testament

'Madame Alfred Carrière', with its beautiful pale tea-rose foliage and loose yellow-white bloom, soon becomes leggy below and is therefore all the more suitable for pushing up through bush and tree. [This rose holds its own today among the newer hybrids, very fragrant and free-flowering throughout the summer.] The Boursaults delight in the same treatment, for it is exactly that of their alpine ancestor that grow on the fringes of woodland and in wild bushy tangles. [It is now thought unlikely that *R. pendulina*, the Alpine rose, is one of the parents, although the Boursaults undoubtedly resemble a double form of this. They have long almost thornless canes, with few leaves, and flowers borne in loose clusters, a good mixture of purples and reds. There is a good form at Cranborne, called 'The Blush', possibly the only one still available today. Graham Stuart Thomas mentions the large-flowered 'Madame Sancy de Parabère'.]

'Bouquet d'Or' is of the same race as the wonderful buff-yellow 'Gloire de Dijon', but seldom seen today. It is dark yellow and very vigorous. Returning to March: Then comes a space of *Clematis montana* and *C. flammula*, and then more roses – 'Madame Plantier', 'Emélie Plantier' (a delightful rose to cut) and some of the grand sweetbriars raised by Lord Penzance.

['Madame Plantier' is a large bush or pillar rose with white flowers, 'Emélie' a free-grower with arching stems and pink-white bloom. Both old roses, the former is grown at Sissinghurst where 'the trailing stems have been encouraged to climb over orchard trees, and then to fall gracefully under the weight of the white flowers' (Graham Stuart Thomas, *Old Shrub Roses*, 1961). 'The neat soft-green leaves are nearly hidden beneath the showers of medium-size well-filled flowers, opening with a creamy-yellow flush in the centre and rapidly turning to pure white. Every flower has a characteristic green point in the centre, enhancing its purity, and its fragrance, rich and sweet, is carried well on the air' (*Old Shrub Roses*).]

The Penzance sweetbriars all have characteristic fragrant foliage, and are large thorny rather tangled shrubs, the best known today being 'Amy Robsart' with pink flowers, 'Lady Penzance' coppery-yellow, 'Lord Penzance' buff-yellow and 'Meg Merrilees' crimson. The modern *rubiginosa* hybrid 'Fritz Nobis' has exquisite scented double-clustered pink flowers and makes a more compact bushy shape. Lord Penzance on retire-

Roses for English Gardens ment took to rose-breeding. Miss Jekyll writes:] 'this eminent lawyer, who in some of the years of his mature practice had to put the law in effect in decreeing the separation of unhappy human couples, had sought mental refreshment in the leisure of his latest days by devoting it to the happy marriage of roses.'

From mid-summer onwards these roses are continually cut for flower, and yield an abundance of quite the most ornamental class of bloom. For I like to have cut roses arranged in a large free way, with whole branches three or four feet long, easy to have from these free-growing kinds, that throw out branches fifteen feet long in one season, even on our poor sandy soil, that contains no particle of that rich loam that roses love. I think this same 'Reine Olga', the grand grower from which come our longest and largest prunings, must be quite the best evergreen rose, for it holds its full clothing of handsome dark-green leaves right through the winter. It seems to like hard pruning. I have one on a part of the pergola, but I have no pleasure from it, as it has rushed up to the top, and nothing shows but a few naked stems.

One has to find how to use all these different roses. How often one sees the wrong roses used as climbers on the walls of a house. I have seen a 'Gloire de Dijon' covering the side of a house with a profitless reticulation of bare stem, and a few leaves and flowers looking into the gutter just under the edge of the roof. What are generally recommended as climbing roses are too ready to ramp away, leaving bare leggy growth where wall-clothing is desired. One of the best is climbing 'Aimée Vibert', for with very little pruning it keeps well-furnished nearly to the ground, and with its graceful clusters of white bloom and healthy looking polished leaves is always one of the prettiest of roses. Its only fault is that it does not shed its dead petals, but retains the whole bloom in dead brown clusters [rather like the modern single yellow 'Mermaid'].

But if a rose wishes to climb, it should be accommodated with a suitable place. The excellent old rose, 'Dundee Rambler', or the still prettier 'The Garland' rose, will find a way up a holly tree, and fling out its long wreathes of tenderly-tinted bloom; and there can be no better way of using the lovely Himalayan *R. brunonis* [*R. brunonii*, now mostly seen in its fine form 'La Mortola'], with its long almost blue leaves and wealth of milk-white flower. A common sweetbriar will also push up among the branches of some dark evergreen yew or holly, and throw out aloft its scented branches and rosy bloom, and look at its very best.

But some of these same free roses are best of all if left in a clear space to grow exactly as they will without any kind of support or training. So placed, they grow into large rounded groups. Every year, just after the young laterals on the last year's branches have flowered, they throw out vigorous young rods that arch over as they complete their growth, and will be the flower-bearers of the year to come.

[There are some problems about growing roses in this way. In a modern garden of limited size it is unlikely that space can be allotted to these roses in flowerbeds. Perhaps they look best in an outlying area, surrounded by semi-rough grass. Mowing around them is done with an air-cushion type of machine, but in order not to cut and wound the long new shoots it is helpful to have two people working together, one to swing the mower, the other to hold the trailing branches high above the blades. Given suitable conditions they are a valuable ornament to any garden, and a welcome contrast to the stiff and awkward formality of modern bush rose beds.]

Two kinds of roses of rambling growth that are rather tender, but indispensable for beauty, are 'Fortune's Yellow' and the Banksias. Pruning the free roses is always rough work for the hands and clothes, but of all roses I know, the worst to handle is 'Fortune's Yellow'. The prickles are hooked back in a way that no care or ingenuity can escape; and whether they have any-thing of a poisonous quality, I do not know; but whereas hands scratched and torn by roses in general heal quickly, the wounds made by 'Fortune's Yellow' are much more painful and much slower to get well. I knew an old labourer who died of a rose-prick. He used to work about the roads and at cleaning the ditches and mending the hedges. For some time I did not see him, and when I asked another old countryman, 'What's gone o' Master Trussler?' the answer was 'He's dead – died of a canker-bush.' The wild dog-rose is still the 'canker' in the speech of the old people, and a thorn or prickle is still a 'bush'. A dog-rose prickle had gone deep into the old hedger's hand – a 'bush' more or less was nothing to him, but the neglected little wound had become tainted with some impurity, blood-poisoning had set in, and my poor old friend had truly enough 'died of a canker-bush'.

The flowering season of 'Fortune's Yellow' is a very short one, but it comes so early, and the flowers have such incomparable beauty, and are so little like those of any other rose, that its value is quite without doubt. Some of the tea-roses approach it in its pink and copper colouring, but the loose, open, rather flaunting form of the flower, and the twisted set of the petals, display the colour better than is possible in any of the more regularly-shaped roses. It is a good plan to grow it through some other wall-shrub, as it soon gets bare below, and the early maturing flowering tips are glad to be a little sheltered by the near neighbourhood of other foliage.

[In *Roses for English Gardens* she further describes this rose:] The beautiful 'Fortune's Yellow' has been with us long enough to take its place among the older garden roses. It is . . . from China and tender, liking a hot wall; but I have observed that it also likes to be led through some other thin wall-shrub that will protect the leaves in May when the late frosts come; this seems to prevent the falling of the leaves in May which so often happens to the unprotected shoots. But it is a rose that cannot always be trusted to bloom well. We have to consider it a capricious flowerer. Sometimes it is loaded with its glorious loose copper-coloured bloom, and sometimes it is almost bare. We have to remember that it is from a climate very different from our own, and that we cannot expect to have it in such complete control as we may be fairly sure of assuming in the case of hardier roses; so that when it does do well we must be all the more thankful.

['Fortune's Double Yellow' is still deservedly popular where shelter and warmth is possible; it is now thought to be a relation of *R. gigantea*, a species discovered in Northeast India in 1882, and later elsewhere, and variable in form. It will grow to forty feet as opposed to 'Fortune's Yellow's' fifteen, and the flowers are creamy-white, four to five inches across.]

I do not think that there is any other rose that has just the same rich butter-colour as the yellow Banksian, and this unusual colouring is the more distinct because each little rose in the cluster is nearly evenly coloured all over, besides being in such dense bunches. The season of bloom is very short but the neat, polished foliage is always pleasant to see throughout the year. The white kind and the larger white are both lovely as to the individual bloom, but they flower so much more shyly that the yellow is much the better garden plant.

[The Banksian rose may be a hybrid of R. *laevigata* and in its cultivated form was brought from Canton as far back as 1803. Named after Sir Joseph Banks's wife, it comes in several forms and colours, single white, single creamy-yellow, strongly scented double-white and double-deeper yellow. Give it a high wall in full sun, and it will grow to thirty feet; regular pruning each year immediately after May-flowering will ensure future flower and vigorous healthy growth. A typical feature seems to be peeling bark.]

But the best of all climbing or rambling plants, whether for wall or arbour or pergola, is undoubtedly the grape-vine [cultivars of *Vitis vinifera*]. Even when trimly pruned and trained for fruit-bearing on an outer wall it is an admirable picture of leafage and fruit-cluster; but to have it in fullest beauty it must ramp at will, for it is only when the fast-growing branches are thrown out far and wide that it fairly displays its graceful vigour and the generous magnificence of its incomparable foliage.

The hardy Chasselas, known in England by the rather misleading name 'Royal Muscadine', is one of the best, both for fruit and foliage. The leaves are of moderate size, with clearly serrated edges and that strongly waved outline that gives the impression of powerful build, and is, in fact, a mechanical contrivance intended to stiffen the structure. The colour of the leaves is a fresh lively green and in autumn they are prettily marbled with yellow. Where a very large-leaved vine is wanted nothing is handsomer than the North American *Vitis labrusca* [the northern fox grape which has produced many varieties cultivated for their fruit] or the Asiatic *V. coignettii* [*V. coignetiae*], whose autumn leaves are gorgeously coloured. For a place that demands more delicate foliage there is the parsley vine [*V. vinifera* 'Apiifolia'] that has a delightful look of refinement, and another that should not be forgotten is the claret vine [*V. vinifera* 'Purpurea'], with autumnal colouring of almost scarlet and purple, and abundance of tightly clustered black fruit, nearly blue with a heavy bloom.

[Another very beautiful ornamental vine is *Vitis davidii*, with smaller leaves than *V. coignetiae* and a less pushing habit, colouring brilliant red in autumn; a useful alternative for a small garden.]

Many an old house and garden can show the far-rambling power of the beautiful *Wistaria chinensis* [now usually spelt *W. sinensis*], and of the large-leaved *Aristolochia sipho* [*A. macrophylla*], one of the best plants for covering a pergola, and of the varieties [species] of Ampelopsis, a near relation of the grape-vine. [The vigorous *A. aconitifolia* with deeply lobed and variable leaves grows luxuriantly. *A. brevidendunculata* looks more like a hoi with strongly outlined lobes, usually in threes. After a hot season it bears exceptionally attractive deep blue fruits.] The limits of these notes only admits of mention of some of the more important climbers; but among these the ever-delightful white jasmine must have a place. It will ramble far and fast if it has its own way, but then gives little flower; but by close winter pruning it can be kept full of bloom and leaf nearly to the ground. [*Jasminum officinale* has coloured leaf forms with gold and silver variegation both of which are much less vigorous than the type. The silver form is difficult to get but worth searching for as its delicate leaf-colouring is charming. (*See* THE PERGOLA for others, also *Gardeners' Testament*, p. 69.)]

The woods and hedges have also their beautiful climbing plants. Honeysuckle in suitable conditions will ramble to great heights – in this district most noticeable in tall hollies and junipers as well as in high hedges. [This is *Lonicera periclymenum*, old-fashioned woodbine; the cultivated forms *L. p.* 'Belgica' and the late-flowering *L. p.* 'Serotina' come in to their full beauty of flower in July and October.]

[Elsewhere Miss Jekyll describes] a large holly, laced through *Colour Schemes* and through with wild honeysuckle. The honeysuckle stems that run up into the tree look like great ropes, and a quantity of the small ends come showering out of the tree-top and over the path, like a tangled veil of small cordage.

The wild clematis [*C. vitalba*] is most frequent on the chalk, where it laces together whole hedges and rushes up trees, clothing them in July with long wreaths of delicate bloom, and *Colour Schemes* in September with still more conspicuous feathery seed . . . One of the many garden possessions that I ardently desire and can never have is a bit of rocky hillside; . . . there would be the place for the yellow winter jasmine [*J. nudiflorum*], for the honey-suckles both bushy and rambling, for the trailing clematises [described earlier] and for the native *C. vitalba*, beautiful both in flower and fruit; for shrubs like *Forsythia suspensa* and *Desmodium penduliflorum*, that like to root high and then throw down cascades of bloom.

Colour Schemes   [Elsewhere, referring to shallow steps, she writes:] During the last year or two some pretty incidents have occurred about these same steps; not important enough to call garden pictures, but charming and interesting and easily enjoyable because they are close to the open garden door of the sitting-room and because they teach me to look out for the desirable things that come of themselves. A seedling of the wild clematis (*C. vitalba*) appeared among the briars [*R. pimpinellifolia*] to the left. As it was too strong a plant to let grow over them unchecked, I pulled it forward toward the steps, training one or two shoots to run along the hollow of the steps and laying on them pieces of stone, invisible among the foliage to keep them from being dislodged by the skirts of visitors or the gambol of my cats.

At the same time, in a crack of the stone just below the upper step there came a seedling of the tall chimney campanula (*C. pyramidalis*). The second year this threw up its tall flower stem and ·was well in bloom when it was wrecked by an early autumn gale, the wind wrenching out the crown and upper root-stock. But a little shred of rooted life remained, and now there is again the sturdy tuft promising more flower-stems for the coming season. Close behind the bell-flower a spreading sheet of wild thyme has crept out of the turf and flowed rather widely over the stone. Luckily I just saved it from the tidying process that threatened it, and as it is now well-established over the stone I still have the pleasure of its bright rosy bloom when the duties of the mowing-machine rob me of the other tiny flowers – hawkweed, milkwort and bedstraw – that bloom so bravely in the intervals between its ruthless but indispensable ministrations.

[Returning to March]: For rapid growth perhaps no English plant outstrips the hop [*Humulus lupulus*], growing afresh from the root every year and almost equalling the vine in beauty of leaf. [The golden form is most effective grown in a shady town garden and easily trained on criss-crossed strings. It is startling on a stretch of pergola and will give thick shade to an arbour.] The two kinds of wild bryony [black bryony is *Tamus communis* and white is *Bryonia dioica*] are also herbaceous climbers of rapid growth, and among the most beautiful of our hedge plants.

The wild roses run up to great heights in hedge and thicket, and never look so well as when among the tangles of mixed growth of wild forest land or clambering through some old gnarled thorn-tree. The common brambles are also best seen in these forest groups; these again in form of leaf show somewhat of a vine-like beauty.

In the end of March, or at any time during the month when the wind is in the east or north-east, all increase and development of vegetation appear to cease. As things are, so they remain. Plants that are in flower retain their bloom, but, as it were, under protest. A kind of sullen dullness pervades all plant life. Sweet-scented shrubs do not give off their fragrance; even the wood-land moss and earth and dead leaves withhold their sweet, nutty scent. The surface of the earth has an arid infertile look; a slight haze of an ugly grey takes the colour out of objects in middle distance, and seems to rob the flowers of theirs, or to put them out of harmony with all things around. But a day comes, or, perhaps, a warmer night, when the wind, now breathing gently from the south-west, puts new life into all growing things. A marvellous change is wrought in a few hours. A little warm rain has fallen, and plants, invisible before, and doubtless still underground, spring into glad life.

What an innocent charm there is about many of the true spring flowers. Primroses of many colours are now in bloom, but the prettiest, this year, is a patch of an early blooming white one, grouped with a delicate lilac. Then comes *Omphalodes verna*, with its flowers of brilliant blue and foliage of brightest green, better described by its pretty north-country name, Blue-eyed

Mary. There are violets of many colours, but daintiest of all is the pale-blue St Helena; whether it is the effect of its delicate colouring, or whether it has really a better scent than other varieties of the common violet, I cannot say, but it always seems to have a more refined fragrance.

APRIL

'Even the better ways of gardening do not wholly escape the debasing influence of fashion. Wild gardening is a delightful, and in good hands a most desirable, pursuit, but no kind of gardening is so difficult to do well, or is so full of pitfalls and of paths of peril. Because it has in some measure become fashionable, and because it is understood to mean the planting of exotics in wild places, unthinking people rush to the conclusion that they can put any garden plants into any wild places, and that that is wild gardening. I have seen woody places that were already perfect with their own simple charm just muddled and spoilt by a reckless planting of garden refuse, and healthy hillsides already sufficiently and beautifully clothed with native vegetation made to look lamentably silly by the planting of a nurseryman's mixed lot of exotic conifers.' *Home and Garden,* p. 269

Woodland spring flowers — Daffodils in the copse — Grape hyacinths and other spring bulbs — How best to plant them — Flowering shrubs — [Other April-flowering shrubs] — Scents of April — Snowy mespilus — Marsh marigolds, and other spring flowers — Primrose garden — Pollen of Scotch fir — Opening seed-pods of fir and gorse — Auriculas — Tulips — Small shrubs for rock-garden — Daffodils as cut flowers — Lent hellebores — Primroses — Leaves of wild arums.

In EARLY APRIL there is quite a wealth of flower among plants that belong half to wood and half to garden. *Epimedium pinnatum* [*E. pinnatum colchicum*], with its delicate orchid-like spike of pale yellow bloom, flowers with its last year's leaves, but as soon as it is fully out the young leaves rush up, as if hastening to accompany the flowers.

[In order best to see the flowers it is worth cutting back the leaves in early March; there is a slight risk of frost damage to the new growth but an annual trim suits this epimedium. The evergreen *E. perralderianum* is larger and strong-growing making a handsome groundcover for problem dry-areas, and needing little attention. How many plants come into this category? The small and choice *E. × rubrum* has crimson flowers, white-spurred, with young leaves tinted reddish-pink each year; it is less vigorous but ideal for the front of borders in shade or sun.]

Dentaria pinnata, a woodland plant of Switzerland and Austria, is one of the handsomest of the white-flowered *cruciferae*, with well-filled heads of twelve to fifteen flowers, and palmate leaves of freshest green. Hard by, and the best possible plant to group with it, is the lovely Virginian cowslip (*Mertensia virginica*), the very embodiment of the freshness of early spring. The sheaf of young leafage comes almost black out of the ground, but as the leaves develop, their dull lurid colouring changes to a full pale green of a curious texture, quite smooth, and yet absolutely unreflecting. The dark colouring of the young leaves now only remains as a faint tracery of veining on the backs of the leaves and stalks, and at last dies quite away as the bloom expands.

The flower is of a rare and beautiful quality of colour hard to describe – a rainbow-flower of purple, indigo, full and pale blue, and daintiest lilac, full of infinite variety and indescribable charm. The flowers are in terminal clusters, richly filled; lesser clusters springing from the axils of the last few leaves and joining with the topmost one to form a gracefully drooping head. The lurid colouring of the young leaves is recalled in the flower stems and calix, and enhances the colour effect of the whole.

Colour Schemes [In a chapter on Colour Miss Jekyll suggests planting this mertensia, the Virginian cowslip, in the front of a spring border] with more double arabis . . . the lovely pale blue of *Myosotis dissitiflora* [the early forget-me-not] and *Mertensia virginica*, and, with sheets of the foam-like *Tiarella cordifolia*, the tender pink of *Dicentra eximia* and pink and rose-red tulips. At the back of this come scarlet tulips, the stately cream-white form of *Camassia leichtlinii* and a bold tuft of Solomon's Seal; then orange tulips, brown wallflowers, orange Crown Imperial [*Fritillaria imperialis*], and taller scarlet tulips of the *gesneriana* class.

[This passage shows the importance of detailed planning of colour associations for every season of the year. Returning to April:] The flower of the common dog-tooth violet [*Erythronium dens-canis*] is over, but the leaves have grown larger and handsomer. They look as if, originally of a purplish-red colour, some liquid had been dropped on them, making confluent pools of pale green, lightest at the centre of the drop. The noblest of the same family (*Erythronium giganteum*) is now in flower – a striking and beautiful wood plant, with turncap-shaped flowers of palest straw-colour, almost white, and large leaves, whose markings are not drop-like as in the more familiar kind, but are arranged in a regular sequence of bold splashings, reminding one of a maranta [*Maranta arundinacea* 'Variegata', a greenhouse herbaceous perennial].

[*Erythronium giganteum* is a confused name, and in the past was used to describe both *E. grandiflorum* and *E. oregonum*. To make matters worse *E. oregonum* is often confused with *E. revolutum*, which has pinkish flowers. Clearly Miss Jekyll means the pale yellow *E. oregonum*. *E. grandiflorum* is rarer and comparatively difficult in average gardens. The flowers, single or in pairs, rise on stems a foot or fifteen inches high; the throat is beautifully marked with flames of rich bay on a yellow ground, and the handsome group of golden-anthered stamens and silvery pistil make up a flower of singular beauty and refinement.

Later in an article she writes:] There are other of the spring bulbs that may be used in happy colour combinations, with some of the earliest shrubs and plants. Dog-tooth violets (*Erythronium dens-canis*) and *Corydalis solida*, the latter a favourite in old cottage gardens, are happy in combination. The corydalis, also known as *Fumaria bulbosa*, has solid little round yellowish tubers that go down a good depth. The flowers of both these plants are of colours nearly alike and that merge pleasantly one into the other; a low-toned purplish pink, very near that of *Daphne mezereum*, which, with *Rhododendron praecox*, may well stand in the background. The picture may be made more complete by the addition of some of the Lent hellebores that have the same kind of purple-pink colouring – hybrids of *H. colchicus*, *H. olympicus* and *H. orientalis*.

'Grouping of Hardy Bulbs' *The Garden*, 1913

There are other beautiful erythroniums that are best treated separately, such as the tall *E. giganteum* [*E. oregonum*] from California and Vancouver Island. This capital plant is at its happiest in the half-shade of thin woodland, where, when a wide patch is well established, it is a sight worth seeing in April. The pale yellow flowers, on stems a foot high, look like little turncap lilies; they are not only beautiful when seen in the mass, but they well repay close examination for the delicate pencillings and markings of the underpart of the flower. The leaves are also handsome, with a whitish marbling on a quiet green. It is with such variations of plants and colour that the floor of the wild garden is mostly suitably covered. It is not enough to say that in a wild garden anything looks well, even indiscriminate planting. Successful planning and grouping of varieties and colour forms will turn even a dull stretch of this woodland into a place of beauty.

[Returning to April:] That valuable Indian primrose, *P. denticulata*, is another fine plant for the cool edge or shady hollows of woodland in rather good deep soil.

But the glory of the copse just now consists in the great stretches of daffodils. Through the wood run shallow parallel hollows, the lowest part of each depression some nine paces apart. Local tradition says they are the remains of old pack-horse roads; they occur frequently in the forest-like heathery uplands of our poor-soiled sandy land, running, for the most part, three or four together, almost evenly side by side. The old people account for this by saying that when one track became too much worn another was taken by its side. Where these pass through the birch copse the daffodils have been planted in the shallow hollows of the old ways, in spaces of some three yards broad by thirty or forty yards long – one kind at a time. Two of such tracks, planted with *N. princeps* and *N. horsfieldii* are now waving rivers of bloom, in many lights and accidents of cloud and sunshine full of pictorial effect. The planting of daffodils in this part of the copse is much better than in any other portions where there are no guiding track-ways, and where they were planted in haphazard sprinklings. The grape hyacinths are now in full bloom. It is well to avoid the common one, *Muscari racemosum* [*M. neglectum*], at any rate in the light soils, where it becomes a troublesome weed. One of the best is *M. conicum* [still listed in the *R.H.S. Dictionary*, but now not often available]; this, with the upright-leaved *M. botryoides*, and its white variety, are the best for general use, but the Plume hyacinth [then *M. comosum* now *Leopoldia comosia*] which flowers later should have a place. *Ornithogalum nutans* is another of the bulbous plants that, although beautiful in flower, becomes so pestilent a weed that it is best excluded.

Where and when the early flowering bulbs had best be planted is a question of some difficulty. Perhaps the mixed border, where they are most usually put, is the worst place of all, for when in flower they only show as forlorn little patches of bloom rather

[Miss Jekyll recommends planting Sweet Cicely, veratrum, *Euphorbia wulfenii*, Solomon's Seal and bergenias in garden areas devoted to spring bulbs, where their important foliage gives a rich sense of permanence.]

'. . . the fern-like Sweet Cicely (*Myrrhis odorata*) with its wide umbels of creamy bloom.' ['Between plants for the spring border', *Gardening Illustrated*, 13 June 1925.]

[Miss Jekyll planted Solomon's Seal, *Polygonatum multiflorum*, under flowering trees and for foliage effect in borders of spring bulbs.] 'In the copse . . . are widely spreading patches of Solomon's Seal and tufts of the woodrush (*Luzula sylvatica*), showing by their happy vigour how well they like their places.' [*Wood and Garden*, Gertrude Jekyll, p. 61.]

[At Munstead Wood much of the garden was laid out before the house was built.]

'The only portion with a definite plan is a small paved court between two wings of the house [to the north] and a double flight of steps enclosing a tank, all forming one design . . . The stairways on each side of the tank are punctuated by eight balls of clipped box. The tank itself has a wealth of ferns growing out of its cool north face.' [*Gardens for Small Country Houses*, Jekyll and Weaver, p. 42.]

far apart, and when their leaves die down, leaving their places looking empty, the ruthless spade or trowel stabs into them when it is desired to fill the space with some other plant. Moreover, when the border is manured and partly dug in the autumn, it is difficult to avoid digging up the bulbs just when they are in full root growth. Probably the best plan is to devote a good space of cool bank to small bulbs and hardy ferns, planting the ferns in such groups as will leave good spaces for the bulbs; then as their leaves are going the fern fronds are developing and will cover the whole space. Another way is to have them among any groups of newly-planted small shrubs, to be left there for spring blooming until the shrubs have covered their allotted space.

Many flowering shrubs are in beauty. *Andromeda floribunda* [*Pieris floribunda*] still holds its persistent bloom, that had endured for nearly two months. The thick, drooping tassel-like bunches of bloom of *A. japonica* [*P. japonica*] are just going over. *Magnolia stellata,* a compact bush some five feet high and wide, is white with the multitude of its starry flowers; individually they look half-double, having fourteen to sixteen petals.

Forsythia suspensa, with its graceful habit and tender yellow flower, is a much better shrub than *F. viridissima,* though, strangely enough, that is the one most commonly planted. [Its great merit is in flowering a few weeks later than the finer *F. suspensa.*] Kerria [*K. japonica* 'Flore-Pleno'] with its bright yellow balls, the fine old rosy ribes [*R. sanguineum*], the Japan quinces [*Chaenomeles speciosa* forms] and their salmon-coloured relative *Pyrus mauleii* [*C. japonica*], *Spiraea thunbergii* with its neat habit and myriads of tiny flowers, these make frequent points of beauty and interest.

[The Bridal Wreath, *Spiraea × arguta,* also flowers in April and like *Osmanthus delavayi* (1890) and the hybrid *O. × burkwoodii* thrives in any soil. I would have expected Miss Jekyll to have treasured the primrose-flowered *Corylopsis pauciflora,* introduced by Messrs Veitch in 1874, but it may not have been available by 1899. It prefers an acid or neutral soil, but the larger and later flowering

[The building of Munstead Wood embodied the perfect understanding which existed between Miss Jekyll and her architect, Edwin Lutyens. This quiet and modest approach to the porch expresses their joint attitude to the house in the wood.]

'The path runs to an arch in the eastern wall of the house, leading into a kind of long porch . . . Anyone entering looks through to the garden picture of lawn and trees and low, broad steps, and dwarf dry wall crowned with the hedge of Scotch briers.' [*Home and Garden*, Gertrude Jekyll, p. 7.]

[*Asplenium trichomanes*, the little spleenwort, grows happily in lime mortar joints in shade or sun.]

'It would be well worth having a bit of cool wall for British plants and ferns alone; its beauty would scarcely be less than that of a wall planted with exotics.' [*Wall and Water Gardens*, Gertrude Jekyll, p. 38.]

C. glabrescens (1905) and *C. spicata* (1863) are not so particular. All are best in semi-woodland with their flower-buds protected from early morning sun. The hybrid *Mahonia* × 'Undulata' flowers in April too, most freely, and is a vigorous bush, happy in shade and poor soil.]

In the rock-garden, *Cardamine trifoliata* [*C. trifolia*; the taller *Dentaria pinnata* is closely related to the cardamine] and *Hutchinsia alpina* are conspicuous from their pure white flowers and neat habit– both have leaves of darkest green, as if the better to show off the bloom. *Ranunculus montanus* fringes the cool base of a large stone; its whole height not over three inches, though its bright yellow flowers are larger than field buttercups. [Usually available today in its garden cultivar, the brightly coloured 'Molten Gold'.] The surface of the petals is curiously brilliant, glistening and flashing like glass. *Corydalis capnoides* is a charming rock-plant, with flowers of palest sulphur colour, one of the neatest and most graceful of its family.

[I think *C. capnoides* must be *C. marshalliana*, which according to Ingwersen may be a sub-species of the more common *C. bulbosa*, with short-stemmed purple flowers. In *Home and Garden* Miss Jekyll suggests growing this little sulphur-flowered corydalis in the wall-joints of a shady part of a garden almost entirely given over to wallflowers of blood-red, yellow, buff-yellow and ivory-white shades. She has arranged the plants in informal drifts, using small spreading Alpine wallflowers at eye-level in wall and bank. She describes *C. capnoides* as] 'most delicate and lovely of the fumitories'.

Border plants are pushing up vigorous green growth; finest of all are the veratrums, with their bold, deeply-plaited leaves of brilliant green. [*Veratrum nigrum* and *V. album*, both admirable plants for early foliage, the former with strange maroon-black flowers.] Delphiniums and Oriental poppies [*see* p. 226 for Gertrude Jekyll's treatment of their untidy habits] have also made strong foliage, and day-lilies are conspicuous from their fresh masses of pale greenery. Flag iris [*I. pseudocorus*] have their leaves three parts grown, and paeonies are a foot or more high,

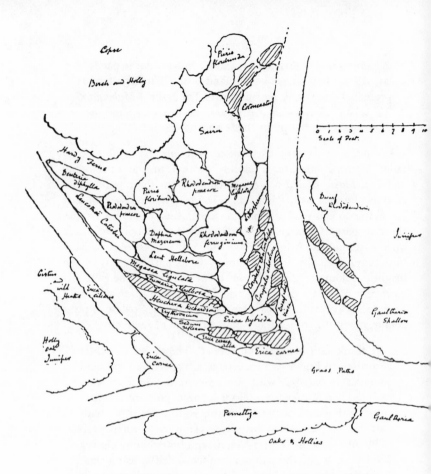

MUNSTEAD WOOD BORDER (Portion)
from *Wood and Garden*.
As described on p. 110.

in all varieties of rich red colouring. It is a good plan, when they
are in beds or large groups, to plant the dark-flowered wallflowers among them, their colour making a rich harmony with
the reds of the young paeony growths. [*See* MAY, p. 122, for
details of paeonies.]

There are balmy days in mid-April, when the whole garden
is fragrant with sweetbriar [*R. rubiginosa*]. It is not 'fast of its
smell' as Bacon says of the damask rose, but gives it so lavishly

that one cannot pass near a plant without being aware of its gracious presence. Passing upward through the copse, the warm air draws a fragrance almost as sweet, but infinitely more subtle, from the fresh green of the young birches; it is like a distant whiff of lily-of-the-valley. Higher still the young leafage of the larches gives a delightful perfume of the same kind. It seems as if it were the office of these mountain trees already nearest the high heaven, to offer an incense of praise for their new life.

Few plants will grow under Scotch fir [*Pinus sylvestris*] but a notable exception is the whortleberry [*Vaccinium myrtillus*] now a sheet of brilliant green, and full of its arbutus-like, pink-tinged flower. This plant also has a pleasant scent in the mass, difficult to localize, but coming in whiffs as it will.

The snowy mespilus (amelanchier) shows like puffs of smoke among the firs and birches, full of its milk-white cherry-like bloom – a true woodland shrub or small tree. It loves to grow in a thicket of other trees, and to fling its graceful sprays about through their branches. It is a doubtful native, but naturalized and plentiful in the neighbouring woods. As seen in gardens, it is usually a neat little tree of shapely form, but it is more beautiful when growing at its own will in the high woods.

[This is probably *Amelanchier lamarckii*, a large shrub or small tree naturalized in northern Europe and in the past frequently wrongly named as *A. canadensis* or *A. laevis*. These two are also confused, the latter being correctly distinguished by the delicate pink young foliage. All species of amelanchier prefer acid moist soil but those from western North America as opposed to those from the east coast are more lime tolerant. For soils containing lime or chalk there are many prunus species (including the Japanese cherries of hybrid origin). For woodland, the wild cherry, *Prunus avium*, with its white cup-shaped flowers in April, is among the most attractive of our native trees. For the garden, forms of *P. subhirtella* (including those which flower in winter) are delightful, with pink-white blossom, and less exotic and less heavy in flower than the highly developed hybrids.]

Marshy hollows in the valleys are brilliant with marsh mari-gold (*Caltha palustris*), damp meadows have them in plenty, but they are largest and handsomest in the alder swamps of our valley bottoms, where their great luscious clumps rise out of pools of black mud and water.

Adonis vernalis is one of the brightest flowers of the middle of April, the flowers looking large for the size of the plant. The bright yellow, mostly eight-petalled blooms are comfortably seated in dense fennel-like masses of foliage. It makes strong tufts, that are the better for division every four years. The spring bittervetch (*Orobus vernus* – [*Lathyrus vernus*]) blooms at the same time, a remarkably clean-looking plant, with its cheer-ful red and purple blossom and handsomely divided leaves. It is one of the toughest of plants to divide, the mass of black root is like so much wire. It is a good plan with plants that have such roots, when dividing time comes, to take the clumps to a strong bench or block and cut them through at the crown with a sharp cold-chisel and hammer. [*L. albo-roseus*, which may simply be a form of *L. vernus*, has bi-coloured flowers of white and pink. They all need damp soils in full sun.] Another of the showiest families of plants of the time is doronicum. *D. austriacum* is the earliest, but it is closely followed by the fine *D. plantagineum*. [The latter is rather taller and its forms 'Excel-sum' or 'Harpur Crewe' carry three or four large yellow daisy-flowers on each stem.] The large form of wood forget-me-not (*Myosotis sylvatica major*) is in sheets of bloom, opening pink and changing to a perfect blue.

[For flowerbeds and under deciduous shrubs, the large heart-shaped-leaved *Brunnera macrophylla* (which would in Miss Jekyll's day have been named *Anchusa myosotidi-flora*) is perhaps a more useful plant, keeping its foliage in greater repair throughout the summer. Various attractive cultivars now exist, but with variegated and spotted leaves; among these is 'Hadspen Cream' which keeps its leaf variegation and does not 'burn' like the better known 'Variegata'. The flowers are vivid blue lasting longer than those of most ordinary forget-me-nots.]

This is a great improvement on the older smaller one. Grouped with it, as an informal border, and in patches running through and among its clumps, is the foam-flower (*Tiarella cordifolia*), whose flower in the mass looks like the wreaths of foam tossed aside by a mountain torrent. By the end of the month the satin-leaf (*Heuchera richardsonii* [*H. americana*]) is pushing up its richly-coloured leaves, of a strong bronze-red, gradating to bronze-green at the outer edge. The beauty of the plant is in the colour and texture of the foliage. To encourage full leaf growth the flower stems should be pinched out, and as they push up rather persistently, they should be looked over every few days for about a fortnight.

The primrose garden is now in beauty, but I have so much to say about it that I have given it a chapter on its own [*see* pp. 267–8].

The Scotch firs are shedding their pollen; a flowering branch shaken or struck with a stick throws out a pale-yellow cloud. Heavy rain will wash it out, so that after a storm the sides of the roads and paths look as if sulphur had been washed up in drifts. The sun has gained great power, and on still bright days sharp *snicking* sounds are to be heard from the firs. The dry cones of last year are opening, and the flattened seeds with their paper-like edges are fluttering down. Another sound, much like it but just a shade sharper and more *staccato*, is heard from the gorse [*Ulex europaeus*] bushes, whose dry pods are flying open, and letting fall the hard, polished little bean-like seeds.

Border auriculas are making a brave show. Nothing in the flower year is more interesting than a bed of good seedlings of the alpine class. I know nothing better for pure beauty of varied colouring among early flowers. Except in varieties of Salpi-glossis, such rich gradation of colour, from pale lilac to rich purple, and from rosy pink to deepest crimson, is hardly to be found in any one family of plants. There are varieties of cloud-ings of smoky-grey, sometimes approaching black, invading, and at the same time enhancing, the purer colours, and numbers of shades of half-tones of red and purple, such as are comprised within the term 'murrey' of heraldry, and tender blooms of one colour, sulphurs and milk-white – all with the admirable texture and excellent perfume that belong to the 'Bear's-ears' of old English gardens. For practical purposes the florist's definition of a good auricula is of little value; that is for the show-table, and, as Bacon says, 'Nothing to the true pleasure of a garden.' The qualities to look for in the bed of seedlings are not the narrowing ones of proportion of eye to tube, of exact circle in the circumference of the individual pip, and so on, but to notice whether the plant has a handsome look and stands up well, and is a delightful and beautiful thing as a whole.

Tulips are the great garden flowers in the last week of April and earliest days of May. In this plant also the rule of the show-table is no sure guide to garden value; for the show tulip, beautiful though it is, is of one class alone – namely, the best of the 'Broken' varieties of the self-coloured seedlings called 'breeders'. These seedlings, after some years of cultivation, change or 'break' into a variation in which the original colouring is only retained in certain flames or feathers of colour, on a ground of either white or yellow. If the flames in each petal are symmetrical and well-arranged, according to the rules laid down by the florist, it is a good flower; it receives a name and commands a certain price. If, on the other hand, the markings are irregular, however beautiful the colouring, the flower is comparatively worthless, and is 'thrown into mixture'. The kinds that are the grandest in gardens are ignored by the florist. One of the best for graceful and delicate beauty is *T. retroflexa*, of a soft lemon-yellow colour, and twisted and curled petals; then Silver Crown, a white flower with a delicate picotee-like thread of scarlet along the edge of the sharply pointed and reflexed petals. A variety of this called Sulphur Crown is only a little less beautiful. Then there is Golden Crown, also with pointed petals and occasional threadings of scarlet. [*T. retroflexa*, probably a cross between *acuminata* and *gesneriana* (*see* below), stems to two feet with recurved flowers, and is easy to grow.] Nothing is more gorgeous than the noble *gesneriana major*, with its great chalice of crimson-scarlet and pools of blue in the inner base of each petal. [The Darwin tulips are self-coloured forms of the species *gesneriana*.] The gorgeously flamed Parrot tulips are indispensable, and the large double 'Yellow Rose' and the early double 'White La Candeur'.

[It is not absolutely certain whether the original garden tulip was developed from one species or from hybridization from more than one. The original May-flowering tulips, called 'breeders' as Miss Jekyll says, though attractive are not now much grown. To avoid confusion, the hybridized tulips have been divided into classes and the following give some idea of those best for average gardening practice: Single Early, Double Early, Cottage, including Lily-flowered, Darwin, Parrot and Late Doubles. Crosses have been made between these groups to get other types and you need to be an expert to understand it all.

Among the species which are mostly early spring flowering there are few which tolerate shade, as most come from areas where there are hot dry summers. The native *T. sylvestris* has grey leaves and carries scented yellow flowers on fifteen-inch stems in April. It is a feature here at Tintinhull, thriving happily among deciduous shrubs. Good drainage and summer baking are essential for the small species such as *T. tarda*, *T. kaufmanniana* and *T. greigii*, the latter with leaves veined bronze and bright scarlet flowers. *T. fosteriana* is taller to eighteen inches, also scarlet-red above grey leaves. The very desirable *T. clusiana*, with white flushed red flowers, and *T. saxatilis*, with pinkish flowers, both need a place at the base of a hot wall (the same sort of site as chosen for *Iris unguicularis*).]

The best thing now in the rock-garden is a patch of some twenty plants of *Arnebia echineides* [now correctly *A. echioides longiflorum*], always happy in our dry soil. It is of the borage family, a native of Armenia. It flowers in single- or double-branching spikes of closely-set flowers of a fine yellow. Just below each indentation of the five-lobed corolla is a spot which looks black by contrast, but is of a very dark, rich, velvety brown. The day after the flower had expanded the spot had faded to a moderate brown, the next day to a faint tinge, and on the fourth day it was gone. The legend, accounting for the spots, says that Mahomet touched the flower with the tips of his fingers, hence its English name of Prophet-flower.

[Though introduced long ago, this little plant, growing to eighteen inches, is still rarely seen. Elsewhere Miss Jekyll recommends it for a dry stone wall, where digging its roots deeply down into earth it gets adequate moisture with excellent drainage. Both it and the small, to six inches, *Hacquetia epipactis*, from the European Alps, like a cool partly shaded site. The latter flowers with its golden heads set above a frill of glossy tri-foliate leaves. E. A. Bowles describes it as having 'a very bright and cheerful appearance in these nippy, cold days, when its glossy green leaves and yellow heads take the place of the winter aconites, but it increases slowly, and so is never seen in profusion'.]

The upper parts of the rock-garden that are beyond hand-reach are planted with dwarf shrubs, many of them sweetly scented either as to leaf or flower – Gaultherias, Sweet gale [*Myrica gale*], Alpine rhododendron [*R. ferrugineum*], skimmias, pernettyas, ledums and hardy daphnes. *Daphne pontica* now gives off delicious wafts of fragrance, intensely sweet in the evening.

In March and April daffodils are the great flowers for house decoration, coming directly after the Lent hellebores. Many people think these beautiful late-flowering hellebores useless for cutting because they live badly in water. But if properly prepared they live quite well, and will remain ten days in beauty. Directly they are cut, and immediately before putting in water, their stalks should be slit up three or four inches, or according to their length, and then put in deep, so that the water comes nearly up to the flowers; and so they should remain, in a cool place, for some hours, or for a whole night, after which they can be arranged for the room. Most of them are inclined to droop; it is the habit of the plant in growth; this may be corrected by arranging them with something stiff like box or berberis.

Anemone fulgens is a grand cutting flower, and looks well with its own leaves only or with flowering twigs of laurustinus. Then there are the pansies, delightful things in a room, but they should be cut in whole branches of leafy stem and flower and bud. At first the growths are short and only suit dish-shaped things but as the season goes on they grow longer and bolder, and graduate first into bowls and then into upright glasses. I think pansies are always best without mixture of other flowers, and in separate colours, or only in such varied tints as make harmonies of one class of colour at a time.

The big yellow and white bunch primroses are delightful room flowers, beautiful, and of sweetest scent. When full-grown the flower-stalks are ten inches long and more. Among the seedlings there are always a certain number that are worthless. These are pounced upon as soon as they show their bloom, and cut up for greenery to go with the cut flowers, leaving the root stock with all its middle foliage, and cutting away the roots and any rough outside leaves. When the first daffodils are out and suitable greenery is not abundant in the garden (for it does not do to cut their own blades) I bring home handfuls of the wild arum leaves so common in roadside hedges, grasping the whole plant close to the ground; then a steady pull breaks it away from the tuber, and you have a fine long-stalked sheaf of leafage held together by its own underground stem. This should be prepared like the Lent hellebores, by putting it deep in water for a time. I always think the trumpet daffodils look better with this than any other kind of foliage. When the wild arum is full grown the leaves are so large and handsome that they do quite well to accompany the white arum lilies from the greenhouse.

[The Italian version of our native arum, *Arum italicum* 'Pictum', has white marbling on the green leaves and is useful in the winter garden as well as for picking. Today, of course, the hardy Crowborough cultivar of the arum, *Zantedeschia aethiopica* 'Crowborough', flowers rather later and in the flower-bed; it is equally beautiful for cutting for house decoration and lovely with branches of the glossy green-leaved shrub *Choisya ternata*. The latter normally flowering in May (and repeating less freely in September) will have finished flowering before the hardy arums come into full beauty.]

MAY

'Anyone who wishes to see silvery-green satin of the highest quality should look at the back of the leaves of *Alchemilla alpina*. Indeed the whole plant, though anything but showy, is full of what one may call interesting incident. I remember finding this out one hot afternoon, when after a hard morning's work I sat down, a good bit tired, on the lowest of the steps leading into the little rock-garden. Just under my hand was a tuft of this lady's mantle, and half-lazily, and yet with a faint prick of the moral spur that urges me against complete idleness, I picked a leaf to have a good look at it, and then found how much, besides the well-known beauty of its satin back, there was to admire in it. The satin lining, as is plain to see, comes up and over the front edge of the leaf with a brightness that looks like polished silver against the dull green surface. The edge of each of the seven leaflets is plain for two-thirds of its length, and then breaks into saw teeth, which increase in size, always silver-edged, till they reach the end and nearly meet . . . The heads of small green flowers, set on lesser stalks that leave the main stem by springing out of a frilled collar half leaf half bract, are not exactly beautiful, but have a curious squareness of plan, still further accentuated by the four stamens also squarely planted at the inner angles of the petals.'

Home and Garden, p. 104

Cowslips — Morells — Woodruff — Felling oak timber —
Trillium and other wood-plants — Lily-of-the-valley
naturalized — Rock-wall flowers — Two good wall shrubs
— Queen wasps — Rhododendrons — Arrangement for
colour — Separate colour-groups — Difficulty of choosing
— Hardy azaleas — Grouping flowers that bloom together
— Guelder-rose as climber — The garden-wall door —
[Terracing — Dry walls] — The paeony garden — Moutans
— Paeony varieties — Species desirable for garden.

WHILE MAY IS still young, cowslips [*Primula veris*] are in beauty
on the chalk lands a few miles distant, but yet within pleasant
reach. They are finest of all in orchards, where the grass grows
tall and strong under the half-shade of the old apple trees, some
of the later kinds being loaded with bloom. The blooming of the
cowslip is the signal for a search for the morell, one of the very
best of the edible fungi. It grows in open woods or where the
under-growth has not yet grown high, and frequently in old
parks and pastures near or under elms. It is quite unlike any
other fungus: shaped like a tall egg, with the pointed end upwards, on a short hollow stalk, and looking something like a
sponge. It has a delicate flavour, and is perfectly wholesome.

The pretty little woodruff [*Asperula odorata*] is in flower;
what scent is so delicate as that of its leaves? They are almost
sweeter when dried, each little whorl by itself, with the stalk
cut closely away above and below. It is a pleasant surprise to
come upon these fragrant little stars between the leaves of a
book. The whole plant revives memories of rambles in Bavarian
wood-lands, and of Maitrank, that best of the 'cup' tribe of
pleasant drinks, whose flavour is borrowed from its flowering
tips.

In the first week of May oak-timber is being felled. The wood

is handsomer, from showing the grain better, when it is felled
in the winter, but it is delayed till now because of the value of
the bark for tanning, and just now the fast-rising sap makes the
bark strip easily. A heavy fall is taking place in the fringes of a
large wood of old Scotch fir.

[By the end of the nineteenth century the value of best
oak bark was about £7 a ton, reduced to about half its
former value by the introduction of foreign bark and other
substances adapted for tanning leather. Oak was the bark
most esteemed by the tanner (birch was used as well) and
its removal and processing was quite a skilled and complicated trade, just nicely balanced to be profitable depending
on local labour and costs. However, oak and other woods
were also grown for 'coppice', harvested and allowed to
re-grow every twenty-five years or so. The best and thickest
pieces of oak-wood, at the root end, were used for the manu-
facture of wheel-spokes and as firewood for smoking fish,
making charcoal etc. and worth about 15 shillings [75p] a
ton. The yield every cutting was probably £20 or £30 an
acre after all expenses. Today oak is of no value as coppice
and bark is no longer used for tanning in this country.]

Where the oaks grow there is a blue carpet of wild hyacinth
[bluebell – Endymion non-scriptus]; the pathway is a slightly
hollowed lane so that the whole sheet of flowers right and left is
nearly on a level with the eye, and looks like solid pools of blue.
The oaks not yet felled are putting forth their leaves of golden
bronze. The song of the nightingale and the ring of the woodman's axe gain a rich musical quality from the great fir wood.
Why I do not know; but so it is. Any sound that occurs within
it is, on a lesser scale, like a sound in a cathedral. The tree itself
when struck gives a musical note. Strike an oak or an elm on the
trunk with a stick, and the sound is mute; strike a Scotch fir, and
it is a note of music.

In the copse are some prosperous patches of the beautiful
North American wood-lily (Trillium grandiflorum). It likes a bed
of deep leaf-soil on levels or cool slopes in woodland, where its
large white flowers and whorls of handsome leaves look quite
at home. Beyond it are widely spreading patches of Solomon's

106

Seal [*Polygonatum × hybridum*] and tufts of the wood-rush (*Luzula sylvatica*) showing by their happy vigour how well they like their places, while the natural woodland carpet of moss and dead leaves puts the whole together. Higher in the copse the path runs through stretches of the pretty little *Smilacina bifolia* [*Maianthemum bifolium*, an acid-loving relation of the lily-of-the-valley; rich green leaves with six-inch cream-white flower spikes], and the ground beyond this is a thick bed of whortleberry [*Vaccinium myrtillus*], filling all the upper part of the copse under oak and birch and Scotch fir. The little flowers of the whortleberry have already given place to the just-formed fruit, which will ripen in July, and be a fine feast for the blackbirds. Other parts of the copse, where there was no heath or whortleberry, were planted thinly with the large lily-of-the-valley. [*Convallaria majalis*; Miss Jekyll is probably referring to Fortin's form which is larger than the type and more robust (Robinson's 8th edition of *The English Flower Garden*, 1900). There are several modern forms but one with pretty striped leaves and single white flowers has been in cultivation since 1835; it is normally considered more choosy than the type and prefers a sunny situation.]

[In recommending plants for the front of borders she writes:] Lily-of-the-valley must not be forgotten, for though we grow it in greater quantity in reserve ground for cutting and in woodland, yet its beautiful foliage and sweetest of sweet bloom must be near the front edge of this border also. [Here she is discussing the north border where many plants do better than in any sunny aspect:] for many of them come to us from woodland places and the cooler sides of mountain ranges. Solomon's Seal is so well known that no description is needed, but where there is a north border, there it will be best in place. Much like it in its general way of growth, and botanically closely allied is *Smilacina racemosa*, a North American plant, but in this, the flowers are in close racemes, not in drooping axillary clusters. It is interesting too in autumn, when the weight of the fruit, like little berries curiously veined and marbled, bends the stem over and makes it sway and swing heavily when moved by wind. The little plant that is commonly called *S. bifolia*, but more correctly *Maianthemum convallaria* [*see* above, *M. bifolium*] is another

'The North Border', *Gardeners' Testament*, p. 99

near relation and one of the loveliest plants for the rock edge of the north border.

[Returning to May and the lily-of-the-valley:] It has spread and increased and become broad sheets of leaf and bloom, from which thousands of flowers can be gathered without making gaps, or showing that any have been removed; when the bloom is over the leaves still stand in handsome masses till they are hidden by the fast-growing bracken. They do not hurt each other, as it seems likely that the lily-of-the-valley, having the roots running just under ground, while the fern-roots are much deeper, the two occupy their respective strata in perfect good fellowship. The neat little smilacina (maianthemum) is a near relation of the lily-of-the-valley; its leaves are of an even more vivid green and its little modest spikes of white flower are charming. It loves the poor sandy soil and increases in it fast, but will have nothing to say to clay. A very delicate and beautiful North American fern (*Dicksonia punctilobulata*) proves a good colonist in the copse. [Now known as *Dennstaedtia punctilobula*, this fern bears no resemblance to true Tree Ferns. Graham Thomas points out that it is often confused with the New Zealand dwarf bracken *Hypolepsis millifolia* which has darker green leaves and is too invasive for most gardens.] It spreads rapidly by creeping roots, and looks much like our native thelypteris, but is of a paler green colour.

> [*T. limbosperma*, the mountain fern, thrives in dry woods, while *T. palustris*, the marsh fern, is useful in damper situations. All these ferns need acid conditions, but some of the most beautiful such as the varieties of *Polystichum setiferum*, the prickly shield-fern, are tolerant of almost any soil.]

In the rock-garden the brightest patches of bloom are shown by the tufts of dwarf wallflowers; of these, *Cheiranthus alpinus* has a strong lemon colour that is of great brilliancy in the mass, and *C. marshalli* is of a dark orange colour, equally powerful. The curiously-tinted *C. mutabilis*, as its name implies, changes from a light mahogany colour when just open, first to crimson then to purple. In length of life *C. alpinus* and *C. marshalli* are rather more than biennials, and yet too short-lived to be called true perennials; cuttings of one year flower the next, and are handsome tufts the year after, but are scarcely worth keeping longer. *C. mutabilis* is longer lived, especially if the older growths are cut right away, when the tuft will generally spring into vigorous new life.

[Usually now classified as erysimums rather than cheiranthus, *Erysimum alpinum* is most often seen as its hybrid 'Moonlight' with paler softer yellow flowers. 'Pamela Pershouse' with deeper coloured bloom is nearer to the old orange hybrid *E. marshalli*. In *My Garden in Spring* (1914) E. A. Bowles suggests that *Cheiranthus mutabilis*, with its changing shades of brown, crimson and purple, is in truth a form of *C. alpinus* and not a separate species.]

Orobus aurantiacus [*Lathyrus aureus*] is a beautiful plant not enough grown, one of the handsomest of the pea family, with flowers of a fine orange colour, and foliage of a healthy-looking golden green.

[This is still true today, neither it nor the forms of *L. vernus* are enough seen; they are tough perennials for full sun and not fussy about soil. Perhaps they do not survive in all gardens as after their spring flowering the leaves and stems rapidly wither and the plant virtually disappears until the following spring. The careless and often hurried gardener overlooks them in making new planting schemes.]

A striking and handsome plant in the upper part of the rockery is *Othonna cheirifolia* [*Othonnopsis cheirifolia*]; its aspect is unusual and interesting, with its bunches of thick blunt-edged leaves of blue-grey colouring, and large yellow daisy flowers.

There is a pretty group of the large white thrift [probably *Armeria maritima* 'Alba' or *A. plantaginea leucantha* 'Alba'. William Robinson describes the latter, then *A. cephalotes* in his earliest edition. *A. plantaginea* grows to eighteen inches with strong evergreen leaves, and there are several good modern colour forms], and near it a spreading carpet of blue veronica [almost certainly *V. prostrata*, then *V. rupestris*, a very easy and showy plant with many named clones, today giving a wide choice of flower-colour from pale to dark blue] and some of the splendid gentian-blue *Phacelia campanularia*, a valuable annual for filling any bare patches of rockery where its brilliant colouring will suit the neighbouring plants, or best of all, in patches among dwarf ferns, where its vivid blue would be seen to great advantage. [Instead of this pretty annual, the] 'glorious *Gentiana acaulis* [might be grown. In general these small gentians are difficult, and seldom] seen at their best in English gardens, but *G. acaulis* is a much more willing colonist, and in some gardens where the soil is rich loam it grows rapidly and flowers abundantly and proves one of the best of plants for a garden edging. Though properly a plant of the pastures . . . it takes kindly to the rock-garden in England.'

Wall and Water

Two wall-shrubs have been conspicuously beautiful during May; the Mexican Orange flower (*Choisya ternata*) has been smothered in its white bloom, so closely resembling orange-blossom. With a slight winter protection of fir boughs it seems quite at home in our hot dry soil, grows fast, and is very easy to propagate by layers. When cut, it lasts for more than a week in water. [Cuttings made of the half-ripened wood will root quite quickly if placed in a rooting medium with gentle heat, and the harder wood can be easily rooted in a cold frame in winter.] *Piptanthus nepalensis* [*P. laburnifolius*] has also made a handsome show, with its abundant yellow pea-shaped bloom and deep-green trefoil leaves. The dark green stems have a slight bloom on a half-polished surface, and a pale ring at each joint gives them somewhat the look of bamboos. [This shrub is easily grown from seed, which is very freely produced in late summer.]

Now is the time to look out for the big queen wasps and to destroy as many as possible. They seem to be specially fond of the flowers of two plants, the large perennial cornflower (*Centaurea montana*) and the common cotoneaster. I have often secured a dozen in a few minutes on one or other of these plants, first knocking them down with a battledore.

Now, in the third week of May, rhododendrons are in full bloom on the edge of the copse. The plantation was made about nine years ago, in one of the regions where lawn and garden were to join the wood. During the previous blooming season the best nurseries were visited and careful observations made of colouring, habit and time of blooming. The space they were to fill demanded about seventy bushes, allowing an average of eight feet from plant to plant – not seventy different kinds, but perhaps ten of one kind, and two or three fives, and some threes, and a few single plants, always bearing in mind the ultimate intention of pictorial aspect as a whole. In choosing the plants and in arranging and disposing the groups these ideas were kept in mind: to make pleasant ways from lawn to copse; to group only in beautiful colour harmonies; to choose varieties beautiful in themselves; to plant thoroughly well, and to avoid overcrowding. Plantations of these grand shrubs are generally spoilt or ineffective, if not absolutely jarring, for want of attention to these simple rules.

The choice of kinds is now so large, and the variety of colouring so extensive, that nothing can be easier than to make beautiful combinations, if intending planters will only take the small amount of preliminary trouble that is needful. Some of the clumps are of brilliant scarlet-crimson, rose and white, but out of the great choice of colours that might be so named only those are chosen that make just the colour-harmony that was intended. A large group, quite detached from this one, and more in the shade of the copse, is of the best of the lilacs, purples and whites. When some clumps of young hollies have grown, those two groups will not be seen at the same time, except from a distance. The purple and white group is at present rather the handsomest, from the free-growing habit of the fine old kind *Album elegans*, which forms towering masses at the back. A detail of pictorial effect that was aimed at, and that has come out well, was devised in the expectation that the purple groups would look richer in the shade, and the crimson ones in the sun. This arrangement has answered admirably.

Before planting, the ground, of the poorest quality possible, was deeply trenched, and the rhododendrons were planted in wide holes filled with peat, and finished with a comfortable 'mulch', or surface-covering of farmyard manure. From this a supply of grateful nutriment was gradually washed in to the roots. This beneficial surface-dressing was renewed every year for two years after planting, and even longer in the case of the slower growing kinds. No plant better repays care during its early years. Broad grass paths leading from the lawn at several points pass among the clumps, and are continued through the upper parts of the copse, passing through zones of different trees . . .

It may be useful to describe a little more in detail the plan I followed in grouping rhododendrons, for I feel sure that anyone with a feeling for harmonious colouring, having once seen or tried some such plan, will never again approve of the haphazard mixtures. There may be better varieties representing the colourings aimed at in the several groups, but those named are ones that I know, and they will serve as well as any others to show what is meant.

[As Miss Jekyll says herself, there are always alternative plants for the different colour groups, and this is of more consequence today when the range of choice is even wider. Her basic colour sense and arrangement may still guide us to effect wise groupings.]

The colourings seem to group themselves into six classes of easy harmonies, which I venture to describe thus:

1. Crimsons inclining to scarlet or blood-colour grouped with dark claret colour and true pink. In this group I have planted 'Nigrescens', dark claret colour; 'John Waterer' and 'James Marshall Brook', both fine red crimsons; 'Alexander Adie' and 'Atrosanguineum', good crimsons, inclining to blood-colour; 'Alarm', rosy-scarlet; and 'Bianchi', pure pink. [Of these only 'John Waterer' and 'James Marshall Brook' are available today.]

2. Light scarlet rose colours inclining to salmon, a most desirable range of colour, but of which the only ones I know well are 'Mrs R. S. Holford' [still available], and a much older kind, 'Lady Eleanor Cathcart' [also available]. These I put by themselves, only allowing rather near them the good pink 'Bianchi'.

3. Rose colours inclining to amaranth.

4. Amaranths or magenta-crimsons.

5. Crimson or amaranth-purples.

6. Cool clear purples of the typical *ponticum* class, both dark and light, grouped with lilac-whites, such as 'Album Elegans'

[available] and 'Album Grandiflorum' [not available]. The beautiful 'Everestianum' comes into this group, but nothing redder among purples. 'Fastuosum Flore-Pleno' is also admitted, and 'Luciferum' and 'Reine Hortense', both good lilac-whites. But the purples that are most effective are merely *ponticum* seedlings, chosen when in bloom in the nursery for their depth and richness of cool purple colour.

[In fact Miss Jekyll herself only planted from Groups 1, 2 and 6, although she admitted that it would have been possible to plant splendidly, particularly by choosing those with fine white trusses. Most of these rhododendrons are described in the 1976 edition of Bean but the importance lies with the choice of colour associations rather than with the named cultivars. As in her flower-beds, Miss Jekyll used massed colours to build up a landscape picture, weaving and blending appropriate shades of reds and purples to create a desired effect.]

[Omitting further descriptions of individual rhododendrons I return to her vivid account of the flowering of hardy azaleas:] The last days of May see hardy azaleas in beauty. Any of them may be planted in company, for all their colours harmonize. [Beware today of this generalization; many of the modern Knap Hill hybrids and the dwarf evergreen Kurumes from Japan must be very carefully chosen. There seem to be many woodland glades made hideous by sparkling mixtures of harsh colours, when care and discrimination could have meant harmonious associations. Of course Miss Jekyll refers mainly to the more restrained Ghent azaleas and the old hardy *Azalea pontica* with its scented yellow flowers. All azaleas are now classified as rhododendrons; her description of grouping for colour can be used as a planting guide.]

In this garden, where care is taken to group plants well for colour, the whites are planted at the lower and more shady end of the group; next come the pale yellows and pale pinks, and these are followed at a little distance by kinds whose flowers are of orange, copper, flame, and scarlet-crimson colourings; this strong-coloured group again softening off at the upper end by strong yellows, and dying away into the woodland by bushes of the common yellow *Azalea pontica* [*Rhododendron luteum*] and its variety with flowers of larger size and deeper colour . . . Azaleas should never be planted among or even within sight of rhododendrons. Though both enjoy a moist peat soil, and have a near botanical relationship, they are incongruous in appearance, and impossible to group together for colour . . . In the case of small gardens, where there is only room for one bed or clump of peat plants, it would be better to have a group of either one or the other of these plants, rather than spoil the effect by the inharmonious mixture of both.

I always think it desirable to group together flowers that bloom at the same time. It is impossible, and even undesirable, to have a garden in blossom all over, and groups of flower-beauty are all the more enjoyable for being more or less isolated by stretches of intervening greenery.

As one lovely group for May I recommend Moutan paeony and *Clematis montana*, the clematis on a wall low enough to let its wreaths of bloom show near the paeony. The old Guelder rose or Snowball tree [*Viburnum opulus* 'Sterile'] is beautiful anywhere, but I think it is best of all on the cold side of a wall. Of course it is perfectly hardy, and a bush of strong sturdy growth, and has no need of the wall either for support or for shelter; but I am for clothing the garden walls with all the prettiest things they can wear, and no shrub I know makes a better show. Moreover, as there is necessarily less wood in a flat wall-tree than in a round bush, and as the front shoots must be pruned close back, it follows that much strength is thrown into the remaining wood, and the blooms are much larger.

I have a north wall eleven feet high, with a Guelder rose on each side of a doorway, and a *Clematis montana* that is trained on the top of the whole. The two flower at the same time, their growths mingling in friendly fashion while their unlikeness of habit makes the companionship all the more interesting. The Guelder rose is a stiff-wooded thing, the character of its main stems being a kind of stark uprightness, though the great white balls hang out with a certain freedom from the newly-grown shoots. The clematis meets it with an exactly opposite way of growth, swinging down its great swags of many-flowered garland masses into the head of its companion, with here and there a single flower streamer making a tiny wreath on its own account.

[Many good shrubs perform superbly when trained back against a wall and gain from the reflected heat of brick or stone. For north-facing walls *Garrya elliptica* and *Viburnum tinus* (its attractive variegated form needs a wall in most gardens) spring quickly to mind, but many of the more tender evergreens can be grown safely with this extra heat, and of course flower more freely as their wood has opportunity to ripen. The enthusiastic gardener today is so often working in a garden of limited size; training and tying-in against available walls increases the capacity as well as increasing flower quality. Most of the deciduous viburnums can be trained in this way; at Sissinghurst the horizontal branching *V. plicatum* 'Mariesii' has had its branches tied against a north wall like an espalier apple, and at Tintinhull the oak-leaved hydrangea, *H. quercifolia*, makes a fine specimen, carefully tied with invisible supports, as the long trusses of flower are heavy and drooping.]

On the southern sides of the same gateway are two bushes of the Mexican Orange-flower (*Choisya ternata*), loaded with its orange-like bloom. Buttresses flank the doorway on this side, dying away into the general thickness of the wall above the arch by a kind of roofing of broad flat stones that lie back at an easy pitch. In mossy hollows at their joints and angles, some tufts of thrift [*Armeria maritima*] and of little Rock pinks [*Dianthus petraeus*] have found a home, and show as tenderly-coloured tufts of rather dull pink bloom. Above all is the same white clematis, some of its abundant growth having been trained over the south side, so that this one plant plays a somewhat important part in two garden scenes.

[More than any previous garden designer Miss Jekyll used low and high walls behind borders to extend and enhance her planting colour schemes. Great drifts of lavender, campanula, *Cerastium tomentosum*, silvery saxifrages, thrift and dianthus in full sun, were matched on the shady side by ferns, sedums and little corydalis. Dry-

walling was so constructed that the stones all leant slightly backwards on a tilt so that every drop of rain tended to run into the joints and reach the roots. Although in the following passage she describes terraced gardening on a scale of magnificence hardly possible today, yet it still remains a statement of an ideal which can be readily (and cheaply) adapted to a modest garden. Although regular labour is expensive and often not available, large machines can alter levels and provide the framework for steps and terraces within a few hours. In a garden such as Tintinhull (admittedly large by modern standards), a completely flat area has been given interest and variety by clever changes of level, allowing the observer to discover sharp illusions of height and depth which turn what could be an attractive conventional garden into one full of concealed mysteries and surprises.

At Hestercombe (*see* plan on pp. 144–5) the grey garden she designed for a large-scale double terrace and walk can be seen today; plants flow and drift in what appear to be free-flowing movements but which are in reality strictly aligned planting schemes. Grey architectural leaves and white and pale blue flowers seemingly stray in drifts against the soft rough local stone (Lutyens used dressed Ashlar stone from Ham Hill near Yeovil for the more formal walls and pillars), contributing to a masterpiece of Lutyens architectural framework and Jekyllian planting principles.]

[*Omphalodes linifolia*, Venus's navelwort, is a worthwhile annual.]
'I always think this daintily beautiful plant is undeservedly neglected, for how seldom one sees it. It is full of the most charming refinement, with its milk-white bloom and grey-blue leaf and neat habit of growth.' [*Wood and Garden*, Gertrude Jekyll, p. 112.]

[*Athrium felix-femina* 'Plumosum' is a particularly good form of the Lady Fern, with light green, elegantly divided fronds.]
'. . . one of the most water-loving of our native kind [of fern]. It is happiest of all when it can be planted at the extreme edge of a pond or any rather still water, or the bank of a wet ditch, so that its outer rootlets are actually in the water.' ['Native ferns in the garden', *Gardening Illustrated*, January 1931.]

[In the opening chapter to *Wall and Water Gardens* Miss Jekyll introduces us to the principles that guided her:] Many a garden has to be made on a hillside more or less steep. The conditions of such a site naturally suggest some form of terracing, and in connection with a house of modest size and kind, nothing is prettier or pleasanter than all the various ways of terraced treatment that may be practised with the help of dry-walling, that is to say, rough wall-building without mortar, especially where a suitable kind of stone can be had locally. It is well in sharply-sloping ground to keep the paths as nearly level as may be, whether they are in straight lines or whether they curve in following the natural contour of the ground. Many more beautiful garden-pictures may be made by variety in planting even quite straightly terraced spaces than at first appears possible, and the frequent flights of steps, always beautiful if easy and well-proportioned, will be of the greatest value . . . Where the stairway cuts through the bank and is lined on each side by the dry-walling, the whole structure becomes a garden of delightful small things. Little ferns are planted in the joints on the shadier side as the wall goes up, and numbers of small saxifrages and stonecrops [sedums], pennywort [*Umbilicus rupestris*] and Erinus [*E. alpinus*], corydalis and sandwort [*Arenaria serpyllifolia*]. Then there will be hanging sheets of aubrietia and Rock pinks [*see* above] and cerastium, and many another pretty plant that finds a happy home in the cool shelter of the rocky joint. In some regions of the walling wallflowers and snapdragons and plants of thrift can be established; as they ripen their seed it drifts into the openings of other joints, and the seedlings send their roots deep into the bank and along the cool backs of the stones, and make plants of surprising health and vigour, that are longer lived than the softer-grown plants in the rich flower borders.

I doubt if there is any way in which a good quantity of plants and of bushes of moderate size can be so well seen and enjoyed as in one of these roughly terraced gardens, for one sees them up and down and in all sorts of ways, and one has a chance of seeing many lovely flowers clear against the sky, and of perhaps catching some sweetly-scented tiny thing like *Dianthus fragrans* at exactly nose-height and eye-level, and so of enjoying its tender beauty and powerful fragrance in a way that had never before been found possible.

[Miss Jekyll continues, by describing the maintenance of sloping banks of mown grass, where she can see the advantages of attractive retaining walls and steps. Financial outlay on mason-work is not always possible, and still less so today. However,] If there must be sloping space . . . it is better to plant the slope with low bushy or rambling things; with creeping cotoneaster, or Japan honeysuckle [*Lonicera japonica*], with ivies, or with such bushes as savin [forms of *Juniperus sabina*], *Pyrus japonica* [*Chaenomeles speciosa*], cistus or berberis; or if it is on a large scale, with the free-growing rambling roses and double-flowered brambles [species of rubus or forms of the ordinary blackberry *Rubus fruticosus*]. I name these things in preference to the rather overdone periwinkle [forms of *Vinca minor*, *V. major* and the rather superior but slightly tender *V. difformis*] and St John's Wort [*Hypericum calycinum*] because periwinkle is troublesome to weed, and soon grows into undesirably tight masses, and the hypericum, though sometimes of good effect, is extremely monotonous in large masses by itself, and is so ground-greedy that it allows of no companionship.

[With modern air-cushion mowing the maintenance of sloping grass banks is no longer a problem, and although in modern municipal planting and in shady areas where grass does not flourish, I would follow her lead – but with suggestions for an increased range of plants not available to her (*see* below) – I cannot entirely agree with the principle of eliminating smooth gently sloping banks. These, if correct in scale and well-kept, can often be exciting and important; sunlight and shadow play on them in a way not possible on horizontal grass. Probably smooth green banks are most appropriate on a largish scale, but they should not be dismissed for the smaller garden. What is undesirable is their too frequent use for spring bulbs, where the untidy uncut turf must remain an eyesore through the weeks following flowering.

To Miss Jekyll's list of shrubs can be added a few suitable for small gardens. There are several forms of prostrate ceanothus, in particular *C. thyrsiflorus repens* and the more tender *C. prostratus* for banks in full sun; for acid soil *Pachysandra terminalis* and species of pernettya make interesting evergreen cover; forms of *Potentilla fruticosa* make dense hummocks for sun or shade in any soil, santolinas prefer full sun, and *Viburnum davidii* makes impenetrable cover in shade. Among herbaceous plants the evergreen epimediums, lamiums (used with caution), creeping ajugas and bergenias all enjoy sloping areas and need little annual attention.]

[Returning to Miss Jekyll's chapter on terrace gardening:] There is another great advantage to be gained by the use of terrace walls; this is the display of many shrubs as well as plants that will hang over and throw their flowering sprays all over the face of the wall. In arranging such a garden I like to have a rather narrow border at the foot of each wall. If the whole width of the terrace is eighteen feet I would have the border at the foot of the wall not more than four feet wide, so as to be near it and near all the pretty things in its face and top. Then there would be the paths, six feet wide, and then the wider border, planted with the bushy things towards its outer edge, which will be the top of the wall of the next terrace below.

[*See* the plan at Hestercombe on pp. 144–5, which is on this vast scale; however, it is still worth listening to her words since one reduces these dimensions while keeping their relationship to each other constant. The new measurements will suit the smaller house, the range of different plants should be less.]

There would be mostly bushes of moderate growth, such as lavender, rosemary, berberis and *Pyrus japonica* [*Chaenomeles speciosa*], with all the things I could think of for partly hanging over the face of the wall. Among them would be *Forsythia suspensa*, *Phlomis fruticosa* (Jerusalem sage), the common barberry [*Berberis vulgaris*], so beautiful with its coral-like masses of fruit in October, and its half-weeping habit of growth and its way of disposing its branches in pictorial masses. There would also be *Desmodium penduliflorum* [*Lespedeza thunbergii*, an arching shrub now rather difficult to obtain. It and others of the genus all like a position in full sun, and bear rose-purple pea-flowers in late summer], and above all the many kinds of roses that grow and flower so kindly in such a position . . . *R. lucida* [*R. virginiana*] and Scotch briars [forms of *R. pimpinellifolia*] come over a wall nearly five feet high, and flower within a foot from the ground; *R. wichuriana* hangs over in a curtain of delicate white bloom and polished leafage.

[Today we might, if space permits, add the huge white-flowered *R.* 'Paulii' or the much more modest-sized pink sport *R.* 'Paulii Rosea'. Both have very thorny stems and make impenetrable groundcover. *R.* 'Max Graf' will trail flat on the ground and send long shoots earthwards from the top of a five-foot wall.]

Where in steep ground the terraces come near together the scheme may comprise some heroic doings with plants of monumental aspect, for at the outer edge of one of the wall tops there may be a great group of *Yucca gloriosa* or *Y. recurva* [*Y. recurvifolia*], some of it actually planted in the wall within a course or two of the top, or some top stones may be left out; or the yuccas may be planted as the wall goes up, with small kinds such as *Y. flaccida* a little lower down . . . When the yuccas are in flower and are seen from below, complete in their splendid dignity of solid leaf and immense spire of ivory bloom, against the often cloudless blue of our summer skies, their owner will rejoice in possessing a picture of perhaps the highest degree of nobility of plant form that may be seen in an English garden . . . In the case of the hot dry sunny aspect, a large proportion of south European plants that are hardy in England . . . can be used. Many of these have greyish foliage, and it would be greatly to the advantage of the planting, from the pictorial point of view, to keep them rather near together . . . a large proportion of them, of shrubby or half-shrubby character, are good winter plants, such as lavender, rosemary, phlomis, othonnopsis and santolina . . . they can be as well planted at the top edge of the wall, at the bottom, or in the face.

With these plants well grouped and the addition of some

common white pinks and the useful hybrids of Rock pinks; with a few grey-leaved Alpines such as cerastium, *Artemisia nana* [probably *A. schmidtiana* 'Nana'], *A. sericea*, the encrusted saxifrages, and *Achillea umbellata* [there is an especially good silver form of this], a piece of wall-gardening can be done that will be as complete and well furnished in winter (but for the bloom of plants) as it is in summer . . . The character of the planting might then change and gradually give way to another grouping that might be mainly of cistuses . . . and in the hottest wall place some of the south European campanulas: *C. isophylla*, both blue and white, *C. garganica* [*C. poscharskyana*, introduced in 1933 is like a *C. garganica* but with longer stems and more rampant and hardier], *C. fragilis* and *C. muralis* [*C. portenschlagiana*]. [She used *C. carpatica*, in a white form, for a terrace wall at Hestercombe in 1908; this is now replaced by the excellent *C. c.* 'Bressingham White'.]

These gems of their kind live and do well in upright walling, whereas they would perish on the more open rockery, or could only be kept alive by some unbeautiful device for a winter protection. [This is, as she points out, because moisture does not accumulate in the crown of a plant as it would when planted on the flat.]

[Returning to May:] Through the gateway again, beyond the wall northward and partly within its shade, is a portion of ground devoted to paeonies, in shape a long triangle, whose proportion in length is about thrice its breadth measured at the widest end. A low cross-wall, five feet high, divides it nearly in half . . . thus the paeonies are protected all round, for they like a sheltered place, and the Moutans do best with even a little passing shade at some time of the day. Moutan is the Chinese name for Tree paeony. For an immense hardy flower of beautiful colouring what can equal the salmon-rose 'Moutan Reine Elizabeth' [*Paeonia suffruticosa* 'Elizabeth']? Among the others that I have, those that give me most pleasure are 'Baronne d'Alès' and 'Comtesse de Tudor', both pinks of a delightful quality, and a lovely white called 'Bijou de Chusan'. The tree paeonies are also beautiful in leaf; the individual leaves are large and important, and so carried that they are well displayed. Their colour is peculiar, being bluish, but pervaded with a suspicion of pink or pinkish-bronze, sometimes of a metallic quality that faintly recalls some of the variously-coloured alloys of metal that the Japanese bronze-workers make and use with such consummate skill.

[In Miss Jekyll's day these grafted plants (generally on the softer stock of *Paeonia lactiflora* or *P. officinalis*) were admirably grown in France, and she had to choose them from catalogue description only. Today all available *suffruticosa* types come grafted from Japan. The best can be seen at Kelway's stands at early summer flower shows or at their nursery; otherwise a colour and flower description must suffice. The easy and popular, but in my opinion rather dull, tree paeony, *P. lutea* 'Ludlowii', is now often grown, and its yellow flowers and plain green leaves make it a useful shrub for edge of woodland, where more exotic planting would be out of place. The kinds of June-flowering paeonies which Miss Jekyll most prefers are planted near the moutans in her gardens. These are] the garden varieties of the Siberian *P. albiflora* [*P. lactiflora*], popularly known as Chinese paeonies. Though among these, as is the case with all the kinds, there is a preponderance of pink or rose-crimson colouring of a decidedly rank quality, yet the number of varieties is so great, that among the minority of really good colouring there are plenty to choose from, including a good number of beautiful whites and whites tinged with yellow.

[Miss Jekyll gives a list of her favourites, some of which are still available, and which cover a range of colour from pure and warm white to pale yellow, pink, salmon-rose and rose, blush and deep claret. Any good nurseryman will have a list of modern named Chinese paeonies with good colour and varying from single to semi-double and double.] Then there are the old garden paeonies, the double varieties of *P. officinalis*. They are in three distinct colourings – full rich crimson, crimson-rose and pale pink changing to dull white. These are the earliest to flower, and with them it is convenient, from the garden point of view, to class some of the desirable species.

Some years ago my friend Mr Barr kindly gave me a set of the paeony species as grown by him. I wished to have them, not for the sake of making a collection, but in order to see which were the ones I should like best to grow as garden flowers. In due time they grew into strong plants and flowered. A good many had to be condemned because of the raw magenta colour of the bloom, one or two only that had this defect being reprieved on account of their handsome foliage and habit. Prominent among these was *P. decora* with bluish foliage handsomely displayed, the whole plant looking strong and neat and well-dressed. [According to the *R.H.S. Dictionary P. decora* is a synonym for *P. peregrina*, but this hardly answers to Miss Jekyll's description. In fact *P. lobata*, see below, with its vivid forms 'Fire King' and 'Sunshine' is correctly *P. peregrina*. In Nicholson (1887) *P. decora* is given as a relation of *P. arietina*, and *P. arietina* is allied to *P. peregrina* – *see* Graham Thomas for further explanation].

Others whose flower-colour I cannot commend, but that seemed worth growing on account of their rich masses of handsome foliage, are *P. triternata* [*P. daurica*] and *P. broteri* [both magenta flowered and very similar]. Though small in size, the light red flower of *P. lobata* [*P. peregrina*] is of a beautiful colour. *P. tenuifolia*, in both single and double form, is an old garden favourite. *P. wittmanniana*, with its yellow-green leaves and tender yellow flower, is a gem; but it is rather rare, and probably uncertain, for mine, alas, had no sooner grown into a fine clump than it suddenly died. [These species paeonies are still difficult to get. To Miss Jekyll's collection can be added the yellow *P. mlokosewitschii* which flowers early and has distinctive soft grey-green leaves. A suckering shrubby paeony *P. potaninii* has small maroon flowers and makes a mass of twiggy stems. There is a white form I have yet to see.]

All paeonies are strong feeders. Their beds should be deeply and richly prepared, and in later years they are grateful for liberal gifts of manure, both as surface dressings and waterings. Friends often ask me vaguely about paeonies, and when I say 'What kind of paeonies?' they have not the least idea. Broadly, and for garden purposes, one may put them into three classes:

1. Tree paeonies (*P. moutan* – [*P. suffruticosa*]) flowering in May. [Also *P. lutea* etc. since Miss Jekyll.]

2. Chinese paeonies (*P. albiflora* [now *P. lactiflora*]).

3. Old garden paeonies (*P. officinalis*), herbaceous, including some other herbaceous species.

[The *P. lactiflora* hybrids which flower in June, and which Graham Thomas calls the Edwardian paeonies, are still incomparable for their range of splendid double and single flowers. However, some new American hybrids are superb, and have recently become available in this country.]

I find it convenient to grow paeony species and caulescent (Lent) hellebores together. They are in a wide border on the north side of the high wall and partly shaded by it. They are agreed in their liking for deeply worked ground with an admixture of loam and lime, for shelter, and for rich feeding; and the paeony clumps, set, as it were, in picture frames of the lower-growing hellebores are seen to all the more advantage.

JUNE

'The garden artist – by which is to be understood the true lover of good flowers, who has taken the trouble to learn their ways and wants and moods, and to know it all so surely that he can plant with the assured belief that the plants he sets will do as he intends, just as the painter can compel and command the colours on his palette – plants with an unerring hand and awaits the sure result. Elgood and Jekyll, p. 112

When one says the "simplest means" it does not always mean the easiest. Many people begin their gardening by thinking that the making and maintaining of a handsome and well-filled flower border is quite an easy matter. In fact it is one of the most difficult problems in the whole range of horticultural practice – wild gardening perhaps excepted. To achieve anything beyond the ordinary commonplace mixture, that is without plan or forethought, and that glares with the usual faults of bad colour-combinations and yawning empty gaps, needs years of observation and a considerable knowledge of plants and their ways as individuals.'

The gladness of June — The time of roses — Garden roses — 'Reine Blanche' — The old white rose — Old garden roses as standards — Climbing and rambling roses — Scotch briars — Hybrid perpetuals a difficulty — Tea roses — Pruning sweet peas, autumn sown — Elder trees — Virginian cowslip — Dividing spring-blooming plants — Two best mulleins — White French willow — [The June border — Colour combinations — Middle and end of June] — Bracken.

WHAT IS ONE TO SAY about June – the time of perfect young summer, the fulfilment of the promise of the earlier months, and with as yet no sign to remind one that its fresh young beauty will ever fade? For my own part I wander up into the wood and say 'June is here – June is here; thank God for lovely June!' The soft cooing of the wood-dove, the glad song of many birds, the flitting of butterflies, the hum of all the little winged people among the branches, the sweet earth-scents – all seem to say the same, with an endless reiteration, never wearying because so gladsome. It is the offering of the Hymn of Praise! The lizards run in and out of the heathy tufts in the hot sunshine, and as the long day darkens the night-jar trolls out his strange song, so welcome because it is the prelude to the perfect summer night; here and there a glow-worm shows its little lamp. June is here – June is here; thank God for lovely June!

And June is the time of roses. I have great delight in the best of the old garden roses; the Provence (cabbage rose – [R. *centifolia*]), sweetest of all sweets, and the Moss rose, its crested variety [probably 'Chapeau de Napoleon', known as the 'Crested Moss' but not a true Moss in modern classification]; the early Damasks [R. *damascena*] and its red and white striped kind [this is 'York and Lancaster' – R. × *damascena versicolor*]; the old, nearly single, 'Reine Blanche' [*R. rubrotincta*, otherwise known as 'Hebe's Lip']. I do not know the origin of this charming rose, but by its appearance it should be related to the Damask. [Later, in *Roses for English Gardens*, she and Mr Mawley came to think that it belonged to the Provins (*gallica*) group.] A good many years ago I came upon it in a cottage garden in Sussex, and thought, 'I have found a white Damask.' The white is a creamy white, the outsides of the outer petals are stained with red, first showing clearly in the bud. The scent is delicate and delightful, with a faint suspicion of magnolia. A few years ago this pretty old rose found its way to one of the meetings of the Royal Horticultural Society, where it gained much praise. It was there that I recognized my old friend, and learned its name.

I am fond of the old *R. alba*, both single and double [*R. alba maxima*, Jacobite rose, the great double white], and its daughter, 'Maiden's Blush'. How seldom one sees these roses except in cottage gardens; but what good taste it shows on the cottager's part, for what rose is so perfectly at home upon the modest wayside porch?

I have also learned from cottage gardens how pretty are some of the old roses grown as standards. The picture of my neighbour, Mrs Edgeler, picking me a bunch from her bush, shows how freely they flower, and what fine standards they make. I have taken the hint, and have now some big round-headed standards, the heads a yard through, of the lovely 'Celeste' [*R. alba* 'Celeste'] and of 'Madame Plantier', that are worth looking at, though one of them is rather badly-shaped this year, for my handsome Jack [donkey] ate one side of it when he was waiting outside the studio door, while his cartload of logs for the ingle fire was being unloaded.

[Since Miss Jekyll's time a great amount of work has been done on the old roses, and thanks to such people as Graham Stuart Thomas their complicated history can be understood by those interested. Many lovely old shrub roses are available from specialist nurseries, and collections can be seen in several gardens as well as at Mottisfont Abbey, owned by the National Trust. Here Mr Thomas has demonstrated their beauty, fragrance and flowering qualities. However, as the old-fashioned nurseryman is superseded by the Garden Centre, these roses may once more become difficult to obtain. Miss Jekyll writes in the early days of the natural movement led by William Robinson – a time when the old garden plants were evocative of earlier gardening periods and were loved for this as much as for their value as flowering plants.]

What a fine thing, among the cluster roses, is the old Dundee rambler. [The wild *R. arvensis* is a parent of the climbing Ayrshire roses such as 'Dundee Rambler' and 'Bennet's seedling', both often planted by Miss Jekyll. Now they are less popular and have been largely superseded by roses which flower more than once.] I trained one to go up a rather upright green holly about twenty-five feet high, and now it has rushed up and tumbles out at the top and sides in masses of its pretty bloom. It is just as good as a 'fountain', giving it a free space where it can spread at will with no training or support whatever. These two ways I think are much the best for growing the free rambling roses. In the case of the fountain, the branches arch over and display the flowers to perfection; if you tie your rose up to a tall post or train it over an arch or pergola, the birds flying overhead have the best of the show. The Garland rose, another old sort [sometimes classified as a hybrid musk, it has medium-sized clustered semi-double scented blush-pink flowers], is just as suitable for this kind of growth as 'Dundee Rambler', and the individual flowers, of a tender blush-colour, changing to white are even more delicate and pretty.

The newer 'Crimson Rambler' is a noble plant for the same use, in sunlight gorgeous of bloom, and always brilliant with its glossy bright-green foliage. Of the many good plants from Japan, this is the best that has reached us in late years [either a *wichuriana* or a *multiflora* hybrid introduced in the 1880s]. The Himalayan *R. brunonis* [*R. brunonii*] is loaded with its clusters of milk-white bloom, that are so perfectly in harmony with its very long, almost blue leaves. But of all the free-growing roses, the most remarkable for rampant growth is *R. polyantha* [*R. multiflora*, and with *R. wichuriana* one of the parents of many of the best ramblers grown today]. One of the bushes in this garden covers a space thirty-four feet across – more than a hundred feet round. It forms a great fountain-like mass, covered with myriads of its small white flowers, whose scent is carried a considerable distance.

Directly the flower is over it throws up rods of young growth eighteen to twenty feet long; as they mature they arch over, and next year their many short lateral shoots will be smothered in bloom.

Two other roses of free growth are also great favourites – 'Madame Alfred Carrière', with long stalked loose-white flowers, and 'Emilie Plantier'. I have them on an east fence, where they yield a large quantity of bloom for cutting; indeed, they have been so useful in this way that I have planted several more, but this time for training down to an oak trellis, like the one that supports the row of 'Bouquet d'Or', in order to bring the flowers within easier reach.

Now we look for the bloom of the Burnet rose (*R. spinosissima* – [*R. pimpinellifolia*]), a lovely native plant, and its garden varieties, the Scotch briars. The wild plant is widely distributed in England, though somewhat local. It grows on moors in Scotland, and on Beachy Head in Sussex, and near Tenby in South Wales, favouring wild places within smell of the sea. The rather dusky foliage sets off the lemon-white of the wild, and the clear white, pink, rose and pale yellow of the double garden kinds. The hips are large and handsome, black and glossy, and the whole plant in late autumn assumes a fine bronzy colouring between ashy black and dusky red.

Other small old garden roses are coming into bloom. One of the most desirable, and very frequent in this district, is *R. lucida* [*R. virginiana*], with red stems, highly-polished leaves, and single fragrant flowers of pure rosy-pink colour. The leaves turn a brilliant yellow in autumn and after they have fallen the bushes are still bright with the coloured stems and the large clusters of bright-red hips. It is the St Mark's Rose of Venice, where it is usually in flower on St Mark's Day, April 25th. The double variety is the old 'Rose d'Amour', now rare in gardens; its half-expanded bud is perhaps the most daintily beautiful thing that any rose can show.

[According to Miss Wilmott (*The Genus Rosa*, 1910), the double form of 'Rose d'Amour' was the true St Mark's Rose and this is now accepted. Miss Jekyll's next few pages are devoted to the methods of growing and pruning Hybrid Perpetuals and Tea roses. Enough has been said to show her taste for the natural free-growing and free-flowering roses and for many of the older kinds with scented heavy heads. The importance today is not in listing her preferred roses but in grasping how she used them and in understanding her preference for clear pink, blush-pink and whites rather than the magenta and purple colourings. I think we can guess that she would have had little sympathy or use for the more vivid modern orange and scarlet roses (or those with salmon shades) in her rose garden or in the wilder woodland glades where 'The Garland' clambered through the hollies. She might have used them in her great colour borders but, in the main, these highly bred modern roses do not sit comfortably next to herbaceous plants. The modern shrub roses, both species such as *R. moyesii* introduced after her gardening days (originally in 1890 but not in general commerce until Wilson's reintroduction of 1903), and recent hybrids, are worthy of places in all mixed borders, many being repeat flowerers and strong and robust when jostled by vigorous herbaceous plants.]

[She describes a rose garden laid out to good effect:] A rose garden may often be made much more delightful by having some point of interest besides the roses, for nothing is more usual than to find that, except in the few weeks of its fullest bloom, the rose garden is rather a dull place. There are several ways in which such an object of interest may be secured; either by a sundial or fountain, or a raised stone flower bed, or a piece of ornamental sculpture in stone or lead, whether central or defining certain points of the circumference in prepared niches in the bounding hedge. In the case of the garden shown [*see* plan on p. 134], this variation of interest is given by a tank for water lilies twenty feet across, giving good space for at least three kinds of beautiful water lilies. The low flat curb, which in an unbroken circle of this size would be a trifle monotonous, is varied on the four

Country Life, August 1919

PLAN OF A ROSE GARDEN WITH LILY POOL IN
THE CENTRE

A   Blanc Double de Coubert
B   Zephyrine Drouhin, or other deep pink
C   Bright red
D   White
E, F Light pink
L   Lavender in round bushes, with edges of China Rose

sides opposite the paths by a square projection, which gives
width enough for the placing of four pots or small tubs of
flowers in pairs. The four beds nearest the tank are also treated
with a certain symmetry, and are planted with lavender and
China rose, thus securing some permanence of effect and good

134

clothing for all seasons, and so also joining in with the enduring and unaltering stonework of the tank. The small circles in the four diagonal angles are trained weeping roses, of such a kind as the pretty pale pink 'Lady Godiva'. [The charming small poly-antha rose 'The Fairy' is a sport of this rambler of the *multiflora* type.]

The large clumps have a middle mass of five plants of the fine rugosa hybrid 'Blanc Double de Coubert'. This is chosen because of its handsome dark green foliage and for its way of forming a dense bushy mass of solid character, quite different to the thinner habit of most roses. The coloured roses will come well in groups as shown, using four kinds in each clump. The names of the actual kinds are not given, because the choice will depend both on the character of the soil and climate and on the taste of the owner. But as a general suggestion as to colour arrangement, it would be well to have in the space B some good rose of a deep pink or a clear rosy-red such as 'Zephyrine Drouhin' [one of the Bourbon roses, practically thornless with fine copper foliage, repeat flowering], in C a bright red, in D a white, and in E and F a light pink. The whole garden is much beautified by a com-plete edging of *Stachys lanata*. The flower stems are cut out when half developed; then the plant at once spreads at the root and forms a silver carpet [a modern form 'Silver Carpet' does not flower]. It is kept fairly even on the side next the turf, but runs freely into the bed where there is space between the roses. The edging is not only most becoming to the roses, but serves a useful purpose by defining the form of the design.

[It may be possible to have attractive paving between rose beds, rather than grass which needs meticulous edging. Then the carpet of grey leaves can be allowed to stray over the stonework. Often a rose garden of this quite large size will have either surrounding hedges which create shade in parts only, or there will be overhanging trees on one side or another. In another rose garden of very similar plan Miss Jekyll uses rosemary, catmint, santolina and dwarf lavenders in full sun, associated with hostas, *Clematis heracleifolia davidiana* (one of her favourite plants), eryngium and echinops in the lightly shaded areas.

Gertrude Jekyll wrote extensively about the rose and how best to use it in the garden. Many of her favourites have been superseded by new hybrids, but the chapter headings used by her in her book *Roses for English Gardens*, written with Edward Mawley and first published in 1902, show a realistic approach to garden planning. She never recommended bush roses alone in beds; always adding softening grey-green shrubs or plants. Some of the chapter titles are: 'Rose pillars', 'The Pergola', 'Rose arches and arbours', 'Rose screens, hedges and trellises', 'Roses as fountains and growing free', 'Roses on walls and houses', 'Roses for converting ugliness to beauty' and 'Rose gardens'. The names of the roses may have changed, but the needs are still similar, in the small as much as in the large gardens about which she wrote.]

[Returning to June:] Within the first days of June we can generally pick some sweet peas from the rows sown in the second week of September. They are very much stronger than those sown in spring. By November they are four inches high, and seem to gain strength and sturdiness during the winter; for as soon as spring comes they shoot up with great vigour, and we know that the spray used to support them must be two feet higher than for those that are spring-sown.

[Today bush varieties need little staking and highly bred long-stemmed sweet peas (often with little scent) are available in a bewildering number of forms and colours. September sowing is best done in seed trays; then pot on and keep in a cold frame over winter, planting out in April. Alternatively sow plants in March outside in the flowering site, or under glass to be transplanted in early May. Sowing directly in September in the permanent site usually leads to problems and it is advisable to cover the young plants with cloches when cold weather is forecast.]

They are sown in shallow trenches; in spring they are earthed up very slightly, but still with a little trench at the base of the plants. A few doses of liquid manure are a great help when they are getting towards blooming strength.

I am very fond of the elder tree [*Sambucus nigra*]. It is a sociable sort of thing; it seems to like to grow near human habitations. In my own mind it is certainly the tree most closely associated with the pretty old cottage and farm architecture of my part of the country; no bush or tree, not even the apple, seems to group so well or so closely with farm buildings. When I built a long thatched shed for so many needs of the garden, in the region of pits and frames, compost, rubbish and burn-heap, I planted elders close to the end of the building and on one side of the yard. They look just right, and are, moreover, every year loaded with their useful fruit. This is ripe quite early in September, and is made into Elder wine, to be drunk hot in winter, a comfort by no means to be despised. My trees now give enough for my own wants, and there are generally a few acceptable bushels to spare for my cottage neighbours.

About the middle of the month the Virginian cowslip (*Mertensia virginica*) begins to turn yellow before dying down. Now is the time to look for the seeds. A few ripen on the plant, but most of them fall while green, and then ripen in a few days while lying on the ground. I shake the seeds carefully out, and leave them lying round the parent-plant; a week later when they will be ripe, they are lightly scratched into the ground. Some young plants of last year's growth I mark with a bit of stick, in case of wanting some later to plant elsewhere, or to send away; the plant dies away completely, leaving no trace above ground, so that if not marked it would be difficult to find what is wanted.

[This is probably the reason why this charming plant with pale blue flowers and grey leaves is not grown more often; the unwary gardener literally loses it by forking over what appears to be bare earth or by planting something else in its site.]

This is also the time for pulling to pieces and replanting that good spring plant, the large variety of *Myosotis dissitiflora*; I always make sure of divisions, as seed does not come true. *Primula rosea* should also be divided now, and planted to grow on in a cool place, such as the foot of a north or east wall, or be put at once in its place in some cool rather moist spot in the rock-garden. Two-year-old plants come up with thick clumps of matted root that is now useless. I cut off the whole mass of old root about an inch below the crown, when it can be easily divided into nice little bits for replanting. Many other spring-flowering plants may with advantage be divided now, such as aubrietia, arabis, auricula, tiarella and saxifrage.

The great branching mullein, *Verbascum olympicum*, is just going out of bloom, after making a brilliant display for a fortnight. It is followed by the other of the most useful tall yellow-flowered kinds, *V. phlomoides*. Both are seen at their best either quite early in the morning, or in the evening, or in half-shade, as, like all their kind, they do not expand their bloom in bright sunshine. Both are excellent plants on poor soils. *V. olympicum*, though classed as a biennial [now classified as perennial, with grey woolly leaves], does not come to flowering strength till it is three or four years old; but meanwhile the foliage is so handsome that even if there were no flower it would be a worthy garden plant. It does well in any waste spaces of poor soil, where, by having plants of all ages, there will be some to flower every year.

Miss Jekyll does not mention *V. vernale* (possibly correctly *V. chaixii*) which makes a most useful mid-summer contribution. Growing to five feet, and rather variable, this perennial has long grey-green leaves covered in white woolly hairs. From the basal rosettes, yellow flowers with very noticeable purple stamens are borne freely on branching stems. There is also a white form 'Album'.] The mullein moth is sure to find them out, and it behoves the careful gardener to look for and destroy the caterpillars, or he may find, instead of his stately mulleins, tall stems clothed with unsightly grey rags. The caterpillars are easily caught when quite small or when rather large; but midway in their growth, when three-quarters of an inch long, they are wary, and at the approach of an avenging gardener, they will give a sudden wriggling jump, and roll down into the lower depths of the large foliage, where they are difficult to find. But by going round the plants twice a day for about a week they can all be discovered.

The white variety of the French willow (*Epilobium angustifolium*) [the French or rose bay willow herb; this is the form 'Album', rather less invasive than the type] is a pretty plant in the edges of the copse, good both in sun and shade, and flourishing in any poor soil. In better ground it grows too rank, running quickly at the root and invading all its neighbours, so that it should be planted with great caution; but when grown on poor ground it flowers at from two feet to four feet high, and its whole aspect is improved by the proportional amount of flower becoming much larger.

[She describes her own border in June:] The big flower border *Colour Schemes* is about two hundred feet long and fourteen feet wide (*see* plan on pp. 260–1). It is sheltered from the north by a solid sandstone wall about eleven feet high clothed for the most part with evergreen shrubs – bay and laurustinus, choisya, cistus and loquat. These show as a handsome background to the flowering plants. They are in a three-foot-wide border at the foot of the wall; then there is a narrow alley, not seen from the front, but convenient for access to the wall shrubs and for working the back of the border.

As it is impossible to keep any one flower border fully dressed for the whole summer, and as it suits me that it should be at its best in the late summer, there is no attempt to have it full of flowers as early as June. Another region belongs to June; so that at that time the big border has only some incidents of good bloom, though the ground is rapidly covering with the strong patches, most of them from three to five years old, of the later-blooming perennials. But early in the month there are some clumps of the beautiful *Iris pallida dalmatica* in the regions of grey foliage, and of the splendid blue-purple bloom of *Geranium ibericum platyphyllum* [*G.* × *magnificum*], the best of the large cranesbills, and the slow-growing *Dictamnus fraxinella* (the white variety), and meadowsweets white and pink, foxgloves and Canterbury bells, and to the front some long-established sheets of *Iberis sempervirens* that have grown right on to the path. The large yuccas, *Y. gloriosa* and *Y. recurva* [*Y. recurvifolia*] are throwing up their massive spikes, though it will be July before they actually flower, and the blooms on some bushes of the great *Euphorbia wulfenii*, although they were flowers of May and their almost yellow colour is turning greener, are still conspicuous and ornamental. Then the plants in the middle of the wall, *Choisya ternata* and *Clematis montana*, are still full of white bloom, and the Guelder rose is hanging out its great white balls. I like to plant the Guelder rose and *Clematis montana* together. Nothing does better on north or east walls, and it is pleasant to see the way the clematis flings its graceful garlands over and through the stiff branches of the viburnum.

The more brilliant patches of colour in the big border in June are of Oriental poppies intergrouped with gypsophila, which will cover their space when they have died down, and the earlier forms of *Lilium croceum* of that dark orange colour that almost approaches scarlet.

The planting of the border is designed to show a distinct scheme of colour arrangement. At the two ends there is a groundwork of grey and glaucous foliage – stachys, santolina, *Cineraria maritima*, sea-kale [*Crambe maritima*] and lyme-grass [*Elymus arenarius*], with darker foliage, also of grey quality, of yucca, *Clematis recta* and rue. With this, at the near or western end there are flowers of pure blue, grey-blue, white, palest yellow and palest pink; each colour partly in distinct masses and partly intergrouped. The colouring then passes through stronger yellows to orange and red. By the time the middle space of the border is reached the colour is strong and gorgeous, but, as it is in good harmonies, it is never garish. Then the colour strength recedes in an inverse sequence through orange and deep yellow to pale yellow, white and palest pink; again with blue-grey foliage. But at this, the eastern end, instead of the pure blues we have purples and lilacs.

Looked at from a little way forward, for a wide space of grass allows this point of view, the whole border can be seen as one picture, the cool colouring at the ends enhancing the brilliant warmth of the middle. Then, passing along the wide path next the border, the value of the colour arrangement is still more strongly felt. Each portion now becomes a picture in itself, and every one is of such a colouring that it best prepares the eye, in accordance with natural law, for what is to follow. Standing for a few moments before the end-most region of grey and blue, and saturating the eye to its utmost capacity with these colours, it passes with extraordinary avidity to the succeeding yellows. These intermingle in a pleasant harmony with the reds and scarlets, blood-reds and clarets, and then lead again to yellows. Now the eye has again become saturated, this time with the rich colouring, and has therefore, by the law of complementary colour, acquired a strong appetite for the greys and purples. These therefore assume an appearance of brilliancy that they would not have had without the preparation provided by their recently received complementary colour.

There are well-known scientific toys illustrating this law. A short word, printed in large red letters, is looked at for half a minute. The eyes are shut and an image of the same word appears, but the lettering is green. Many such experiments may be made in the open garden. The brilliant orange African marigold has leaves of a rather dull green colour. But look steadily at the flowers for thirty seconds in sunshine and then look at the leaves. The leaves appear to be bright blue!

[In a later article she suggests a colour scheme for a separate *Country Life* June border:] The middle days of June bring the perfect bloom of the flag irises and the perennial lupins. Where a space can be given to these and a few other kinds of flowers of the season a complete picture of flower beauty may be had . . . in a border carefully arranged for colour . . . on the left it begins with a bold patch of *Anchusa* 'Opal' [clear pale blue] with the white bloom masses of *Olearia gunnii* [*O. phlogopappa*. Today, for its larger greater flowers, one might use the hybrid *O. × scilloniensis*. I would expect this or the species to be flowering by the end of May and to be a bit dingy by the middle of June.]

These are followed by blue and white lupins in separate patches; then pink China roses, blue-purple and white irises and masses of blue cranesbill [*Geranium × magnificum*, often called *G. ibericum*; violet-blue flowers in June over a very long period] and catmint [nepeta], with white pinks [*Dianthus* 'Mrs Sinkins'?] and pansies to the front. Next come tall pale yellow irises to the middle and back, grouped with Lupine Somerset [obviously a yellow tree lupin] and gold privet [*Ligustrum ovalifolium* 'Aureum'], a capital thing for clever use in this way.

The colouring then passes by deeper yellows to some of the irises of the *squalens* section of rich red-purples, with red-purple lupins, a harmonious quality of colour being provided towards the front by a grouping of *Incarvillea delavayii*, with a setting of the deep reddish leaved *Heuchera richardsonii* [*H. americana*].

By now the end of the border is reached, and there is a group of white tree lupin with tall spires of asphodel [*A. albus*] and pink China roses [I would use 'Nathalie Nypels', one of the best of the old pink Chinas]. At the beginning of the return border on the right is the fine pink *Iris pallida* 'Queen of the May', with white and rosy perennial lupin and a front planting of pink pinks, and so on again through pale yellows to clear lilacs and purples, pinks and whites.

Towards the end of June the bracken [*Pteris aquilina*, usually an indication of acid soil] that covers the greater part of the ground of the copse is in full beauty. No other manner of under-growth gives to the woodland in so great a degree the true forest-like character. This most ancient plant speaks of the old untouched land of which large stretches still remain in the south of England – land too poor to have been worth cultivating, and that has therefore for centuries endured human contempt.

In the early part of the present [19th] century William Cobbett, speaking of the healthy headlands and vast hollow of Hindhead in Surrey, calls it 'certainly the most villainous spot God ever made'. This gives expression to his view, as farmer and political economist, of such places as were incapable of cultivation, and of the general feeling of the time about lonely roads in waste places, as the fields for the lawless labours of smuggler and high-wayman. Now such tracts of natural wild beauty, clothed with stretches of heath and fern and whortleberry, with beds of sphagnum moss, and little natural wild gardens of curious and beautiful sub-aquatic plants in the marshy hollows and un-drained wastes, are treasured as such places deserve to be, especially when they still remain within fifty miles of a vast city.

The height to which bracken grows is a sure guide to the depth of the soil. On the poorest, thinnest ground it only reaches a foot or two; but in hollow places where leaf-mould accumulates and surface soil has washed in and made a better depth, it grows from six feet to eight feet high, and when straggling up through bushes to get to the light a frond will sometimes measure as much as twelve feet. Country people who have always lived on the same poor land say 'where the fern grows tall any-thing will grow'; but that only means that there the ground is somewhat better and capable of cultivation, as its presence is a sure indication of a sandy soil. The timber merchants are shy of buying oak trees felled from it, the timber of trees grown on the wealden clay being so much better.

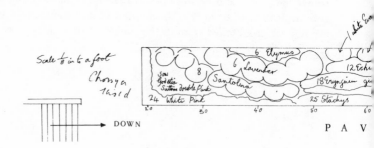

Santolina [*S. chamaecyparis*]

Lavender [*Lavandula* 'Munstead']

Sow *Godetia* 'Suttons Pink' [*now Dianthus* 'Excelsior']

White pink [*Dianthus* 'Mrs Sinkins]

Elymus [*E. arenarius*]

White everlasting pea [*Lathyrus latifolius* 'Albus']

Clematis jackmanii

Echinops ritro

Clematis davidiana

Eryngium giganteum

Nepeta

Lavender 'Munstead'

White tree lupin [*Lysimachia clethyoides*]

Eryngium olivuanum

Cineraria maritima

Sedum spectabile

Achillea 'The Pearl'

Gypsophila paniculata

Stachys lanata [*now S. lanata* 'Silver Carpet']

THE GREY BORDER AT HESTERCOMBE

[Miss Jekyll herself had a garden mainly of plants with grey and silver foliage, but was enthusiastic about the possibilities of other restricted colour schemes. At Hestercombe she designed her grey border on four different planes. The double border on a raised walk was backed by a five-foot wall in which the drifts of plants from the bed directly in front were extended. Similarly below the double walk a much higher bed dropping to another south-facing border below continued the theme of the bed above and of that below. Lavender, santolina and eryngiums stretched in to the wall planting (not as difficult as it sounds if done as the wall was being built); after a few years plants seed themselves in the crevices and regenerate. Smaller trailing plants such as cerastium, *Campanula carpatica*, *Achillea argentea*, dianthus crept over the edges of the paved walk and over the front of the main wall. Other vigorous spreading plants such as lyme grass (*Elymus arenarius*) and *Saponaria officinalis* carpeted the earth between and round grand foliage plants such as *Yucca flaccida* and *Y. gloriosa*. The predominant theme was held together by the grey, silver and almost white foliage, but the flower

144

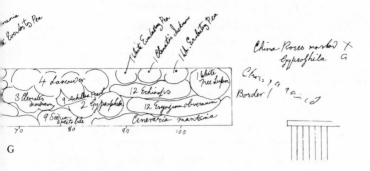

colour varied between the pure white of *Dianthus* 'Mrs Sinkins', and *Achillea* 'Pearl', pale pink of *Sedum spectabile*, double pink godetia (the pink *Dianthus* 'Excelsior' now takes the place of this annual) and blues and mauves of rosemary, ceratostigma, catmint and lavender. For the more creamy white of tree lupin, a valuable softening influence, a spreading clump of *Lysimachia clethroides* has been substituted.

The complete plan of the upper inner border is shown. On raised beds at either end groups of *Choisya ternata* balance the whole scheme and give bulk and border, with glossy healthy green leaves and sweet-smelling white flowers in early summer. The white pea is designed to be brought forward over the stems of *Echinops ritro* for late summer display, as she did in her own garden. On the southern side of the paved path the bed is twice as wide and the planting is more substantial. Shrubs such as cistus, lavender, *Phlomis fruticosa*, rosemary, santolina and scattered groups of a pink China rose ('Natalie Nypels' has been used in the modern replanting scheme) are mixed with herbaceous. At the western end the strong yucca foliage and *Olearia gunnii* (*O* × *scilloniensis*, a more recent garden hybrid has been substituted) dominates, and is admirable against the rough local stone.

At the base of the deep wall there are more plantings of drifts of rosemary, catmint, *Clematis recta* and *C. heracelifolia davidiana*, more groups of rose 'Natalie Nypels', *Gypsophila paniculata* and groups of cistus. *Stachys lanata* is used as front edging throughout; Miss Jekyll recommended cutting off the flower stems to encourage spreading, but today the non-flowering type 'Silver Carpet' saves labour and quickly establishes itself. Perhaps in these borders the greatest problem is control of the rampant creeping roots of the lyme grass and the saponaria, and every spring a certain number are dug out. Although it is difficult to match the blue-grey colour of the grass I think I would use another non-spreading grass, *Helictotrichon sempervirens* (*Avena candida* of gardens). The pendulous form arches gracefully and the foliage is steely grey. Instead of the saponaria I might experiment with a group of *Phuopsis stylosa*, whose lax flopping stems carry dense heads of tiny pink flowers through middle and late summer. *Phlomis italica* has silvery-grey, very hairy leaves and pale pink flowers and although woody rather prefers to be cut to ground-level each year. Its pale leaves and flowers would fade gently into the colour scheme.]

[In the Dutch Garden at Hestercombe, beds of pink roses are intermingled with drifts of catmint, lavender and rosemary. The edging is grey-leaved *Stachys lanata*, in its modern, non-flowering form, 'Silver Carpet'.]
'The whole garden is much beautified by a complete edging of *S. lanata*. The flower stems are cut out when half developed; then the plant at once spreads at the root and forms a silvery carpet . . . This edging is not only most becoming to the roses, but serves a useful purpose by defining the form of the design.' ['Designing a rose garden', *Country Life*, 23 August 1919.]

[The east rill at Hestercombe. In the borders between clumps of tall iris, groups of orange and yellow flowers fade into pale mauves and blues of lavender and globe thistle. The central water rill contained forget-me-not, arum lily, water-plantain and arrowhead.]
'The planted rill may be considered the invention of Mr E. L. Lutyens. The one in the garden at Hestercombe shows the most typical form. The wide, paved ledges make pleasant walking ways; at even intervals they turn, after the manner of the gathered ribbon strapwork of ancient needlework, and enclose circular tanklets, giving the opportunity of a distinct punctuation with important plants.' [*Wall and Water Gardens*, Gertrude Jekyll, p. 176.]

[The hanging terraces at Hestercombe from the Plat. Plantings in the grey walk above are extended in drifts from the upper levels to unite with grey and silver plants at the base of the wall. Lavenders and campanulas originally planted in the vertical faces seed and spread informally.]

'As an example, on a sunny wall there may be a colour scheme of grey with purple of various shades, white and pale pink, composed of dwarf lavender, nepeta, aubretia, cerastium, helianthemums of the kinds that have grey leaves and white and pale pink bloom, rock pinks, stachys, the dwarf artemisias and *Achillea umbellata* [*A. argentea*], and in the border above, yuccas, lavender, rosemary, the larger euphorbias, China roses, phlomis and santolina with white and pink snapdragons.' [*Gardens for Small Country Houses*, Jekyll and Weaver, p. 121.]

[Looking north-east from the west end of the pergola, across the Plat to Lutyen's orangery. The main beds are edged with Miss Jekyll's favourite *Bergenia × schmidtii*, and planted with a pink China rose, 'Natalie Nypels', paeonies, lilies and late-flowering aconitums.]

'The great quantity [of plants] we have now to choose from is itself a danger, for in the best and most refined kinds of formal gardening one is more than ever bound to the practice of the most severe restraint in the choice of kinds, and to accept nothing that does not in its own place and way satisfy the critical soul with the serene contentment of an absolute conviction.' [*Formal Gardens Journal* of the RHS, vol. xxvii, 1902.]

[Brick piers, alternating circular and square, with cross stretchers of Spanish chestnut, are used for the pergola at Hestercombe.]

'As to the best plants for pergolas, there is nothing more delightful than grape vines, or for other good foliage aristolochia and Virginia creeper. Where flowering plants are desired, there are wisteria, clematis and preferably the kinds near the species such as *montana*, *flammula* and *vitabla*, white jasmine, Japan honeysuckle, Dutch honeysuckle, *Bignonia radicans* [*Campsis radicans*] and climbing roses.' [*Gardens for Small Country Houses*, Jekyll and Weaver, p. 188.]

JULY

'As far as my own understanding of the colour-requirements of flowers went, it was better to treat blues with contrasts rather than with harmonies. And I have observed, when at one point, from a little distance, I could see in company the pure deep orange of the herring lilies (*L. croceum*) with the brilliant blue of some full-blue delphiniums, how splendid, although audacious, the mixture was, and immediately noted it, so as to take full advantage of the observation when planting-time came. In the autumn, two of the large patches of lilies were therefore taken up and grouped in front of, and partly among, the delphiniums; and even though neither had come to anything like full strength in the past summer (the first year after removal), yet I could see already how grandly they went together, and how well worth doing and recommending such a mixture was. The delphiniums should be of a full deep-blue colour, not perhaps the very darkest, and not any with a purple shade.' *Home and Garden,* p. 83.

Scarcity of flowers — Delphiniums — Yuccas — Cottager's way of protecting tender plants — Alströmerias — [Eryngiums] — Carnations — Gypsophila — [Herbaceous clematis] — *Lilium giganteum* [*Cardiocrinum giganteum* — Seasonal and colour borders — Penstemons — Division of border plants — Use of shrubs in border to save labour — Free-growing roses] — Cutting of fern pegs.

AFTER THE WEALTH OF BLOOM of June, there appear to be but few flowers in the garden; there seems to be a time of comparative emptiness between the earlier flowers and those of autumn. It is true that in the early days of July we have delphiniums, the grandest blues of the flower year. They are in two main groups in the flower border, one of them nearly all of the palest kind – not a solid clump but with a thicker nucleus, thinning away for several yards right and left. Only white and pale-yellow flowers are grouped with this, and pale, fresh-looking foliage of maize [*Zea mays*, Indian corn, an annual] and funkia [hosta, probably *H. fortunei* 'Albo-picta' and *H. f.* 'Aurea'].

The other group is at some distance, at the extreme western end. This is of the full and deeper blues, following a clump of yuccas, and grouped about with things of important silvery foliage, such as globe artichoke [*Cynara scolymus*; the cardoon, *Cynara cardunculus*, has even greyer leaves, long and silvery] and silver thistle (eryngium [probably *E. giganteum*]). I have found it satisfactory to grow delphiniums from seed, choosing the fine strong 'Cantab' as the seed-parent, because the flowers were of a medium colour – scarcely so light as the name would imply – and because of its vigorous habit and well-shaped spike. It produced flowers of all shades of blue, and from these were derived nearly all I have in the border. I found them better for the purpose in many cases than the named kinds of which I had a fair collection.

[Today there are even more named varieties available as well as seed strains which can produce excellent plants if time and space can be given to selection.]

Delphiniums are greedy feeders, and pay for rich cultivation and for liberal manurial mulches and waterings. In a hot summer, if not well cared for, they get stunted and are miserable objects, the flower distorted and cramped into a clumsy-looking, elongated mop-head.

Though weak in growth the old *Delphinium belladonna* has so lovely a quality of colour that it is quite indispensable; the feeble stem should be carefully and unobtrusively staked for the better display of its incomparable blue. [*See* COLOUR, pp. 290–1 for more descriptions of delphiniums.]

Some of the yuccas will bloom before the end of the month. I have them in bold patches the whole fifteen-feet depth of the border at the extreme ends, and on each side of the pathway, where, passing from the lawn to the paeony ground, it cuts across the border to go through the arched gateway. The kinds of yucca are *gloriosa, recurva* [*recurvifolia*], *flaccida*, and *filamentosa*. They are good to look at at all times of the year because of their grand strong foliage, and are the glory of the garden when in flower. One of the *gloriosa* threw up a stout flower spike in January. I had thought of protecting and roofing the spike, in the hope of carrying it safely through till spring, but meanwhile there came a damp day and a frosty night, and when I saw it again it was spoilt. The *Y. filamentosa* that I have I was told by a trusty botanist was the true plant, but rather tender, the one commonly called that name being something else. I found it in a cottage garden, where I learnt a useful lesson in protecting plants, namely, the use of thickly-cut peaty sods. The goodwife had noticed that the peaty ground of the adjoining common, covered with heath and gorse and mossy grass, resisted frost much better than the garden or meadow, and it had been her practice for many years to get some thick dry sods with the heath left on and to pack them close round to protect tender plants. In this way she had preserved her fuchsias of greenhouse kinds, and calceolarias, and the yucca in question.

The most brilliant mass of flower in early July is given by the beds of *Alströmeria aurantica*; of this we have three distinct varieties, all desirable. There is a four feet wide bed, some forty feet long, of the kind most common in gardens, and at a distance from it a group grown from selected seed of a paler colour; seedlings of this remain true to colour, or, as gardeners say, the variety is 'fixed'. The third sort is from a good old garden in Ireland larger in every way than the type, with petals of great width, and extremely rich in colour. *A. chilensis* is an equally good plant, and beds of it are beautiful in their varied colourings, all beautifully harmonious, and ranging through nearly the same tints as hardy azaleas. These are the best of the alströmerias for ordinary garden culture; they do well in warm sheltered places in the poorest soil, but the soil must be deep, for the bunches of tender, fleshy roots go far down. The roots are extremely brittle, and must be carefully handled. Alströmerias are easily raised from seed, but when the seedlings are planted out the crowns should be quite four inches under the surface, and have a thick bed of leaves or some other mild mulching material over them in winter to protect them from frost, for they are Chilean plants, and demand and deserve a little surface comfort to carry them safely through the average English winter. [Perhaps the most widely grown alströmeria today is from a group of hybrids formed from *A.* × *ligtu* and *A. haemantha* in which colour blends from pink and salmon to orange. It is a less rapid colonizer than *A. aurantiaca*, and the pale variable colours look well in a massed planting.]

Sea-holly (eryngium) is another family [genus] of July-flowering plants that does well on poor, sandy soils that have been deeply stirred. Of these the more generally useful is *E. oliverianum*, the *E. amethystinum* of nurserymen, but so named in error, the true plant being rare and scarcely known in gardens. The whole plant has an admirable structure of a dry and nervous quality, with a metallic colouring and dull lustre that are in strong contrast to softer types of vegetation. The black-coated roots go down straight and deep, and enable it to withstand almost any kind of drought. Equalling it in beauty is *E. giganteum*, the silver thistle, of the same metallic texture, but whitish and almost silvery. This is a biennial, and should be sown every year. A more lowly plant, but hardly less beautiful, is the wild sea-holly of our coasts (*E. maritimum*), with leaves almost blue, and a handsome tuft of flower nearly matching them in colour. It occurs on wind-blown sandhills, but is worth a place in any garden. It comes up rather late, but endures, apparently unchanged, except for the bloom, throughout the late summer and autumn.

[To these we might add *E. agavifolium* and its near relation *E. serra*, which both make rosettes of sharply toothed leaves from which flower-heads on four- or five-foot stems rise in late summer. The rosettes are evergreen and attractive in winter. Another eryngium which has attractive winter foliage is *E. varifolium*, which quickly makes a mass, with white-veined green leaves and flower-heads to eighteen inches, thriving in light shade and useful under spring-flowering deciduous shrubs. *E. tripartitum*, probably a hybrid, is reputedly similar to the true, but elusive, *E. amethystinum*. It produces widespread branches to three feet, with blue heads and dark blue spiky bracts; the flowers are most striking but the leaves perhaps less so than others. The Mexican *E. proteiflorum* is remarkable with spiny leaves and flowers of steely white, but, although now available as seed, is difficult and fussy, even when given full sun and fine drainage. *E. giganteum*, known as Miss Wilmott's Ghost, will self-seed freely so there is little need to gather and sow; it is easily transplanted before it has time to develop its long tap roots. Miss Jekyll used it in her blue garden where its steely grey-blue complemented the pure blue flowers of anchusa, lobelias etc. In her July border she places *E. oliverianum* behind the darker blue *Tradescantia virginica*, with *Thalictrum flavum* behind and flanked by the stronger yellow of *Coreopsis lanceolata*, *Achillea* (*filipendulina*) and yellow cannas.]

But the flower of this month that has the firmest hold of the gardener's heart is the carnation – the glove gilliflower of our ancestors. Why the good old name 'gilliflower' has gone out of use it is impossible to say, for certainly the popularity of the flower has never waned. Indeed in the seventeenth century it seems that it was the best-loved flower of all England; for John Parkinson, perhaps our earliest writer on garden plants, devoted to it a whole chapter in his 'Paradisus Terrestris', a distinction shared by few other flowers. He describes no less than fifty kinds, a few of which are still to be recognized, though some are lost. For instance, what has become of the 'gret gray Hulo', which he describes as a plant of the largest and strongest habit? The 'gray' in this must refer to the colour of the leaf, as he says the flower is red; but there is also a variety called the 'Blew Hulo', with flowers of a 'purplish murrey' colouring, answering to the slate colour that we know of not unfrequent occurrence. The branch of the family that we still cultivate as 'Painted Lady' is named by him 'Dainty Lady', the present name being no doubt an accidental and regrettable corruption. But though some of the older sorts may be lost, we have such a wealth of good known kinds that this need hardly be a matter of regret. The old red clove always holds its own for hardiness, beauty, and perfume; its newer and dwarfer variety, 'Paul Englehart', is quite indispensable, while the beautiful salmon-coloured 'Raby' is perhaps the most useful of all, with its hardy constitution and great quantity of bloom. But it is difficult to grow carnations on our very poor soil; even when it is carefully prepared they still feel its starving and drying influence, and show their distaste by unusual shortness of life.

[Carnations and garden pinks are some of the oldest flowers in cultivation, the former mainly descended from *Dianthus caryophyllus* and the latter from *D. plumarius*. Some of the old border carnations are now difficult to locate, but named garden pinks of kinds such as 'Brympton Red' and 'Bat's Double Red' can be found. The famous 'Mrs Sinkins' (1868) has a fine double white flower. The pinks flower in June and the border carnations later, probably in July. The popular *D. × allwoodii* hybrids of the early twentieth century are more or less perpetual flowering, and are basically obtained from crossing the old fringed white pink with the perpetual flowering carnation. The small and mainly alpine Dianthus species are really separate from the above and can be grown on the edge of rockeries, in dry walls etc.

Among the easiest and most attractive are *D. caesius*

159

(Cheddar pink) and *D. deltoides*. The border carnations and Garden pinks like a fairly rich garden loam in a bed raised above ordinary ground level, and top dressings of good well-rotted farmyard manure in March and thorough watering after hot dry days in summer. Miss Jekyll's sandy soil would prevent any possibility of water-logged roots but would require careful feeding. They are easily increased by layering or from heeled 'slips' as cuttings. Miss Jekyll frequently used white pinks for edging and then may have planted both the old fringed type as well as the more recent hybrid 'Mrs Sinkins'.]

Gypsophila paniculata is one of the most useful plants of this time of year; its delicate blooms are like clouds of flowery mist settled down upon the flower borders. Shooting up behind and among it is a salmon-coloured gladiolus, a telling contrast both in form and manner of inflorescence. Nothing in the garden has been more satisfactory and useful than a hedge of the white everlasting pea [*Lathyrus latifolius* 'Albus']. The thick black roots that go down straight and deep have been undisturbed for some years, and the plants yield a harvest of strong white bloom for cutting that seems almost inexhaustible. They are staked with stiff branching spray, thrust into the ground diagonally, and not reaching up too high. This supports the heavy mass of growth without encumbering the upper blooming part.

Hydrangeas are well in flower at the foot of a warm wall, and in the same position are spreading masses of the beautiful *Clematis davidiana* [*C. heracleifolia davidiana*], a herbaceous kind, with large, somewhat vine-like leaves and flowers of a pale-blue colour of a delicate and uncommon quality. [This clematis now has some splendid cultivars or hybrids. 'Cote d'Azur' would have been known to Miss Jekyll, and was very popular until superseded by 'Wyevale' with clear China-blue flowers over a very long period. *C. × jouiniana* makes a woody stem and will clamber vigorously to seven feet; its milky blue flowers are fragrant. 'Praccos' is an early-flowering cultivar. Another species *C. integrifolia* has been hybridized with *C. × jackmanii* to form the beautiful August-flowering *C. × durandii*, which combines herbaceous character with the large flowers from the latter parent. The flowers are indigo-blue.]

The blooming of the *Lilium giganteum* [*Cardiocrinum giganteum*; *see also* OCTOBER, p. 229] is one of the great flower events of the year. It is planted in rather large straggling groups just within the fringe of the copse. In March the bulbs, which are only just underground, thrust their sharply pointed bottle-green tips out of the earth. These soon expand into heart-shaped leaves looking much like arum foliage of the largest size, and of a bright green colour and glistening surface. The groups are so placed that they never see the morning sun. They require a slight sheltering of fir-bough, or anything suitable till the third week of May, to protect the young leaves from the late frosts. In June the flower-stem shoots up straight and tall, like a vigorous young green-stemmed tree . . . The upper part of the stem bears the gracefully drooping great white lily flowers, each bloom some ten inches long, greenish when in bud, but changing to white when fully developed. Inside each petal is a purplish-red stripe.

In the evening the scent seems to pour out of the great white trumpets, and is almost overpowering, but gains a delicate quality by passing through the air, and at fifty yards away is like a faint waft of incense . . . The flowers only last a few days, but when they are over the beauty of the plant is by no means gone, for the handsome leaves remain in perfection till the autumn, while the growing seed-pods rising into an erect position, become large and rather handsome objects . . . The original bulb is, of course, gone, but when the plants that have flowered are taken up at the end of November, offsets are found clustered round the root; these are carefully detached and replanted. The great growth of these lilies could not be expected to come to perfection in our very poor shallow soil, for doubtless in their mountain home in the eastern Himalayas they grow in deep beds of cool vegetable earth. Here, therefore, their beds are deeply excavated, and filled to within a foot of the top with any of the vegetable rubbish of which only too much is accumulated in the late autumn . . . the upper foot of the soil is of good compost, and when the young bulbs are planted, the whole is covered with some inches of dead leaves that join in with the natural woodland carpet.

[Miss Jekyll arranges much of her garden for consecutive

161

[Miss Jekyll planted this biennial thistle, *Eryngium giganteum*, in her grey borders where flowers were mainly of white, pink and light and dark purple.]

'. . . the silver thistle of . . . metallic texture, but whitish and almost silvery.' [*Wood and Garden*, Gertrude Jekyll, p. 93.]

[*Lathryus latifolius* 'White Pearl'. Miss Jekyll used this free-flowering pea in many border schemes, particularly for training forward over thistle and delphinium stalks in late summer.]

'The white everlasting pea notched into the back of the echinops is meant to be trained over and among the branches of the globe thistle as this goes out of flower.' ['Border plants that succeed best on light soils', *The Garden*, 12 March 1921.]

flowering seasons.] The earliest of the season gardens will be for April and early May; the one next to follow for May and June. Then will come the main display for July, August and September . . . Every border should be carefully considered for colour effect. Without such preparatory care the result will be a mere jumble, of no value to the cultivated eye. For a border of some length it is found best to keep the ends cool in colouring, with a large amount of grey foliage, and to approach the middle through flowers and foliage of increasingly warm colour, with a gorgeous climax of strong reds nearly midway in the length. Thus taking the July to September border month by month, one end in July – to name some of the more important flowers – would have delphinium, white lily [probably Madonna lily, but possibly *L. regale*, which was introduced in 1908 and thereafter very widely grown], white foxglove and eryngium, with foamy masses of the bushy *Clematis recta* and white tree lupin, passing to the pale yellow of thalictrum, mullein [verbascum], the tall oenothera and the pale yellow day-lily; then onwards in strength of colour in alströmeria, orange day-lily and the fine *L. croceum* to the scarlet of *Lychnis chalcedonica*.

'The Hardy Flower Border', *Country Life*, 6 April 1912

The sequence of colour would then again proceed by orange and yellow to the far end, where there would be galega white and purple, *Chrysanthemum maximum*, the tall white campanulas, *macrantha* and *persicifolia*, and white everlasting pea [*see above*] with the splendid purple of *Campanula macrocarpa* [could she mean a form of *C. glomerata*; if so, *C. glomerata* 'Superba' (1910) may well be the one? It is an excellent plant with typical leafy stems and intense violet-purple flowers, massed in a rounded head at the top eighteen inches] and the noble cranesbill, *Geranium ibericum* [probably *G.* × *magnificum*, which has violet-blue flowers and handsome hairy rounded leaves]. These will be followed in August by *Anemone japonica*, white and pink; echinops, erigeron, gypsophila, *Lilium longiflorum* at the cool ends, and hollyhock, helenium, penstemon, red phlox etc. in the middle.

Among the best flowers of July that have a place . . . are the penstemons planted last year. We grow them afresh from cuttings every autumn, planting them out in April. They are not quite hardy, and a bad winter may destroy all the last year's plants.

Colour Schemes

But if these can be saved they bloom in July, whereas those planted in the spring of the year do not flower till later. So we protect the older plants with fir-boughs and generally succeed in saving them.

[One of Miss Jekyll's penstemons was 'Spitzberg' of palest pink colouring, a name not now found in modern lists. These half-hardy border plants have colourings from dark red *P. campanulatus* 'Garnet', rose-pink *P.c.* 'Evelyn', scarlet *P. hartwegii* and *P. gloxinioides* 'Schoenholzeri', which is a brilliant scarlet and larger than *P. hartwegii*. *P.g.* 'Sour Grapes' and *P. gentianoides* 'Alice Hindley' are blue-purple and cool lilac respectively.]

[Of course other herbaceous plants, although completely hardy, may need replanting every few years.]

There are a number of plants in a well-established flower border that can only rarely be moved – deep-rooting things like everlasting pea, gypsophila, eryngiums, paeonies, Oriental poppies and clematis species – and a certain number that require replanting every two or three years, such as echinops, *Salvia virgata* [now a form of *S. nemorosa*, the best known being 'Superba', for a central position, growing to three feet, or the dwarf 'Lubeca' for the front of a border], delphiniums, hollyhocks, phloxes and iris. But the greater number of the good hardy perennials are the better for a yearly shift. In light soil this is best done in autumn, but in many gardens, and especially those on stiff soils, it is either more convenient or more salutary to renew them in the spring . . . the ground is freshly manured, the plants divided and carefully replaced according to their needs. Delphiniums will be one of the first cares; the clumps that have stood for three years come up and are carefully divided with a sharp knife into pieces with two or three crowns. Phloxes soon become woody at the base; three-year-old plants will cut up into a number, and though young plants from spring cuttings, with single shoots, give the handsomest blooms, yet the divisions from the older clumps are too good to be discarded. *Chrysanthemum maximum* increases about three-fold in the year, and is divided so as to have three or four crowns to each piece. *Artemisia lactiflora*, a plant of quick increase, divides in about the same way and is replanted in anticipation of its pleasant association with the pale primrose-coloured annual sunflower [*Helianthus annuus*]. The tall *H. orgyalis*, so useful for pegging down for an autumn display over earlier plants that have gone out of bloom, is also a plant of ready increase . . . The thalictrums are left in place for three years. Two kinds are favourites in the border – the tall *T. flavum* [*T. speciosissimum*] and the purple-coloured form of *T. aquilegifolium*. It is interesting to cut down the tall, hollow stems of *T. flavum* while they are still green, each cut gives a distinct musical note . . . *Anthemis tinctoria* may stand for two years, but is rather better if yearly divided.

This good plant is in several shades of yellow; the paler is the better and more refined, and is the more desirable because there are so many more flowers of the deeper yellow. Oenotheras of the fruticosa section are best divided yearly, also that useful front edge plant *Rudbeckia speciosa*, which in all soils is best replanted in spring. [*See* OCTOBER, pp. 221–7 for more on dividing and replanting.]

'Spring Planting for the Summer', *Gardening Illustrated*, 14 March 1926

[Generally speaking Miss Jekyll's replanting times can be much extended. She wrote in a period of cheap available labour. It may be easier too to take cuttings of the doubtfully hardy types of plants, such as penstemons, and thus ensure annual renewing, than to grow too many of the so called hardy perennials, which need dividing and replanting on a yearly basis.

Flowering shrubs, among them old favourites such as lavender, can be substituted for herbaceous plants which tend to demand constant replanting. In July *Buddleia davidii*, if hard-pruned in February, starts to flower and its many forms cover colour from white to lilac-pink, deep red-purple, deep violet to violet-blue. The hybrid *B.* × 'Loch Inch' has grey leaves and scented blue flowers with a deep orange eye. Escallonias such as 'Apple Blossom' with pink and white flowers and the larger 'Donard Seedling' would enhance borders based on pink, white and purple. Grey-leaved cistus such as 'Peggy Sannons', 'Silver Pink' and *Cistus* × *skanbergii* have pale pink flowers and thrive in a

hot border. The deciduous hoherias *H. glabrata* and
H. lyalli have white flowers in July, and forms of *Potentilla
fruticosa* have white, cream, pale yellow and orange-
tangerine bloom over a long period. Hardy fuchsia and
Phygelius capensis have strong red flowers which combine
with *Monarda didyma* to give body and colour when
annuals, dahlias and half-hardy cannas cause too much
work. *Crocosmia masonorum* with fiery orange flowers and
Curtonus paniculatus with dark red, both have decorative
arching sword-shaped leaves. Day-lilies make splendid
grassy clumps with flowers of pale yellowy lemon to
mahogany-red and apricot-pink. Chosen carefully they
will cover similar colour ranges to helianthus and heleniums, and need less staking and attention. When shrubs
are grown in the border a strong purple-blue clematis such
as *C. jackmanii* can be trained over them or up a tripod to
give the effect of the blue-purple which looks so fine with
grey foliage.]

[From the middle of June until the middle of July some of Miss
Jekyll's favourite roses are in flower. She describes the use of]
'roses as fountains and growing free'.

Among the many ways of worthily using the free Ayrshire
roses, one of the best is to leave them to their own way of
growth, without any staking or guiding whatever. Due space
must be allowed for their full size, which will be a diameter of
some ten feet. Of these useful garden roses none is more beautiful
than 'The Garland', with its masses of pretty blush-white bloom.
It is well worth getting up at 4 a.m. on a mid-June morning to
see the tender loveliness of the newly opening buds; for, beautiful though they are at noon, they are better still when just
awaking after the refreshing influence of the short summer
night . . . A grassy space where they may be seen all round, or a
place where the great bush may be free at least on two sides, are
the most suitable, or they may be used as central or symmetric-
ally recurring points in a rose garden of some size. The young
growths that show above the mass when the bloom is waning
are the flowering branches of next year; they will arch over and

bear the clusters of flowers on short stems thrown out at each joint. The way these young main branches spring up and bend over when mature is exactly the way that best displays the bloom.

Each little flower of the cluster is shown in just the most beautiful way; and it is charming to see, when light winds are about, how the ends of the sprays, slightly stirred by the active air, make pretty curtseying movements arising from the weight of the crowded bloom and the elasticity of the supporting stem. There is a whole range of these beautiful roses, from this free fountain shape without any artificial support, to association with trees and bushes in shrub clumps and wood edges, and from that to clambering into the trees themselves . . . when these free roses rush up into trees, instead of throwing out their new growths from close to the earth, they are formed upon the older wood higher up, and the stem or stems that supports them goes on growing till sometimes they attain a considerable thickness . . .

For spaces between garden and wild, for sloping banks, for broken ground, as of an old gravel pit or other excavation, for all sorts of odds and ends of unclassified places about the home grounds, the rambling and free-growing roses seem to be offered us by a specially benevolent horticultural providence. A well-prepared hole is all they need at first. About four years after planting, if the best they can do for us is desired, they should be looked to in the way of removing old wood. This should be done every two years, but beyond this they need no pruning and no staking whatever. When they begin to grow freely among bushes or trees, if it is desired to lead the far-reaching growths one way rather than another, it is easily done with a long forked stick, and a very pleasant and interesting job it is. It is like painting a picture with an immensely long-handled brush, for with a fourteen-foot pole with a forked end one can guide the branches into yew or holly or tall thorn very nearly into such forms of upright spring or downward swag as one pleases. It is pleasant, too, in such rough places, to see the behaviour of one of these roses on the ground without support, and to watch the different way of its own brother plant climbing into a neighbouring tree.

[Another advantage of these roses is] their great usefulness for *Colour Schemes* forming lines of arch and garland as an enclosure to some definite place. I have them like this forming the boundary on two sides of a garden of long beds, whose other two sides are a seven-foot wall and the back of a stable and loft. [Miss Jekyll used roses such as 'The Garland', a *multiflora* hybrid, 'Dundee Rambler', an Ayrshire hybrid, 'Félicité et Perpetué', a *sempervirens* hybrid and so-called Musk Ramblers such as *R. brunonii* which were then available. To these we can add the species *R. filipes*, which is mainly grown as its giant form 'Kiftsgate', the late-flowering *R. longicuspis* (recently correctly named *R. mulliganii*) with attractive clusters of orange-brown hips, *R. helenae* and the scented hybrid 'Bobby James'. All have superficially the same type of clustered small flower and tend to come into bloom as the first flush of June bush and climbing roses ceases, and are a useful addition to a July garden. The pink seedlings of *filipes* known as 'Gardener's Pink' and 'Brenda Colvin' (there seems to be little difference between these two seedlings) make particularly attractive mounds with fresh green glossy leaves and small cupped pink flowers, yellow centred. Today when apple and pear trees are often neglected in favour of the more easily picked bushes, roses can be encouraged to clamber into the old orchard trees.]

Wood and Garden [Returning to July:] In the end of July we have some of the hottest of the summer days, only beginning to cool between six and seven in the evening. One or two evenings I go to the upper part of the wood to cut some fern pegs for pegging carnation layers, armed with a fag-hook and knife and rubber, and a low rush-bottomed stool to sit on. The rubber is the stone for sharpening the knife – a long stone of coarse sandstone grit, such as is used for scythes. Whenever I am at work with a knife there is sure to be a rubber not far off, for a blunt knife I cannot endure, so there is a stone in each department of the garden sheds, and a whole series in the workshop, and one or two to spare to take on outside jobs. The bracken has to be cut with a light hand as the side-shoots that will make the hook of the peg are easily broken at the important joint. The fronds are of all sizes, from two to eight feet long; but the best for the pegs are the moderate-sized, that have not been weakened by growing too close together. Where they are crowded the main stalk is thick, but the side ones are thin and weak; whereas, where they get light and air the side branches are carried on stouter ribs, and make stronger and better balanced pegs. The cut fern is lightly laid in a long ridge with the ends all one way, and the operator sits at the stalk end of the ridge, a nice cool shady place having been chosen. Four cuts with a knife make a peg, and each frond makes three pegs in about fifteen seconds. With the fronds laid straight and handy it goes almost rhythmically, then each group of three pegs is thrown into the basket, where they clash on to the others with a hard ringing sound. In about four days the pegs dry to a surprising hardness; they are better than wooden ones, and easier and quicker to make.

People who are not used to handling bracken should be careful how they cut a frond with a knife; they are almost sure to get a nasty little cut on the second joint of the first finger of the right hand – not from the knife, but from the cut edge of the fern. The stalk has a silicious coating, that leaves a sharp edge like a thin flake of glass when cut diagonally with a sharp knife; they should also beware how they pick or pull off a mature frond, for even if the part of the stalk laid hold of is bruised and twisted, some of the glassy structure holds together and is likely to wound the hand.

[I suppose today this job will be done with a sharp pair of secateurs; pegs are just as important and although the bracken may be further afield than up in the woodland garden, the fern fronds still make the best and cheapest pegs for all garden uses.]

AUGUST

'How well an artist knows the value of grey-leaved plants, and their use in pictorial gardening in the way of giving colour-value by close companionship, to tender pinks and lilacs, and above all to whites. A patch of white bloom is often too hard and sudden and inharmonious to satisfy the trained eye, but led up to and softened and sweetened by masses of neighbouring tender grey it takes its proper place and comes to its right strength in the well-ordered scheme. Lavender, lavender-cotton (santolina), catmint, pinks and carnations and the woolly woundwort (stachys) with some other plants of hoary foliage, do this good work.' Elgood, about his garden, p. 59

Leycesteria — Early recollections — Bank of choice shrubs — [Alternatives for lime] — Bank of briar roses — Hollyhocks — Lavender — Lilies — Bracken and Heath — The fern walk — Late blooming rock plants — Autumn flowers — [The August border — Devices for more flowers — August borders of pink and white with grey foliage] — Tea roses — Fruit of *Rosa rugosa* — Fungi — Chanterelle.

LEYCESTERIA FORMOSA is a soft-wooded shrub, whose beauty, without being showy, is full of charm and refinement. I remember delighting in it in the shrub wilderness of the old home, where I first learnt to know and love many a good bush and tree long before I knew their names. There were towering rhododendrons (all *ponticum*) and ailanthus and hickory and magnolias, and then spirae and snowball tree [*Viburnum opulus* 'Sterile'] and tall yellow azalea [*Rhododendron luteum*] and Buttercup bush [*Kerria japonica*] and the shrubby andromedas, and in some of the clumps tall cypresses and the pretty cut-leaved beech [*Fagus sylvatica heterophylla*], and in the edges of others some of the good old garden roses, double cinnamon [*R. cinnamomea*] and *R. lucida* [*R. virginiana*], and Damask and Provence, Moss rose and sweetbriar [*R. rubiginosa*], besides tall-grown lilacs and syringa [*philadelphus*]. It was all rather overgrown, and perhaps all the prettier, and some of the wide grassy ways were quite shady in summer. And I look back across the years and think what a fine lesson book it was to a rather solitary child; and when I came to plant my own shrub clump I thought I would put rather near together some of the old favourites, so here again we come back to leycesteria, put in rather a place of honour, and near it a buttercup bush and andromeda and magnolias and old garden roses.

I had no space for a shrub wilderness, but have made a large clump for just the things I like best, whether new friends or old.

It is a long, low bank, five or six paces wide, highest in the middle, where the rather taller things are planted. These are mostly junipers and magnolias; of the magnolias the kinds are [×] *soulangiana, conspicua* [*denudata*], *purpurea* [*liliflora* 'Nigra'] and *stellata*. One end of the clump is all of peat earth; here are andromedas, skimmias, and on the cooler side the broad-leaved gale [*Myrica gale*], whose crushed leaves have almost the sweetness of myrtle [*M. communis*]. One long side of the clump faces south-west, the better to suit the things that love the sun. At the farther end is a thrifty bush of *Styrax japonica*, which flowers well in hot summers, but another bush under a south wall flowers better. It must be a lovely shrub in the south of Europe and perhaps in Cornwall; here the year's growth is always cut at the tip, but it flowers well on the older wood, and its hanging clusters of white bloom are lovely. At its foot on the sunny side, are low bushy plants of *Cistus florentinus*. I am told that this specific name is not right; but the plant so commonly goes by it that it serves the purpose of popular identification. [Whatever the correct nomenclature for this cistus, generally considered a natural hybrid between *C. monspeliensis* and *C. salviifolius*, a better and hardier plant is *C.* × *corbariensis*, very similar with white flowers and faintly crinkly leaves. At Hestercombe it has been used instead of *C.* × *florentinus*.]

Then comes *Magnolia stellata*, now a perfectly-shaped bush five feet through, a sheet of sweet-scented bloom in April. Much too near it are two bushes of *Cistus ladaniferus* [*C. ladanifer*]. They were put there as little plants to grow for a year in the shelter and comfort of the warm bank, but were overlooked at the time they ought to have been shifted and are now nearly five feet high, and are crowding the magnolia. I cannot bear to take them away to waste, and they are much too large to transplant, so I am driving in some short stakes diagonally and tying them down by degrees, spreading out their branches between neighbouring plants. It is an upright growing cistus that would soon cover a tallish wall-space, but this time it must be content to grow horizontally, and I shall watch to see whether it will flower more freely, as so many things do when trained down.

Next comes a patch of the handsome *Bambusa ragamowski*, dwarf, but with strikingly-broad leaves of a bright yellow colour. [Now *Sasa tessellata*, this hardy bamboo creates an almost tropical effect with large leaves and low stature. A very dramatic garden plant but with a dangerously spreading root system.] It seems to be a slow grower, or more probably it is slow to grow at first; bamboos have a good deal to do underground. It was planted six years ago, a nice little plant in a pot, and now is eighteen inches high and two feet across. Just beyond is the mastic bush (*Caryopteris mastacanthus*) [now *C. incana*, the dominant parent of the hybrid *C. × clandonensis*, which together with its improved garden forms such as 'Ferndown' and 'Heavenly Blue' is most frequently seen today], a neat, grey-leaved small shrub, crowded in September with lavender-blue flowers, arranged in spikes something like a veronica; the whole bush is aromatic, smelling strongly like highly refined turpentine. Then comes *Xanthoceras sorbifolia* [*X. sorbifolium*], a handsome bush from China, of recent introduction, with saw-edged pinnate leaves and white flowers earlier in the summer, but now forming its bunches of fruit that might easily be mistaken for walnuts with their green shucks on. Here a wide bushy growth of *Phlomis fruticosa* lays out to the sun, covered in early summer with its stiff whorls of hooded yellow flowers – one of the best of plants for a sunny bank in full sun in a poor soil.

A little further along, and near the path, comes the neat little *Deutzia parvifolia* [later confirmed as *D. amurensis*] and another little shrub of fairy-like delicacy, *Philadelphus microphyllus*. Behind them is *Stephanandra flexuosa* [*S. incisa*], beautiful in foliage, and two good St John's worts, *Hypericum aureum* [*H. frondosum*] and *H. moserianum*, and again in front a cistus of low, spreading growth, *C. halimifolius* [*Halimium halimifolium*], or something near it. One or two favourite kinds of tree paeonies, comfortably sheltered by lavender bushes, fill up the other end of the clump next to the andromedas. In all spare spaces on the sunny side of the shrub-clump is a carpeting of *Megasea ligulata* [*Bergenia ciliata ligulata*] a plant that looks well all the year round, and gives a quantity of precious flower for cutting in March and April. I was nearly forgetting *Aesculus macrostachya* [*A. parviflora*], now well established among the choice shrubs. It is like a bush horse-chestnut, but more refined, the white spikes standing well up above the handsome leaves. [This old bush is still at Munstead Wood, but alone now in an expanse of lawn where the bank has been smoothed down and turfed over.] On the cooler side of the clump is a longish planting of dwarf andromeda, precious not only for its beauty of form and flower, but for the fine winter colouring of the leaves, and those two useful spiraeas, *S. thunbergii*, with its countless little starry flowers, and the double *prunifolia*, the neat leaves of whose long sprays turn nearly scarlet in autumn. Then there comes a long stretch of *Artemisia stelleriana*, a white-leaved plant much like *Cineraria maritima* [*Senecio bicolor*], answering just the same purpose, but perfectly hardy. It is so much like the silvery cineraria that it is difficult to remember that it prefers a cool and even partly-shaded place.

[Miss Jekyll had built her bank up using well-manured loam and peat to give a richness and depth not naturally present in the poor sandy soil of Munstead Wood, but ideal for magnolias and the attractive acid-loving styrax. Forms of the hybrid *Magnolia × soulangiana* such as 'Lennei', and a hybrid such as *M. × loebneri* 'Leonard Messel', would do well in calcareous soils. *M. stellata* is small and compact with very pretty white many-petalled flowers in March and April; most suitable for small town gardens and undemanding in cultivation. June-flowering shrubs to plant instead of *Styrax japonica* might be the small almost tree-like *Malus trilobata*, viburnums such as *V. betulifolium* or *V. dilatatum*, which are also attractive in autumn with bronze foliage and magnificent clusters of red-currant-like fruit.

The low evergreen andromedas and skimmias (the latter is reasonably lime-tolerant) can be replaced by shrubs such as *Nandina domestica*, with neat bamboo-like stems and small terminal panicles of white flowers in summer, prostrate box (*Buxus sempervirens* 'Prostrata'), *Prunus laurocerasus* 'Otto Luyken' and a selection of ground-hugging cotoneaster.

Some new phlomis might replace the old-fashioned *P. fruticosa*. *P. chrysophylla* is as hardy and has larger leaves and pale yellow flowers, a shrub which quickly loses shape unless regularly pruned in spring. A recent introduction, *P. anatolica*, seems reliably hardy and has large grey furry leaves; most desirable. Miss Jekyll frequently used the hybrid bergenia *B.* × *schmidtii*, which has toothed margins and early clear pink flowers on stems up to one foot. The more recent cultivar 'Silberlicht' has pure white flowers ageing to pink, and very handsome robust foliage. *Aesculus parviflora* can grow to twelve feet across and six to seven high, and is an excellent late-summer shrub, not seen often enough. The drifts of bergenia and *Artemisia stelleriana* will effectively control weeds but the latter grows woody with age, so a grey-leaved prostrate hebe such as *H. pinguifolia* 'Pagei' might be a useful alternative. A good-coloured foliage plant which quickly carpets the ground in shade is *Lamium maculatum* 'Beacon Silver', with glowing grey-green pinkish leaves. *L. maculatum* itself spreads and seeds with too much abandon and has a poor mauve flower, but the pale pink ar.d the white varieties are very pretty and much less vigorous and prolific. I have seen the white *L. maculatum* 'Album' used with great effect as a thick carpet inside a box-edged bed. *L. galeobdolon*, now correctly *Galeobdolon luteum* 'Variegatum', is only for the larger garden, or for real problem areas under shady trees.]

Beyond the long ridge that forms the shrub-clump is another, parallel to it and only separated from it by a path, also in the form of a long low bank. On the crown of this is the double row of cob-nuts that forms one side of the nut-alley. It leaves a low sunny bank that I have given to various briar roses and one or two other low bushy kinds. Here is the wild Burnet rose [*R. pimpinellifolia*], with its yellow-white single flowers and large black hips, and its garden varieties, the Scotch briars, double white, flesh coloured, pink, rose and yellow, and the hybrid briar, 'Stanwell Perpetual'. [The latter with soft pink flowers and grey-green leaves flowers spasmodically all summer. More recent *spinosissima* or *pimpinellifolia* hybrids are the splendid arching 'Frühlingsgold' with semi-double creamy-yellow flowers and 'Frühlingsduft' with double Hybrid Tea-type apricot-cream flowers in May, both very fragrant, bushes to six feet.]

Here also is the fine hybrid of *R. rugosa* 'Madame Georges Bruant' [not available today but similar in type to 'Agnes' and 'Mrs Anthony Waterer'], and the double *R. lucida* [*R. virginiana* 'Rose d'Amour', a lovely spreading late-flowerer from America], and one or two kinds of small bush roses from out-of-the-way gardens, and two wild roses that have for me a special interest, as I have collected them from their rocky home in the island of Capri. One is a sweetbriar [*R. rubiginosa*], in all ways like the native one, except that the flowers are nearly white, and the hips are larger. Last year the bush was distinctly more showy than any other of its kind, on account of the size and unusual quantity of its fruit. The other is a form of *R. sempervirens*, with large white flowers faintly tinged with yellow.

Hollyhocks have been fine, in spite of the disease, which may be partly checked by very liberal treatment [presumably rich feeding]. By far the most beautiful is one of a pure pink colour, with a wide outer frill. It came first from a cottage garden, and has always since been treasured. I called it 'Pink Beauty'. The wider outer petal (a heresy to the florist) makes the flower infinitely more beautiful than the all-over full-double form that alone is esteemed on the show-table. I shall hope in time to come upon the same shape of flower in white, sulphur, rose-colour and deep blood-crimson, the colours most worth having in hollyhocks.

[Describing the cutting of lavender spikes (probably *L. angustifolia* 'Munstead'):] to reap its fragrant harvest is one of the many joys of the flower year. If it is to be kept and dried, it should be cut when only a few of the purple blooms are out on the spike; if left too late the flower shakes off the stalk too readily.

Some plantations of *Lilium harrisi* [*L. longiflorum*] and *L. auratum* have turned out well. Some of the *harrisi* were grouped among tufts of the bright foliaged *Funkia grandiflora* [*Hosta plantaginea grandiflora*] on the cool side of a yew hedge. Just at the foot of the hedge is *Tropaeolum speciosum*, which runs up into it and flowers in graceful wreaths some feet above the ground. The masses of pure white lily, and cool green foliage below are fine against the dark, solid greenery of the yew, and the brilliant flowers above are like little jewels of flame. The Bermuda lilies (*harrisi*) are intergrouped with *L. speciosum*, which will follow them when their bloom is over.

[Even reference to Miss Jekyll's own book on lilies, published in 1901, is hardly helpful, since the most easily cultivated and deservedly popular *L. regale* was not introduced until 1905. Many lilies grown in gardens today are American hybrids and have been bred to resist disease and flower freely; a selection must be made to suit each type of soil and site. What is important is Miss Jekyll's grouping of lilies, in flowering succession, with hosta leaves, against a background of dark yew.]

The *L. auratum* were planted among groups of rhododendrons; some of them are between tall rhododendrons, and have large clumps of lady fern (*Felix foemina* [now *Athyrium filix-femina*, with bipinnate fresh green fronds]) in front, but those that look best are between and among bamboos (*B. metake* [*Arundinaria japonica*, the hardiest bamboo for English gardens]); the heavy heads of flower borne on tall stems bend gracefully through the bamboos, which just give them enough support.

Here and there in the copse, among the thick masses of green bracken, is a frond or two turning yellow. This always happens in the first or second week of August, though it is no indication of the approaching yellowing of the whole. But it is taken as a signal that the fern is in full maturity, and a certain quantity is now cut to dry for protection and other winter uses. Dry bracken lightly shaken over frames is a better protection than mats, and is almost as easily moved on and off.

The ling [*Calluna vulgaris*] is now in full flower, and is more beautiful in the landscape than any of the garden heaths [but of course needs a lime-free soil]; the relation of colouring, of greyish foliage and low-toned pink bloom with the dusky spaces of purplish-grey shadow, are a precious lesson to the colour-student.

The fern-walk is at its best. It passes from the garden upwards to near the middle of the copse. The path, a wood-path of moss and grass and short-cut heath, is a little lower than the general level of the wood. The mossy bank, some nine feet wide, and originally cleared for the purpose, is planted with large groups of hardy ferns, with a preponderance (due to preference) of dilated shield fern [*Dryopteris dilatata*] and lady fern [*Athyrium filix-femina*].

Home and Garden

[She describes her favourite hardy native ferns:] Where the wild heathland has been partly tamed and adjoins cultivation, and ditches have been cut, there is the place to look for the large and lovely lady fern. Clear and fresh of colour, stately of port, admirable in the perfect 'set' of the large twice pinnate fronds and in their grace of carriage, arched as they are with a plume-like bending towards the tips – to the lady fern must be accorded the place of honour for beauty among our native kinds. This lovely plant seems most at home when growing at the edge of water with its roots taking up their fill of moisture. To see it thus, with its noble fronds mirrored in the face of the still pool, is to see a picture of fern-beauty that can hardly be surpassed.

The only other of our wild ferns that in my opinion comes at all near the lady fern is the dilated shield fern (*Lastrea dilatata* – [*Dryopteris dilatata*, also called broad buckler fern]), slightly stiffer in form and perhaps all the better for it, for the only defect of the lovely *Filix-femina* is a slightly succulent weakness of aspect. The broad shoulder and equality of plane in the whole frond are distinctive features in this handsome shield fern, and the toothing at the edge has a look of well-finished design that is vigorous without being overhard. The fronds are not many, but are well displayed, and the whole plant conspicuously handsome.

Once or twice in the length of the banks are hollows, sinking at their lowest part to below the path-level, for Osmunda [*O. regalis*, the Royal fern, for moist peaty soil] and Blechnum [*B. spicant*, hard fern, making a good clump with shining evergreen fronds and completely hardy; it also needs lime-free soil]. When the rain is heavy enough to run down the path it finds its way into these hollow places.

Among the groups of fern are a few plants of true wood-character – *Linnaea, Trientalis, Goodyera* and *Trillium*. [*Linnaea*

180

borealis, named after the great Linnaeus, is a prostrate creeping plant with bell-shaped pink flowers. *Trientalis europaea*, with nine-inch stems carrying starry white flowers, is a native of Europe, including Great Britain, but Miss Jekyll may have grown the more robust but very similar *T. borealis*. *Goodyera repens*, the creeping lady's tresses, is an uncommon small native orchid. *Trillium grandiflorum*, the North American Wake Robin, flowers in May and there are species and forms with white, pink and rusty-red flowers. This woodland group is composed of northerners, which prefer cold winters and cool shaded summers. All of them, although not tender, need care in cultivation and are apt to disappear so should not be planted and then ignored; other more vigorous natives will quickly swamp them. [*See also* MARCH and APRIL for other woodlanders such as erythroniums.]

Most of the alpines and dwarf-growing plants, whose home is the rock-garden, bloom in May or June, but a few flower in early autumn. Of these one of the brightest is *Ruta patavina*, a dwarf plant with lemon-coloured flowers and a very neat habit of growth [now *Haplophyllum patavinum*, with aromatic grey leaves, flowering in summer]. It soon makes itself at home in a sunny bank in poor soil. *Pterocephalus parnassi* is a dwarf scabious, with small grey foliage keeping close to the ground, and rather large flowers of a low-toned pink. The white thyme [probably *T. serpyllum*] is a capital plant, perfectly prostrate, and with leaves of a bright yellow-green, that with the white bloom give the plant a particularly fresh appearance. It looks at its best when trailing about little flat spaces between the neater of the hardy ferns, and hanging over little rocky ledges. Somewhat farther back is the handsome dwarf *Platycodon mariesi* [*P. grandiflorus* 'Mariesii' with bud-shaped blooms which expand into soft blue flowers], and behind it the taller platycodons [all forms of *P. grandiflorus*], among full-flowered bushes of *Olearia hastii* [*O.* × *hastii*].

By the middle of August the garden assumes a character distinctly autumnal. Much of its beauty now depends on the many non-hardy plants, such as gladiolus, canna, and dahlia, on tritomas [kniphofias] of doubtful hardiness and on half-hardy annuals – zinnia, helichrysum, sunflower [*Helianthus annuus*] and French and African marigold [*Tagetes patula* and

T. erecta]. Fine as are the newer forms of hybrid gladiolus, the older strain of *gandavensis* hybrids are still the best for border flowers. In the large flower border, tall, well-shaped spikes of a good pink one look well shooting up through and between a wide-spreading patch of the smaller yuccas, *Tritoma caulescens* [*Kniphofia caulescens*], *Iris pallida* and *Funkia sieboldii* [*Hosta sieboldiana*], while scarlet and salmon-coloured kinds are among groups of paeonies that flowered in June, whose leaves are now taking a fine reddish colouring.

[Hybrid gladioli mostly derive from *gandavensis* or *brenchleyensis* and all corms need lifting in autumn and careful frost-free storage. Rather than growing the rather coarse large-flowered hybrids available today I prefer a species such as *G. callianthus*, formerly *Acidanthera murielae*, which has arching flowers, white with dark blotches at the throat and sweetly scented.]

Between these and the edge of the border is a straggling group some yards in length of the dark-foliaged *Heuchera richardsonii* [*H. americana*], that will hold its satin-surfaced leaves till the end of the year. Farther back in the border is a group of the scarlet-flowered *Dahlia* 'Fire King', and behind these, *D.* 'Lady Ardilaun' and 'Cochineal', of deeper scarlet colouring. [The numerous hybrids available are best selected when seen in flower or from reliable lists; forms of the scarlet species *D. coccinea* such as 'Laciniata', 'Purpurea' and 'Bishop of Llandaff' have fierce red flowers and metallic dark coppery-purple foliage.] The dahlias are planted between groups of Oriental poppy [*Papaver orientalis*], that flower in May and then die away till late in the autumn. Right and left of the scarlet group are tritomas [kniphofias], intergrouped with dahlias of moderate height, that have orange and flame-coloured flowers. This leads to some masses of flowers of strong yellow colouring; the old perennial sunflower [*Helianthus atrorubens*] in its tall single form, and the best variety of the old double one of moderate height, the useful *H. laetiflorus* and the tall 'Miss Mellish', the giant form of *H. rigidus*. [These are probably hybrids of the species *H. decapetalus*, and the cultivar 'Miss Mellish' is still in gardens.] *Rudbeckia newmannii* [*R. fulgida*, and particularly the form 'Goldsturm', is the modern equivalent] reflects the same strong colour in the front part of the border, and all spaces are filled with orange zinnias and African marigolds (*see* above) and yellow helichrysum [the half-hardy annual *H. bracteatum*].

As we pass along the border the colour changes to paler yellow by means of a pale perennial sunflower [*Helianthus decapetalus* 'Capenoch Star' would be good] and the sulphur-coloured annual kind (*H. annuus* 'Autumn Beauty'], with Paris daisies [a pale yellow *Chrysanthemum frutescens*], *Oenothera lamarckiana* [a hardy biennial now correctly *O. erythosepala*] and *Verbascum phlomoides*. [This is a good biennial but a perennial might be preferred today. *V. chaixii* grows to three feet, and the hybrid 'Golden Bush' to two feet, making an ideal bushy plant for the front of a border.] The last two were cut down to about four feet after their earliest bloom was over, and are now again full of profusely-flowered lateral growths.

At the further end of the border we come again to glaucous foliage and pale-pink flower of gladiolus and Japan anemone [*A. × hybrida*]. It is important in such a border of rather large size, that can be seen from a good space of lawn, to keep the flowers in rather large masses of colour. No one who has ever done it, or seen it done, will go back to the old haphazard sprinkle of colouring without any thought of arrangement, such as is usually seen in a mixed border.

There is a wall of sandstone backing the border, also planted in relation to the colour massing in the front space. This gives a quiet background of handsome foliage with always in the flower season some show of colour in one part or another of its length. Just now the most conspicuous of its clothing shrubs or of the somewhat tall growing flowers at its foot are a fine variety of *Bignonia radicans* [*Campsis radicans*], a hardy fuchsia, the claret vine [*Vitis vinifera* 'Purpurea'] covering a good space, with its red-bronze leaves and clusters of blue-black grapes, the fine hybrid crinums [*C. × powellii*] and *Clerodendron foetidum* [*C. bungei*, a semi-woody suckering shrub with heart-shaped leaves, carrying terminal corymbs of rosy-red fragrant flowers in August and September].

[In *The Garden* (1929) Miss Jekyll provides a plan and description of 'A Little August Garden'. If we combine the detail with earlier descriptions of the August flower border in *Colour Schemes*, leave out some of the labour-intensive annuals, substituting flowering shrubs (many of which were not readily available and some not yet introduced) we can still create a 'Jekyll' type planting scheme.]

Colour Schemes [For her large border:] The western grey end, with its main planting of hoary and glaucous foliage – yucca, sea-kale [*Crambe maritima*], rue [*R. graveolens*], elymus [*E. arenarius*], santolina, stachys etc. – now has *Yucca flaccida* in flower . . . a grand plant for late summer . . . White everlasting pea [*Lathyrus latifolius* 'Albus'], planted about three feet from the back, is trained on stout pea-sticks over the space occupied earlier by the delphiniums and the spiraeas [*Aruncus dioicus*, more fami-

---

[Known to her as Eulalia japonica, Miss Jekyll planted the graceful *Miscanthus sinensis* (and the form *M.s.* 'Zebrinus' with yellow-banded blades) in many schemes, including the Michaelmas daisy border.]
'The giant grasses from Japan . . . do grandly, and when after a year or two they have grown into strong plants, are very handsome and combine extremely well with many kinds of flowers.' [*Home and Garden*, Gertrude Jekyll, p. 195.]

[Miss Jekyll recommends planting the handsome meadow-sweet, *Aruncus dioicus*, (syn. *A. Sylvester*) in borders and in woodland margins where the fern-like leaves and creamy plumes merge into a quiet background of greens.]
'. . . in a cool, retired place in a shrubbery margin, away from other flowers, the misty red-grey-purple of *Thalictrum aquilegifolium* 'Purpureum' with the warm white foam-colour of *Spirea aruncus* [*Aruncus dioicus*].' [*Colour Schemes*, Gertrude Jekyll, p. 50.]

[Miss Jekyll framed the doorway in her long border with choisya, yuccas, bergenias and *Stachys lanata*, all with excellent year-round foliage.]
'*Choisya ternata* is one of the best of wall shrubs.' 'Evergreens on walls in winter', *Country Life*, 13 February 1915.'

liarly *A. sylvester*]. A little of it runs into a bush of golden privet [*Ligustrum ovalifolium* 'Aureum']. This golden privet is one of the few shrubs that have a place in the flower border. Its clean, cheerful, bright yellow gives a note of just the right colour all through the summer. It has also a solidity of aspect that enhances by contrast the graceful lines of the foliage of a clump of the great Japanese striped grass *Eulalia* [*Miscanthus sinensis*], which stands within a few feet of it, seven feet high, shooting upright, but with the ends of the leaves recurved.

[We may now tend to use more good foliage shrubs in our mixed borders but Miss Jekyll's ideas are as valuable as when conceived and remain our guide lines. She herself uses sunken pots containing hydrangeas or lilies in flower to extend the flowering seasons, yet she understands fully how difficult this may be if no area exists for 'growing on' and preparation.]

'Some problems of the flower border', *Gardening Illustrated*, 16 August 1924

In a border that is carefully planted and devoted to the season that extends from the middle of July to the end of September the fine *Eryngium oliverianum* will be one of the first to go. To fill its place we have one or two alternative ways of treatment. At the back of the border there is a group of the tall *Helianthus orgyalis* [*H. salicifolius*], a plant that, if left to itself, shoots up to a height of seven or eight feet and carries a bunch of small yellow flowers at the top. If it did only this it would not be worth having, but in the early days of August we pull it down and peg it across the border, so that a yard of its upper end comes over the eryngiums. As with some other plants, this pulling down to a horizontal position causes the plant to throw up a short flowering shoot from each axil, so that the whole becomes a sheet of pale yellow bloom . . . In another part of the border a second batch of this eryngium has a white everlasting pea trained over it, and as this goes out of bloom, a strong growing hybrid clematis at the back is, in its turn, trained over the pea.

Another useful device is to plant *Clematis flammula* at the back of a group of delphiniums. When the bloom is over and seed pods are forming we cut away all the seeding part, leaving the stems standing about four and a half feet high. The clematis is trained over this and rests on the delphinium stems and gives a mass of bloom in early September.

The pale primrose sunflower [*Helianthus decapetalus*] is planted in happy companionship with *Artemisia lactiflora*. The chief faults of the artemisia are in its rigid uprightness and its considerable show of half-naked stem. The sunflowers are planted behind. Some of them are left to grow to their full height . . . but some are cut back in July, so that they branch and give a number of flowers at a lower height. These are pulled through the stems of the artemisia and hide their lankiness. By watching a flower border carefully and noting the ways and wants of its occupants one may invent and practise many such devices, both to the benefit of its appearance and also much to one's own interest and amusement.

[Elsewhere she suggests:] The white everlasting pea notched into the back of the echinops is meant to be trained over and among the branches of the globe thistle as this goes out of flower. [Miss Jekyll's border] is backed by a stone wall eleven feet high, *Colour Schemes* now fully clothed with shrubs and plants that take their place in the colour scheme, either for tint of bloom or mass of foliage . . . *Robinia hispida* stands where its pink clusters will tell rightly; choisya and *Cistus cyprius* where their dark foliage and white bloom will be of value; the greyish foliage and abundant pale lilac blossom of *Abutilon vitifolium* in the grey and purple region, and the pale green foliage of the deciduous *Magnolia conspicua* [*M. denudata*] showing as a background to the tender blue of a charming pale delphinium.

[At Munstead Wood there was enough space to allow for seasonal borders:] There are comparatively few shrubs that flower in autumn, so that it is quite a pleasant surprise to come upon a group of them all in bloom together . . . the satisfactory effect of a group of *Aesculus parviflora* and *Olearia hastii* . . . all the better for some plants of the beautiful blue-flowered *Perovskia atriplicifolia* and for *Caryopteris mastacanthus* [*C. incana, see* p. 175] in front.

[We may place these shrubs in the actual border or in the narrow bed against the wall behind and can add the small evergreen abelias, both *A. × grandiflora* with glossy leaves and pinky white flowers through August and September and the lilac-flowered *A. schumannii. Bupleurum fruticosum* has glaucous leaves and yellow flowers and seed-heads from July to October and makes a lovely mounded shape, ideal with straggling herbaceous plants. *Deutzia setchuensis* grows to six feet with flat corymbs of white star flowers through July and August, a good alternative to white snap-dragons or white dahlias. Eucryphias with white flowers and yellow stamens make elegant pyramids and enhance any autumn border, preferring an acid loam. *E. × nymansay* is the most lime-tolerant. The small *E. milliganii* has neat evergreen leaves and flowers freely as a two-foot shrub, never exceeding twelve feet but seldom achieving this. *Escallonia* 'Iveyi' has handsome glossy leaves which are attractive all year and carries large panicles of white flowers in August; it grows alarmingly fast but responds to fierce cutting and shaping.

Hydrangea villosa is one of the loveliest late-summer shrubs, with large flowers of lilac-blue or lilac-pink depending on the soil. Hypericums make shapely evergreen mounds in winter and their freely borne flowers cover shades of golden-yellow to pale sulphur. *H. × inodorum* 'Elstead' extends the season with brilliant salmon-red fruits. *Indigofera gerardiana* behaves as a sub-shrub, shooting from the base each year, and with elegant pinnate leaves and purple-rose pea flowers is valuable for foliage and flower. *Itea ilicifolia* is perhaps at its best if grown back against a wall, has holly-like evergreen glossy leaves and bears long catkins of fragrant yellowish flowers from August into autumn.

Some of the hardier olearias, besides the hybrid *O. × hastii*, flower in August. *O. solandri* has dense heath-like golden foliage and sweetly scented flowers. 'Waikariensis' has grey-green leaves and white flower-heads over a long period from July to September, and makes a particularly good mound of flower and foliage in a mixed border. Miss Jekyll recommends 'the clear-cut refinement of myrtle on . . . a wall surface', and in mild areas the shining leaves of *Myrtus communis* are an admirable foil to the duller foliage of perennials.]

In order to use both blue and purple in the flower border, this *Colour Schemes* cool western, grey-foliaged end has the blues and the further eastern end the purples. For although I like to use colour as a general rule in harmonies rather than contrasts, I prefer to avoid, except in occasional details, a mixture of blues and purples. At this end, therefore, there are flowers of pure blue – delphiniums, anchusa, salvia, Blue Cape daisy [*Felicia amelloides*] and lobelia, and it is only when the main mass of blue, of delphiniums and anchusas, is over that even the presence of the pale grey-blue of *Campanula lactiflora* is made welcome. Near the front is another pale grey-blue, that of *Clematis davidiana*, just showing a few blooms [*C. heracleifolia davidiana*] but not yet fully out.

[At an end of the border, where a cross path leads to a gateway in the wall, the mound of grey planting is repeated but here] besides some plants with white, pink and palest yellow colour- *Colour Schemes* ing, the other flowers are not blues, but purples, light and dark . . . in the middle spaces pale pink gladiolus, double *Saponaria officinalis* and pale pink penstemon [possibly *P. barbatus* 'Carnea' or *P. campanulatus* 'Evelyn' would be satisfactory]. At the back, also, there is a clump of globe-thistle (echinops) and a grand growth of *Clematis × jackmanii*, following in season of bloom, and partly led over, a white everlasting pea that in the earliest summer was trained to conceal the dying stems of the red-orange lilies that bloomed in June.

[In a double border specially devoted to August] the scheme of colouring has a ground of grey foliage, with flowers of pink, white, and light and dark purple . . . Next the path is the silvery white of Stachys [*S. lanata*], *Cineraria maritima* [*Senecio bicolor*] and *Artemisia stelleriana*, with the grey foliage and faint purple of the second bloom of catmint [*Nepeta × faassenii*]. Its normal flowering time is June, but if it is cut half back, removing the first bloom . . . it at once makes new flowering shoots. Then bushy masses of lavender and gypsophila, and between them *Lilium longiflorum*, *Godetia* 'Double Rose', and white snapdragons. Behind and among these are groups of the clear white

Achillea 'The Pearl' and the round purple heads of globe-thistle
Here and there, pushing to the front, is a silver thistle (*Eryngium giganteum*).

[In her early borders Miss Jekyll used hollyhocks for pink
flowers in August, but after several years of disappointment she
tried *Lavatera olbia*, which combines well with *Ceanothus*
Colour Schemes 'Gloire de Versailles',] and *Clematis jackmanii*, which is trained
into supporting clumps of the grey-leaved sea buckthorn [*Hippo-phaë rhamnoides*] that is kept trained to a suitable height and
gives the setting of grey foliage. In this garden the *Clematis
jackmanii* is in all cases the plant in the original fine purple
colouring, not the so-called improved of a deeper and more
reddish tint. Here we want the clearer purple of cooler tone. Of
lavender hedges there are several, of varying ages, in different
parts of the garden. Lavender for cutting should be from plants
not more than four to five years old, but for pictorial effect the
bushes may be much older. When they are growing old it is a
good plan to plant white and purple clematises so that they can
be trained freely through and over them.

Tea roses have been unusually lavish of autumn bloom, and
some of the garden climbing roses, hybrids of China and Noisette,
have been of great beauty, both growing and as room decoration.
Many of them flower in bunches at the end of the shoots; whole
branches cut nearly three feet long, make charming arrangements
in tall glasses or high vases of Oriental china. Perhaps their great
autumnal vigour is a reaction from the check they received in
the early part of the year, when the bloom was almost a failure
from the long drought and the accompanying attacks of blight
and mildew.

[A similar drought in 1976, probably longer and of
greater severity, was followed in September, when the rain
finally came, by an amazing flush of flowers, particularly
from shrubs and roses, which almost days before had looked
unable to survive. Most local councils had banned water-ing, but I cannot guess what Miss Jekyll's source of water
was; at least she had plenty of gardeners to do it.

Tea roses first came to Europe in the eighteenth century,

not as hardy as the Chinas, and with long pointed buds and large leaves. Although rather tender they were healthy roses reaching their peak of popularity by the end of the next century; crossing and breeding had of course began much earlier, usually with the Bourbons and Hybrid Perpetuals, ultimately producing a new race of Hybrid Teas which completely ousted the more delicate Tea parent. One of the hardiest is the fragrant pale apricot-yellow 'Lady Hillingdon', which can still be found in bush and climbing form. There is no colour quite like it and it will flourish on a south or west wall. 'Niphetos', with a fragrant white pointed bud opening to creamy-white and globular, is hardier than originally supposed and thrives too on a warm brick wall, flowering off and on all summer. Miss Jekyll might have been growing both of these as well as the pale rose 'Madame Cusin', the pale pink 'Madame Cochet', the new 1899 'Mrs Edward Mawley' (she was probably one of the first to try this rose) and the 'White Maman Cochet', which was vigorous and fairly hardy. Crossed with Noisettes in the nineteenth century a climbing rose was produced.]

The great hips of the Japanese *R. rugosa* are in perfection; they have every ornamental quality – size, form, colour, texture, and a delicate waxlike bloom, their pulp is thick and luscious and makes an excellent jam.

[Returning to August:] The quantity of fungoid growth this year is quite remarkable. The late heavy rains coming rather suddenly on the well-warmed earth have no doubt brought about their unusual size and abundance; in some woodland places one can hardly walk without stepping upon them. Many spots in the copse are brilliant with large groups of the scarlet-capped Fly Agaric (*Amanita muscaria*). It comes out of the ground looking like a dark scarlet ball, generally flecked with raised whitish spots; it quickly rises on its white stalk, the ball changing to a brilliant flat disc, six or seven inches across, and lasting several days in beauty. But the most frequent fungus is the big brown *Boletus*, in size varying from a small bun to a dinner-plate.

Some kinds are edible, but I have never been inclined to try
them, being deterred by their coarse look and uninviting coat of
slimy varnish. And why eat doubtful *Boletus* when one can
have the delicious Chanterelle (*C. cibarius*) also now at its
best? In colour and smell it is like a rich apricot, perfectly
wholesome, and, when rightly cooked, most delicate in flavour
and texture. It should be looked for in cool hollows in oakwoods;
when once found and its good qualities appreciated, it will never
again be neglected.

[Hollyhocks at Blyborough.] 'Then see how well the groups have been
placed; the rosy group leading to the fuller red, with a distant sulphur-
coloured gathering at the far end; its tall spires of *bloom* shooting up
and telling well against the distant tree masses above the wall. And how
pleasantly the colour of the rosy group is repeated in the Phlox in the
opposite border. And what a capital group that is, near the Hollyhocks
of that fine summer flower, the double Crown Daisy (*Chrysanthemum
coronarium*), with the bright glimpses of some more of it beyond. Then
the Pansies and Erigerons give a mellowing of grey-lilac that helps the
brighter colours, and is not overdone.' GJ

SEPTEMBER

'In the teaching and practice of good gardening the fact can Elgood and Jekyll p. 112 never be too persistently urged nor too trustfully accepted, that the best effects are accomplished by the simplest means. The garden artist or artist gardener is for ever searching for these simple pictures; generally the happy combination of some two kinds of flowers that bloom at the same time, and that make either kindly harmonies or becoming contrasts.

In trying to work out beautiful garden effects, besides those purposely arranged, it sometimes happens that some little accident – such as the dropping of a seed, that has grown and bloomed where it was not sown – may suggest some delightful combination unexpected and unthought of. At another time some small spot of colour may be observed that will give the idea of the use of this colour in some larger treatment.

It is just this self-education that is needed for the higher and more thoughtful gardening, whose outcome is the simply conceived and beautiful pictures, whether they are pictures painted with the brush on paper or canvas, or with living plants in the open ground. In both cases it needs alike the training of the eye to observe, of the brain to note, and of the hand to work out the interpretation.'

[Phlox and Daisy.] 'The picture showing autumn Phloxes grandly grown, tells of good gardening and of a strong, rich loamy soil. This is also proved by the height of the Daisies (*Chrysanthemum maximum*). But the lesson the picture so pleasantly teaches is above all to know the merit of one simple thing well done. The quiet background of evergreen hedge admirably suits both figures and flowers.' GJ

Sowing sweet peas — Autumn-sown annuals — Dahlias —
Worthless kinds — Staking — Planting the rock garden —
Growing small plants in a wall — The old wall — Dry-
walling — How built — How planted? — Hyssop — A
destructive storm — Berries of water-elder — Beginning
ground-work.

IN THE SECOND WEEK of September we sow sweet peas in shallow
trenches. The flowers from these are larger and stronger and
come six weeks earlier than from those sown in the spring; they
come too at a time when they are especially valuable for cutting.
Many other hardy annuals are best sown now. Some indeed,
such as the lovely *Collinsia verna* and the large white iberis
only do well if autumn sown. [This is probably the annual
candytuft *Iberis umbellata*, but also might be the handsome
I. onoraria (*I. amara*), with its bold upstanding spikes . . . not
so often seen as it deserves. It may be that it is overlooked,
because for its best development it requires to be sown in
autumn. Another iberis, the sub-shrubby *I. gibraltarica*, is
rather tender and is best planted out in the spring.] Among others,
some of the most desirable are nemophila [elsewhere she calls
this the pretty blue *Nemophila menziesii*], platystemon [*P. californicus*], which has flattish cup-shaped flowers of a pleasant
cream colour, with a spreading habit something like that of the
better known *Limnanthes douglasii* [the poached-egg flower],
love-in-the-mist [*Nigella damascena*], larkspur [annual *Delphinium consolida*], pot-marigold (calendula), Virginian stock
[*Malcolmia maritima*] and the delightful Venus's navel-wort
(*Omphalodes linifolia*). I always think this daintily beautiful
plant is undeservedly neglected, for how seldom one sees it. It
is full of the most charming refinement, with its milk-white
bloom and grey-blue leaf and neat habit of growth. [This little
plant is still rarely seen, but to those of us who have it it is a

constant spring surprise and delight. It seeds quite freely after flowering *in situ*, or seed is easily taken.] A single plant of nemophila [the Californian bluebell] will often cover a square yard with its beautiful blue bloom, and then what a gain it is to have these pretty things in full strength in spring and early summer, instead of waiting to have them in a much poorer state later in the year, when other flowers are in plenty.

[Today we rather shy away from the extra work involved in raising annuals, and prefer to plan our borders with mixed planting of shrubs, hardy herbaceous plants and bulbs. Biennials are popular if they seed themselves freely where we want them. However, if you take over a new garden or one where some work has to be done on cleaning and replanning before permanent planting is possible, then annuals are useful for a season. In the 1920s Miss Jekyll wrote various articles about annuals.]

'The Garden', January 1921 — There is not always in a garden an opportunity for having special borders for annuals yet such a chance occurs from time to time, especially when ground is being slowly restored from unavoidable neglect, or when there are regions infested with couch or some other troublesome weed, such as cannot be entirely got rid of by one forking over. Here is the opportunity for the bed of annuals, to be used as what gardeners call a cleaning crop. The ground is cleared of weeds as well as maybe during the early part of the year or the previous winter, so as to be ready for sowing in March. The annuals will cover it all the summer, and in the autumn when their beauty is over, it will receive its final cleaning.

[Today with modern contact herbicides it is hardly possible to agree with Miss Jekyll; indeed when digging was the only possible way to exterminate troublesome perennial weed, covering the ground with annuals during a whole growing season was scarcely radical enough, and the plants would not have been sufficiently vigorous. However today, if you can use Glyphosate or Paraquat/Dignat in March when weeds such as couch, ground elder and creeping buttercup appear it may be possible to use the

196

later flowering annuals as weed smotherers. Glyphosate is almost totally effective, after only one application, and any stray weeds can be taken out by hand.]

[Returning to September:] Dahlias are now at their full growth. To make a choice for one's own garden, one must see the whole plant growing. As with many another kind of flower nothing is more misleading than the evidence of the show-table, for many that there look the best, and are indeed lovely in form and colour as individual blooms, come from plants that are of no garden value. For however charming in humanity is the virtue of modesty, and however becoming is the unobtrusive bearing that gives evidence of its possession, it is quite misplaced in a dahlia. Here it becomes a vice, for the dahlia's first duty is to swagger and to carry gorgeous blooms well above its leaves, and on no account to hang its head. Some of the delicately-coloured kinds lately raised not only hang their heads, but also hide them away among masses of their coarse foliage, and are doubly frauds looking everything that is desirable in the show, and proving worthless in the garden. It is true that there are ways of cutting out superfluous green stuff and thereby encouraging the blooms to show up, but at a busy season, when rank leafage grows fast, one does not want to be every other day tinkering at the dahlias.

Careful and strong staking they must always have, not forgetting one central stake to secure the main growth at first. It is best to drive this into the hole made for the plant before placing the root, to avoid the danger of sending the point of the stake through the tender tubers. Its height out of the ground should be about eighteen inches less than the expected stature of the plant. As the dahlia grows, there should be at least three outer stakes at such distance from the middle one as may suit the bulk and habit of the plant; and it is a good plan to have wooden hoops to tie to these, so as to form a girdle round the whole plant, and for tying out the outer branches. The hoop should be only loosely fastened – best with roomy loops of osier, so that it may be easily shifted up with the growth of the plant. We make the hoops in the winter of long straight rent rods of Spanish chestnut, bending them while green round a tub and tying them with tarred twine or hosier bands. They last several years. All this care in staking dahlias is labour well bestowed, for when autumn storms come the wind has such a power of wrenching and twisting, that unless the plant, now grown into a heavy mass of succulent vegetation, is braced by firm fixing at the sides, it is in danger of being broken off short just above the ground, where its stem has become almost woody, and therefore brittle.

Now is the moment to get to work on the rock-garden; there is no time of year so precious for this work as September. Small things planted now, while the ground is still warm, grow at the root at once, and get both anchor-hold and feeding-hold of the ground before frost comes. Those that are planted later do not take hold, and every frost heaves them up, sometimes right out of the ground. Meanwhile those that have got a firm root-hold are growing steadily all the winter, underground if not above; and when the first spring warmth comes they can draw upon the reserve of strength they have been hoarding up, and make good growth at once.

Except in the case of a rockery only a year old, there is sure to be some part that wants to be worked afresh, and I find it convenient to do about a third of the space every year. Many of the indispensable alpines and rock-plants of lowly growth increase at a great rate, some spreading over much more than their due space, the very reason of this quick-spreading habit being that they are travelling to fresh pasture; many of them prove it clearly by dying away in the middle of the patch, and only showing vigorous vitality at the edge.

Such plants as *Silene alpestris* [the Alpine catchfly with six-

---

[A view of Munstead Wood today from the doorway leading into the spring garden. The silver birch and mature specimen of *Aesculus parviflora* were originally part of the autumn-flowering shrubbery bank.]

'I was nearly forgetting *Aesculus macrostachys* [*A. parviflora*], now well established among the choice shrubs. It is like a bush horse-chestnut, but more refined, the white spikes standing well up above the handsome leaves. [*Wood and Garden*, Gertrude Jekyll, p. 103.]

inch white fringed flowers over narrow glossy leaves], *Hutchinsia alpina* [a tiny perennial for cool positions, carrying starry white flowers], *Pterocephalus* [*P. parnassi*, a dwarf tufted perennial with purple-pink flowers in summer], the dwarf alpine kinds of achillea and artemisia, veronica and linaria, and the mossy saxifrages, in my soil want transplanting every two years, and the silvery saxifrages every three years.

[Among the dwarf achilleas *A. argentea* and *A. clavenae* are almost synonymous, making dense mats of very pretty filigree silvery foliage with pure white marguerite flowers on four-inch stems. *A. clyopeolata* is taller to eighteen inches and has hairy pinnate leaves and white or pink flowers. *A. tomentosa* is popular and most easily obtainable, with ferny hairy leaves growing in dense mats with flat yellow heads on six-inch stems. The hybrid between *A. argentea* and *A. tomentosa*, *A.* × 'King Edward', is an excellent carpeting plant with grey-green leaves and lemon-yellow flowers on four-inch stems.

The rock-garden artemisias are grown mainly for their silver leaves. *A. canescens* now seems a doubtful name but nevertheless many of us still use it, being uncertain if it is correct; it makes a slightly untidy mound of very silvery filigree leaves up to twelve inches. *A. lanata* (*A. pedemontana?*) makes a small humped cushion of silver and the dwarf form *A. schmidtiana* has rounded rosettes of very finely divided silver-grey leaves. The woody *A. stelleriana* stays quite low but is rather too pushing a plant for the rock-garden with almost white, deeply lobed leaves. I find it best to renew it every few years; cuttings are easy to strike, they can be rooted in late summer and planted out immediately.

In the early 1900s hebes, parahebes and veronicas were all classed as the last-named genus. Without attempting any true botanical explanation of the differences the amateur can loosely class the hebe as a woody shrub, the parahebe as semi-woody, usually dying down to the ground in winter, and the veronica as herbaceous. Although there are many dwarf shrubby hebes suitable for a rock-garden it is probable that Miss Jekyll was referring to the perennial herbs such as *V. teucrinum* and *V. prostrata*, which make dense herbaceous mats of glossy green. There are flower forms of deep blue, pale blue and rose-pink, flower-heads held just above the leafy hummocks, from nine to fifteen inches. The parahebe, *P. catarractae*, with both mauve and white flowers, in time makes a spreading mass, with flowers up to eight inches. The unusual *P. perfoliata* has long arching stems with grey oval leaves clasping the stem, and attractive violet-blue flowers. If given good drainage in full sun this plant will sucker and spread; it is from Australia and probably not known by Miss Jekyll.

Some of the linarias are very invasive, the ivy-leaved *L. cymbalaria* is best left for the wilder bits of rough walling, but *L. alpina* is worthwhile though usually short-lived, with trailing blue-grey leaves and small orange and violet flowers carried all through the summer. *Cymbalaria aequitriloba* and *C. hepaticifolia* (formerly linarias) are both prostrate scramblers for walls and between crevices.]

As in much else, one must watch what happens in one's own garden. We practical gardeners have no absolute knowledge of the constitution of the plant, still less of the chemistry of the soil, but by the constant exercise of watchful care and helpful sympathy we acquire a certain degree of instinctive knowledge, which is as valuable in its own way, and probably more applicable to individual local conditions, than the tabulated formulas of more orthodox science.

One of the best and simplest ways of growing rock-plants is in a loose wall. In many gardens an abrupt change of level makes a retaining wall necessary, and when I see this built in the usual way as a solid structure of brick and mortar – unless there be any special need of the solid wall – I always regret that it is not built as a home for rock-plants. An exposure to north and east and the cool backing of a mass of earth is just what most alpines delight in. A dry wall, which means a wall without mortar, may be anything between a wall and a very steep rock-work, and may be built of brick or of any kind of local stone. I have built and planted a good many hundred yards of dry walling with my own hands, both at home and in other gardens, and can speak with some confidence both of the pleasure and interest of the actual making and planting, and of the satisfactory results that follow.

The best example I have to show in my own garden is the so-called 'Old Wall' before mentioned. It is the bounding and protecting fence of the paeony ground on its northern side, and consists of a double dry wall with earth between. An old hedge bank that was to come away was not far off, within easy wheeling distance. So the wall built up on each side, and as it grew, the earth from the hedge was barrowed in to fill up. A dry wall needs very little foundation; two thin courses underground are quite enough. The point of most structural importance is to keep the earth solidly trodden and rammed behind the stones of each course and throughout its bulk, and every two or three courses to lay some stones that are extra long front and back, to tie the wall well into the bank. A local sandstone is the walling material. In the pit it appears in separate layers with a few feet of hard sand between each. The lowest layer, sometimes thirty to forty feet down, is the best and thickest but that is good building stone, and for dry stone walling we only want 'tops' or 'seconds', the later and younger formations of stone in the quarry. The very roughness and almost rotten state of much of this stone makes it all the more acceptable as nourishment and root-hold to the tiny plants that are to grow in its chinks, and that in a few months will change much of the rough rock-surface to green growth of delicate vegetation. Moreover, much of the soft sandy stone hardens by exposure to weather; and even if a stone or two crumbles right away in a few years' time, the rest will hold firmly, and the space left will make a little cave where some small fern will live happily.

The wall is planted as it is built with hardy ferns – blechnum [*B. spicant*], polypody [*P. vulgare*], hartstongue [*Asplenium scolopendrium*], adiantum [*A. pedatum*], ceterach [later *Asplenium ceterach* but now again a ceterach, *C. officinarum*], Asplenium [*A. scolopendrium*] and *A. rutamuraria*. The last three like lime, so a barrow of old mortar rubbish is at hand, and the joint where they are to be planted has a layer of their favourite soil. Each course is laid fairly level as to its front top edge, stones of about the same thickness going in course by course. The earth backing is then carefully rammed into the spaces at the uneven backs of the stones, and a thin layer of earth over the whole course, where the mortar would have been in a built wall, gives both a 'bed' for the next row of stones and soil for the plants that are to grow in the joints.

The face of the wall slopes backward on both sides, so that its whole thickness of five feet at the bottom draws in to four feet at the top. All the stones are laid at a right angle to the plane of the inclination – that is to say, each stone tips a little down at the back, and its front edge, instead of being upright faces a little upward. It follows that every drop of gentle rain that falls on either side of the wall is carried into the joints, following the backward and downward pitch of the stones, and then into the earth behind them. The mass of earth in the middle of the wall gives abundant root-room for bushes, and is planted with bush roses of three kinds, of which the largest mass is of *R. lucida* [*R. virginiana*]. Then there is a good stretch of berberis [probably *Mahonia aquifolium*]; then Scotch briars [*R. pimpinellifolia*], and in one or two important places junipers; then more berberis, and the common barberry, and neat bushes of *Olearia hastii*.

The wall was built seven years ago, and is now completely clothed. It gives me a garden on the top and a garden on each side, and though its own actual height is only four and a half feet, yet the bushes on the top make it a sheltering hedge from seven to ten feet high. One small length of three or four yards at the top has been kept free of larger bushes, and is planted on its northern edge with a very neat and pretty dwarf kind of lavender, while on the sunny side is a thriving patch of the hardy cactus (*Opuntia raffinesquii*). [This is probably a dwarf form of *O. ficus-indica*, with larger yellow flowers, growing only to twelve inches.] Just here is a group of *Crinum powelli*, while a white jasmine [*J. officinale*] clothes the face of the wall right and left, and rambles into the barberry bushes just beyond. It so happened that these things had been planted close together because the conditions of the place were likely to favour them, and not, as is my usual practice, with any intentional idea of harmonious grouping. I did not even remember that they all flower in July, and at nearly the same time; and one day seeing them all in bloom together, I was delighted to see the success of the chance arrangement, and how pretty it all was, for I should never have thought of grouping together pink and lavender, yellow and white.

The northern face of the wall beginning at its eastern end, is planted thus: for a length of ten or twelve paces there are ferns, polypody and hartstongue and a few *Adiantum nigrum* [I suppose this is *A. pedatum*; this American maidenhair is the hardiest of the genus, and the conditions offered here will make survival likely] with here and there a Welsh poppy [*Meconopsis cambrica*]. There is a clump of the wild stitchwort that came by itself [*Stellaria holostea*, the greater stitchwort, or *S. graminea*, the lesser], and is so pretty that I leave it. At the foot of the wall are the same, but more of the hartstongue; and here it grows best, for not only is the place cooler, but I gave it some loamy soil, which it loves. Farther along the hartstongue gives place to the wild iris (*I. foetidissima*), a good long stretch of it.

Nothing to my mind looks better than these two plants at the base of a wall on the cool side. In the upper part of the wall àre various ferns, and that interesting plant, wall-pennywort (*Cotyledon umbilicus* – [*C. simplicifolia*]). It is a native plant, but not found in this neighbourhood; I brought it from Cornwall, where it is so plentiful in the chinks of the granite stone-fences. It sows itself and grows afresh year after year, though I always fear to lose it in one of our dry summers. Next comes the common London Pride [*Saxifraga umbrosa*], which I think quite the most beautiful of the saxifrages of this section. If it was a rare thing, what a fuss we should make about it. The place is a little dry for it, but all the same, it makes a handsome spreading tuft hanging over the face of the wall. When its pink cloud of bloom is at its best, I always think it is the prettiest thing in the garden.

Home and Garden

[In a passage on flowers in midsummer Miss Jekyll continues to sing the praises of this well known and much loved plant:] One of the happiest mixtures it has ever been my good fortune to hit on is that of St Bruno's Lily [*Paradisea liliastrum*] and London Pride, both at their best about the second week of June. The lovely little mountain lily – fit emblem of a pure-souled saint – stands upright with a royal grace of dignity, and bears with an air of modest pride its lovely milk-white blooms and abundant sheaves of narrow blue-green leaves. It is not a real lily but an *Anthericum* [no longer so, now a *paradisea*; St Bernard's lily, *A. liliago*, is considered by some gardeners a better plant]; no plant, however, better deserves the lily-name, that, when used in its broader significance, denotes some plant that bears bloom of lily-shape, and bears them so worthily that the name is in no danger of dishonour.

The well-grown clumps of this beautiful plant (it is the large kind and nearly two feet high [probably 'Magnificum']) are on a narrow westward-facing bank that slopes down to the lawn. The place would be in the full blaze of the late afternoon sun, but that it is kept shaded and cool by a large Spanish chestnut whose bole is some ten yards away. Between and among the little lilies is a wide planting of London Pride, the best for beauty of bloom of its own branch of the large family of saxifrage. Its healthy-looking rosettes of bright pale leaves and delicate clouds of faint pink bloom seem to me to set off the quite different way of growth of the anthericum [paradisea] so as to display the very best that both can do, making me think of any two people whose minds are in such a happy state of mutual intelligence, that when talking together bright sparks of wit or wisdom flash from both, to the delight of the appreciative listener. The only other flower that bears its part in this pretty show is a cloudy mass of Venus's navel-wort (*Omphalodes linifolia*). [This little group has a near dark backing of shrubs and shadow.] Nothing to distract the eye from the easy grouping and charming tenderness of colour of the simple little summer flowers.

[Returning to September:] Then there is the yellow everlasting (*Gnaphalium orientale* – [now *Anaphalis nubigena*]), a fine plant for the upper edge of the wall, and even better on the sunny side, and the white form of *Campanula caespitosa*, with its crowd of delicate little white bells rising in June from the neatest foliage of tender but lively green. [Then probably *C. cochlearifolia*, but the two species are very similar. *C. cochlearifolia* (sometimes called *C. pulsilla*) has freely running underground roots to form spreading masses of shining green leaves above which three-inch stems carry small dangling bells from pure white to soft lavender

and blue. The several garden named cultivars are all excellent.]
Then follow deep-hanging curtains of yellow alyssum [*A. saxatile*],
and of hybrid rock pinks [*Dianthus petraeus*]. The older plants of
alyssum are nearly worn out, but there are plenty of promising
young seedlings in the lower joints.

Throughout the wall there are patches of polypody fern [*see*
p. 57] one of the best of cool wall-plants, its creeping root-stock
always feeling its way along the joints, and steadily furnishing
the wall with more and more of its neat fronds; it is all the more
valuable for being at its best in early winter, when so few ferns
are to be seen. Every year, in some bare places, I sow a little seed
of *Erinus alpinus*, always trying for places where it will follow
some other kind of plant, such as a place where rock pink or
alyssum has been. All plants are the better for this sort of change.
In the seven years that the wall has stood, the stones have
weathered, and on most of the north side are hoary with mosses,
and look as if they might have been standing for a hundred years.

The sunny side is nearly clear of moss, and I have planted very
few things in its face, because the narrow border at its foot is so
precious for shrubs and plants that like a warm sheltered place.
Here are several choisyas and sweet verbenas [*Lippia citriodora* –
the shrubby lemon-scented verbena], also escallonia, stuartia
and styrax, and a long straggling group of some very fine penstemons. In one space that was fairly clear I planted a bit of
hyssop [*H. officinalis*], an old sweet herb whose scent I
delight in; it grows into a thick bush-like plant full of purple
flower in the late summer, when it attracts quantities of bumble-
bees. It is a capital wall-plant and has sown its own seed till
there is a large patch on the top and some in its face, and a
broadly spreading group in the border below. It is one of the
plants that was used in the old Tudor gardens for edgings; the
growth is close and woody at the base, and it easily bears clipping
into shape.

The fierce gales and heavy rains of the last days of September
wrought sad havoc among the flowers. Dahlias were virtually
wrecked. Though each plant had been tied to three stakes, their
masses of heavy growth could not resist the wrenching and
twisting action of the wind, and except in a few cases where
they were well sheltered, their heads lie on the ground, the

stems broken down at the last tie. If anything about a garden could be disheartening it would be its aspect after such a storm of wind. Wall-shrubs, only lately made safe, as we thought, have great gaps torn out of them, though tied with tarred string to strong iron staples, staples and all being wrenched out. Everything looks battered and whipped and ashamed; branches of trees and shrubs lie about far from their source of origin; green leaves and little twigs are washed up into thick drifts; apples and quinces, that should have hung till mid-October, lie bruised and muddy under the trees.

Newly-planted roses and hollies have a funnel-shaped hole worked in the ground at their base, showing the power of the wind to twist their heads, and giving warning of a corresponding disturbance of the tender roots. There is nothing to be done but to look round carefully and search out all disasters and repair them as well as may be, and to sweep up the wreckage and rubbish, and try to forget the rough weather, and enjoy the calm beauty of the better days that follow, and hope that it may be long before such another angry storm is sent. And indeed a few quiet days of sunshine and mild temperature work wonders. In a week one would hardly know that the garden had been so cruelly torn about. Fresh flowers replace bruised ones, and wholesome young growths prove the enduring vitality of vegetable life. Still we cannot help feeling, near the end of September, that the flower year is nearly over, though the end is a gorgeous one, with its strong yellow masses of the later perennial sunflowers [perennial species and hybrids of helianthus] and marigolds [tagetes and calendulas, all annuals], golden rod [solidago] and a few belated gladioli; the brilliant foliage of Virginian creepers [*Parthenocissus quinquefolia* is the true Virginian creeper, the Boston Ivy, *P. tricuspidata*, is very similar and its form 'Veitchii' is often seen], the leaf-painting of *Vitis coignettii*, and the strong crimson of the Claret vine [*V. vinifera* 'Purpurea'].

The water-elder (*Viburnum opulus*) now makes a brave show in the edge of the copse. It is without doubt the most beautiful berry-bearing shrub of mid-September. The fruit hangs in ample clusters from the point of every branch and of every lateral twig, in colour like the brightest of redcurrants, but with a translucent lustre that gives each separate berry a much brighter look; the whole bush shows fine warm colouring, the leaves having turned to a rich red. Perhaps it is because it is a native that this grand shrub or small tree is generally neglected in gardens, and it is almost unknown in nurserymen's catalogues. It is the parent of the well-known Guelder rose [*V. opulus* 'Sterile'; actually the Guelder rose is the wild species], which is merely its globe-flowered form. But the round flower leaves no berry, its familiar white ball being formed of the sterile part of the flower only, and the foliage of the garden kind does not assume so bright an autumn colouring.

The nights are growing chilly, with even a little frost, and the work for the coming season of dividing and transplanting hardy plants has already begun. Plans are being made for any improvements or alterations that involve ground-work. Already we have been at work on some broad grass rides through the copse that were roughly levelled and laid with grass last winter. The turf has been raised and hollows filled in, grass seed sown in bare patches, and the whole beaten and rolled to a good surface, and the job put out of hand in good time before the leaves begin to fall.

[As September proceeds many borders begin to get overblown and tatty, especially after storms such as Miss Jekyll has described. All the more important are the cool quiet colours to be found in a border of silver and grey. She describes such an area *Colour Schemes* in her own garden:] Perhaps the grey garden is seen at its best by reaching it through the orange borders. Here the eye becomes filled and saturated with the strong red and yellow colouring ... This filling with the strong rich colouring has the natural effect of making the eye eagerly desirous for the complementary colour, so that, standing by the inner yew arch and suddenly turning to look into the grey garden, the effect is surprisingly – quite astonishingly – luminous and refreshing. One never knew before how vividly bright ageratum could be, or lavender or nepeta; even the grey-purple of echinops appears to have more positive colour than one's expectation would assign to it. The purple of the clematises of the Jackmanii class becomes piercingly brilliant, while the grey and glaucous foliage looks strangely cool and clear.

It is not the first time that attention has been drawn to the importance of grey and silver foliage in the arrangement of flower borders for the late summer; but this aspect of gardening has of late aroused so much interest among amateurs, and such unqualified encouragement from artists, that some notes about its planting may be helpful to those who desire to make their gardens pictorially beautiful. The best season for such an arrangement is the six weeks during the months of August and and the first half of September. It is unfortunate that these weeks coincide with the time when so many are away on holiday, and when the owners of large gardens are absent; afloat, or fishing, or on the Scottish grouse moors; but there are many good gardeners who are at home and able to enjoy not the grey garden alone, but all the splendid border flowers whose best effect seems to culminate at just the same season; for it is the time of dahlias and hollyhocks, penstemons, snapdragons, zinnias, salpiglossis, the grand French and African marigolds, and the rest of the good plants that are glorious in the late summer. Of these the most important in the grey garden are hollyhocks and dahlias, those whose colouring is right with the other flowers of purple, pink and white, in the complete setting of silvery-white foliage that is the keynote of the grey garden's harmony . . . *Echinops ruthenicus* is of use, not only from its abundant heads of purplish bloom, but also because the foliage is of so quiet a green that it goes well with the grey plants. Eryngiums would be of much use, but the best kind, *E. oliverianum*, the silver thistle, is just too early in season; but *E. planum*, though less showy, is just right in time and should be included. [Today I should use the hybrid *E. tripartitum* or forms of the hybrid *E. × zabellii*, both late-flowering and with heads of steely blue.]

There are not too many pink flowers available, but among the best are some of the phloxes, especially the cooler of the pink-toned varieties, and one or two of the lilacs. It is best to avoid any pink flowers inclining to salmon tints; the cool colours are best with the purple flowers. [I might add the pink-flowering Japanese anemones, *A. japonica* or *hupehensis* of gardens but correctly now *A. × hybrida*. 'Prinz Heinrich' (1902) is a darker pink; it flowers splendidly at Tintinhull from mid-August. A garden form of *Penstemon campanulatus*, 'Evelyn', is a bushy plant with just the right rose-pink colouring.] A bush of *Lavatera olbia* should be in the background, for though it flowers naturally a little too soon, yet if it is cut back early in June it makes a quantity of flowering shoots for the right time. Also in the background are some bushes of sea buckthorn [*Hippophaë rhamnoides*], valuable not only for their own silvery foliage but also as supports for purple clematises which ramble over them in delightful fashion. This was a valuable hint from an artist.

Another precious bush for the back of the grey border is *Ceanothus* 'Gloire de Versailles'. Cut hard back, it makes a quantity of flowering shoots for the middle of August [I also recommend 'Topaz' with deeper flowers] . . . There should be both kinds of ageratums, one of the good dwarfs [*A. houstonianum* is a dwarf compact species with many good named cultivars] and the tall *A. mexicanum* where it shows as a diffuse purple cloud.

[Further back in the border:] there are groups of lavender with large-flowered clematises placed so that they may be trained close to them and partly over them. There are the . . . monumental yuccas . . . other white flowers are *Lilium longiflorum* and *L. candidum*, the clear white *Achillea*. 'The Pearl' and the grey-white clouds of *Gypsophila paniculata*. The pink flowers are Sutton's Godetia Double Rose, sown in place early in May, the beautiful clear pink hollyhock 'Pink Beauty' [try to find one of clear pink in the modern lists] and the pale pink double soapwort [*Saponaria officinalis* 'Flore Pleno']. Clematis and white everlasting sweet pea [*Lathyrus latifolius* 'Albus'] are planted so that they can be trained to cover the gypsophila when its bloom is done and the seed-pods are turning brown . . . Elymus [*E. arenarius*] is the blue-green lyme grass, a garden form of the handsome blue-leaved grass that grows on the seaward edges of many of our sea-shore sandhills.

The soapwort next to it is the double form of *Saponaria officinalis* [*see* above] found wild in many places. [These are two of the most vigorous travelling plants, quickly covering the soil with running roots. Both very beautiful, Miss Jekyll may have found that they made ideal neighbours, each perhaps controlling the other, but I still would doubt their use except in the larger garden, or if prepared to tackle their control most ruthlessly each year, in autumn and in spring when the new shoots appear.]

[The grey garden has a cool grey setting] of *Stachys lanata* and *Artemisia stelleriana* at the front, with *Cineraria maritima* [*Senecio bicolor*] and santolina; the yellow bloom of the santolina is cut away. But the most effective of the grey plants is *Artemisia ludoviciana*. It is a most accommodating thing, for at the back it may be left to grow to its whole length of four feet or more; in the middle spaces it is cut back to any height required, and it may even be reduced to four inches, when, as often happens, a plant strays to the front edge.

[There is a new form of this, *A. ludoviciana* 'Latifolia', less spreading and invasive and with much broader and paler grey leaves. It is still quite hard to get, but worth the trouble of a search.]

OCTOBER

'And when the day's work is done, and the light just begins to Elgood, p. 62 fail, no one knows better than the artist that then is the best moment in the garden – when the colours acquire a wonderful richness of "subdued splendour" such as is unmatched throughout the lighter hours of the long summer day. Then it is that the flowers of delicate texture, that have grown faint in the full heat, raise their heads and rejoice; that the tall evening primrose opens its pale wide petals and gives off its faint perfume; that the little lilac cross-flowers of the night-scented stock open out and show their modest prettiness and pour forth their enchanting fragrance. The early evening hour is indeed the best of all; the hour of loveliest sight, of sweetest scent, of best earthly rest and fullest refreshment of body and spirit.'

Michaelmas daisies — Arranging and staking — Spindle tree — Autumn colour of azaleas — Quinces — Medlars — Advantage of early planting of shrubs — Careful planting — Pot-bound roots — Cypress hedge — Planting in difficult places — Hardy flower border — Lifting dahlias — Dividing hardy plants — Dividing tools — Plants difficult to divide — Periwinkles — Sternbergia — Czar violets — Deep cultivation for *Lilium giganteum* [*Cardiocrinum giganteum*].

THE EARLY DAYS of October bring with them the best bloom of the Michaelmas daisies, the many beautiful garden kinds of the perennial asters. They have, as they well deserve to have, a garden to themselves.

[Although few of us today have gardens of sufficient size to allow of devoting each section to a season, and in this case to one genus alone, yet the descriptions Miss Jekyll gives of the visual effects of her Michaelmas daisy border make it worth quoting much of her writing on it. I have omitted the detailed description of maintenance and retained that part which seems to me to add to our knowledge of her colour sense and sure feeling for contrasts (*see also* COLOUR, pp. 297–8).]

Passing along the wide path in front of the big flower border, and through the pergola that forms its continuation, with eye and brain full of rich warm colouring of flower and leaf, it is a delightful surprise to pass through the pergola's last right-hand opening, and to come suddenly upon the Michaelmas daisy garden in full beauty. Its clean, fresh pure colouring of pale and dark lilac, strong purple and pure white, among masses of pale-green foliage, forms a contrast almost startling after the warm colouring of nearly everything else; and the sight of the region where the flowers are fresh and newly opened, and in glad spring-like profusion, when all else is on the verge of death and decay, gives an impression of satisfying refreshment that is hard to be equalled throughout the year. Their special garden is a wide border on each side of a path, its length bounded on one side by a tall hedge of filberts and on the other side by clumps of yew, holly and other shrubs . . .

The dwarf *Aster amellus* [now best represented by its more modern hybrid *A. frikartii* 'Mönch', a first-class plant for any border] is used in rather large quantity, coming right to the front in some places, and running in and out between the clumps of other kinds . . . The only other plants admitted are white dahlias, the two differently striped varieties of *Eulalia japonica* [*Miscanthus sinensis* and *M. s.* 'Zebrinus'], the fresh green foliage of Indian corn [*Zea mays*], and the brilliant light green leafage of *Funkia grandiflora* [*Hosta plantaginea grandiflora*, a plant which, with *H. sieboldiana*, Miss Jekyll used frequently for tubs, also recognizing its value as a late flowerer in a border] . . . The fresh-looking pale-green leaves are delightful. [A hybrid 'Royal Standard' is even better, and carries almost pure white flowers above heart-shaped rich green leaves in October, very fragrant.]

The bracken in the copse stands dry and dead, but when leaves are fluttering down and the chilly days of mid-October are upon us, its warm rust colouring is certainly cheering; the green of the freshly grown mossy carpet below looks vividly bright by contrast. Some bushes of spindle tree (*Euonymus europaeus*) are loaded with their rosy seed-pods; some are already burst, and show the orange-scarlet seeds – an audacity of colouring that looks all the brighter for the even, lustreless green of the leaves and of the green-barked twigs and stems. [Some of the Asian species euonymus are also very fine, and one useful quality is their ready adaptability to chalk; they thrive in almost any soil. *E. alatus* is distinguished by corky wings borne on the branches and has brilliant autumn colour. Both *E. sachalinensis* and *E. yedoensis* are strong growing with large orange-scarlet split berries, as well as vivid colouring. The twining climber *Celastrus orbiculatus* bears fruit with a similar appearance; brown capsules borne after insignificant flowers suddenly split open to reveal a yellow inner lining in which rest scarlet seeds.

It is a useful and decorative plant for growing through shrubs or small trees.]

The hardy azaleas are now blazing masses of crimson, almost scarlet leaf; the old *A. pontica* [*Rhododendron luteum*, still much loved for its richly fragrant yellow flowers, superb autumn colour and readiness to thrive in poor soil] with its large foliage, as bright as any. With them are grouped some of the North American vacciniums and andromedas with leaves almost as bright. The ground between the groups of shrubs is knee-deep in heath. The rusty-coloured withered bloom of the wild heath on its purplish-grey masses and the surrounding banks of dead fern make a groundwork and background of excellent colour-harmony.

[Autumn colour is always brighter from trees and shrubs on acid rather than calcareous soils. Some acers, euonymus, *Parrotia persica*, berberis, ceratostigma and viburnum all colour well in alkaline conditions.]

How seldom does one see quinces [*Cydonia oblonga*] planted for ornament, and yet there is hardly any small tree that better deserves such treatment. Some quinces planted about eight years ago are now perfect pictures, their lissom branches borne down with the load of great, deep-yellow fruit, and their leaves turning to a colour almost as rich and glowing. The old English rather round fruited kind with the smooth skin is the best for flavour and beauty – a mature tree without leaves in winter has a remark-ably graceful arching, almost weeping growth. The other kind is of a rather more rigid form, and though its woolly coated pear-shaped fruits are larger and strikingly handsome, the whole tree has a coarser look, and just lacks the attractive grace of the other. They will do fairly well almost anywhere, though they prefer a rich loamy soil and a cool damp, even swampy, place.

[In fact it is not all that easy to grow quince trees success-fully. They dislike heavy clay soil, need a sunny open situation and considerable training upward if a good habit is required. Fruit does not ripen in the north of England; in the south the fruits must be gathered before frosts and allowed to ripen indoors or in a cool store. Although in the early years of this century three different quince trees were listed, one with apple-shaped fruit, another with pear-shaped and the third from Portugal with rather larger fruit, it is doubtful if more than one form is now obtainable with any certainty.]

The medlar [*Mespilus germanica*] is another of the small fruiting trees that is more neglected than it should be, as it well deserves a place among ornamental shrubs. Here it is a precious thing in the region where garden melts into copse. The fruit-laden twigs are now very attractive, and its handsome leaves can never be passed without admiration.

[This picturesque tree has brown apple-shaped fruit, not to everyone's taste for eating even as jelly, but its habit alone puts it in the same category as a mulberry (usually in Great Britain the black mulberry, *Morus nigra*), a tree for every garden and orchard, with a cottage-garden quality very different from exotic trees and shrubs from other continents.]

Close to the medlars is a happy intergrowth of the wild Guelder rose, still bearing its brilliant clusters, a strong-growing and far-clambering garden form of *R. arvensis* [the common hedgerow species], full of red hips, sweetbriar, and holly – a happy tangle of red-fruited bushes, all looking as if they were trying to prove, in friendly emulation, which can make the bravest show of red-berried wild flung wreath, or bending spray, or stately spire; while at their foot the bright colour is repeated by the bending berried heads of the wild iris [*I. foetidissima*], opening like fantastic dragons' mouths, and pouring out the red bead-like seeds upon the ground; and, as if to make the picture still more complete, the leaves of the wild strawberry [*Fragaria vesca*] that cover the ground with a close carpet have also turned to a crimson, and here and there to an almost scarlet colour.

During the year I make careful notes of any trees or shrubs that will be wanted either to come from the nursery or to be transplanted within my own ground, so as to plant them as early as possible. Of the two extremes it is better to plant too early than too late. I would rather plant deciduous trees before their leaves are off than wait till after Christmas, but of all planting times the best is from the middle of October till the end of November, and the same time is the best for all hardy plants of large or moderate size.

I have no patience with slovenly planting. I like to have the ground prepared some months in advance, and when the proper time comes, to do the actual planting as well as possible. The hole in the already prepared ground is taken out so that the tree shall stand exactly right for depth, though in this dry soil it is well to make the hole an inch or two deeper, in order to leave the tree standing in the centre of a shallow depression, to allow of a good watering now and then during the following summer. The hole must be made wide enough to give easy space for the most outward-reaching of the roots; they must be spread out on all sides, carefully combing them out with the fingers, so that they all lay out to the best advantage. Any roots that have been bruised, or have broken or jagged ends, are cut off with a sharp knife on the homeward side of the injury. Most gardeners when they plant, after the first spadeful or two have been thrown over the root, shake the bush with an up and down juggling movement. This is useful in the case of plants with a lot of bushy root, such as berberis, helping to get the grains of earth well in among the root; but in tree planting, where the roots are laid out flat, it is of course useless. In our light soil the closer and firmer the earth is made round the newly planted tree the better, and strong staking is most important, in order to save the newly-planted root from disturbance by dragging.

Some trees and shrubs one can only get from nurseries in pots. This is usually the case with ilex, escallonia and cydonia. Such plants are sure to have the roots badly matted and twisted. The main root curls painfully round and round inside the imprisoning pot, but if it is a clever root it works its way out through the hole in the bottom, and even makes quite nice roots in the bed of ashes it has stood on. In this case, as these are probably its best roots, we do not attempt to pull it back through the hole, but break the pot to release it without hurt. If it is possible to straighten the pot-curled root it is best to do so; in any case, the small fibrous ones can be laid out. Often the potful of roots is so hard and tight that it cannot be disentangled by the hand; then the only way is to soften it by gentle bumping on the bench, and then to disengage the roots by little careful digs all round with a blunt-pointed stick. If this is not done, and the plant is put in in its pot-bound state, it never gets on; it would be just as well to throw it away at once.

[Miss Jekyll's excellent instructions cannot be improved upon. However, most shrubs and some trees today come in containers and even if we still prefer and recommend autumn planting, in fact many people are busy planting all year having got their plants, already packed, from a neighbouring garden centre. With new methods of propagation and 'growing on' techniques and specially prepared soil mixtures, with added slow-acting fertilizers, the problems are rather different from those in her period. On the whole the standard is very high, but plants do need frequent potting-on into larger containers and in a busy season this can be overlooked, especially when the retailer is only a handler of the plants and in no sense a true nurseryman. If the plant is pot-bound, as Miss Jekyll describes above, follow her advice. A well-grown young tree should be carefully wrenched each year in its nursery to prevent formation of permanent roots and to encourage the growth of the small fibrous root system which will be such a help to a tree in establishing itself in its permanent site.]

Nine years ago a hedge of Lawson's cypress [*Chamaecyparis lawsoniana*] was planted on one side of the kitchen garden. Three years later, when the trees had made some growth, I noticed in the case of three or four that they were quite bare of branches on one side all the way up for a width of about one-sixth of the circumference, leaving a smooth, straight upright strip. Suspecting the cause, I had them up and found in every case that the root just below the bare strip had been doubled under the stem, and had therefore been unable to do its share of the work. Nothing could have pointed out more clearly the defect in the planting.

There are cases where ground cannot be prepared as one would wish, and where one has to get cver the difficulty the best way one can. Such a case occurred when I had to plant some yews and savins [*Juniperus sabina*] right under a large birch tree. The birch is one of several large ones that nearly surround the lawn. This one stands just within the end of a large shrub-clump, near the place of meeting of some paths with the grass, and with some planting; here some further planting was wanted of dark green evergreens. There is no tree more ground-robbing than a birch, and under the tree in question the ground was dust-dry, extremely hard, and nothing but the poorest sand. Looking at the foot of a large tree one can always see which way the main roots go, and the only way to get down to any depth is to go between these and not many feet away from the trunk. Further away the roots spread out and would receive more injury. So the ground was got up the best way we could, and the yews and savins planted. Now, after some six years, they are healthy and dark-coloured, and have made good growth. But in such a place one cannot expect the original preparation of the ground, such as it was, to go for much. The year after planting they had some strong, lasting manure just pricked in over the roots – stuff from the shoeing-forge, full of hoof-parings. Hoof-parings are rich in ammonia, and decay slowly. Every other year they have either a repetition of this or some cooling cow manure. The big birch no doubt gets some of it, though its hungriest roots are further afield, but the rich colour of the shrubs shows that they are well nourished.

[Of course, now it is possible to buy Hoof and Horn, dried blood and any other necessary nutrients in powder form, which makes application swift and easy. Cow manure (or the even more nutritious horse manure) is not so easily obtainable, but brand products of organic and artificial fertilizers can be used, as long as some form of bulk humus is also applied regularly.]

As soon as may be in November the big hardy flower border has to be thoroughly looked over. The first thing is to take away all 'soft stuff'. This includes all dead annuals and biennials and any tender things that have been put in for the summer, also Paris daisies [*Chrysanthemum frutescens*], zinnias, French and African marigolds [tagetes species], helichrysums, mulleins and a few geraniums [presumably she means the tender pelargoniums]. Then dahlias are cut down. The waste stuff is laid in

221

big heaps on the edge of the lawn just across the footpath, to be loaded into the donkey cart and shot into some large holes that have been dug in the wood, whose story will be told later.

The dahlias are now dug up from the border, and others collected from different parts of the garden. The labels are tied on to the short stumps that remain, and the roots are laid for a time on the floor of a shed. If the weather has been rainy just before taking them up, it is as well to lay them upside down, so that any wet there may be about the bases of the large hollow stalks may dry out. They are left for perhaps a fortnight without shaking out the earth between the tubers, so that they may be fairly dry before they are put away for the winter in a cellar.

Then we go back to the flower border and dig out all the plants that have to be divided every year. It will also be the turn for some others that only want division every two or three or more years, as the case may be. First, out come all the perennial sunflowers [Helianthus]. These divide themselves into two classes; those whose roots make close clumpy masses, and those that throw out long stolons ending in a blunt snout, which is the growing crown for next year. To the first division belong the old double sunflower (*H. multiflorus* – [now *H. decapetalus* and its hybrids]) of which I only keep the well-shaped variety 'Soleil d'Or' [still available, flowers of vivid deep yellow] and the much taller large-flowered single kind [probably *H. scaberrimus* syn. *rigidus*, or a hybrid] and a tall pale-yellow flowered one with a dark stem, whose name I do not know. It is not one of the kinds thought much of, and as usually grown has not much effect; but I plant it at the back and pull it down over other plants that have gone out of flower, so that instead of having only a few flowers at the top of a rather bare stem eight feet high, it is a spreading cloud of pale yellow bloom; the training down, as in the case of so many other plants, inducing it to throw up a short flowering stalk from the axil of every leaf along the stem.

Colour Schemes   [Elsewhere Miss Jekyll names this sunflower as *H. orgyalis*, now *H. salicifolius*, which bears bunches of small yellow flowers, naturally growing to ten feet, but admirably suited to use in this sensible way.] The kinds with the running roots are *H. rigidus* [*see* above], and its giant variety 'Miss Mellish' [listed now under

H. decapetalus] and *H. laetiflorus* [another hybrid of *H. decapetalus*]. I do not know how it may be in other gardens, but in mine these must be replanted every year.

Phloxes must also be taken up. They are always difficult here, unless the season is unusually rainy; in dry summers, even with mulching and watering, I cannot keep them from drying up. The outside pieces are cut off and the woody middle thrown away. It is surprising what a tiny bit of phlox will make a strong flowering plant in one season. The kinds I like best are the pure whites and the salmon-reds; but two others that I find very pretty and useful are 'Eugénie', a good mauve, and 'Le Soleil', a strong pink, of a colour as near a really good pink as in any phlox I know. Both of these have a neat and rather short habit of growth. I do not have many Michaelmas daisies in the flower border, only some early ones that flower within September; of these there are the white-flowered *Anthemis paniculatus, shortii* [flowers violet-blue, two to four feet], *A. acris* [lilac-mauve, two feet], and *A. amellus* [purple flowers, two feet, one of the parents of the very desirable and long-flowering *A. frikartii* 'Mönch', lavender-blue and to three feet]. These of course come up, and any patches of gladiolus are collected, to be dried for a time and then stored.

[We must mention here another of her favourites, *A. divaricatus* then *A. corymbosus*, which has strange wiry dark stems holding a profusion of white flowers:] There is a small-growing *Colour Schemes* perennial aster, *A. corymbosa*, from a foot to eighteen inches high, that seems to enjoy close association with other plants and is easy to grow anywhere. I find it, in conjunction with megasea [bergenia], one of the most useful of these filling plants for edge spaces that just want some pretty trimming but are not wide enough for anything larger . . . The little starry flower is white and is borne on branching heads; the leaves are lance-shaped and sharply pointed; but when the plant is examined in the hand its most distinct character is the small fine wire-like stem, smooth and nearly black, that branches about in an angular way of its own.

[Returning to October:] The next thing is to look through the border for the plants that require occasional renewal. In the front I find that a longish patch of *Heuchera richardsonii*

[*H. americana*] has about half the plants overgrown. These must come up, and are cut into pieces. It is not a nice plant to divide; it has strong middle crowns, and though there are many side ones, they are attached to the main ones too high up to have roots of their own; but I boldly slice down the main stocky stem with straight downward cuts, so as to give a piece of the thick stock to each side bit. I have done this both in winter and in spring, and find the spring rather the best, if not followed by drought. Groups of *Anemone japonica* [now *A. hupehensis japonica* or simply *A. × hybrida*] and of *Polygonum compactum* [*P. cuspidatum* 'Compactum'] are spreading beyond bounds and must be reduced. Neither of these need be entirely taken up. Without going into further detail, it may be of use to note how often I find it advisable to lift and divide some of the more prominent plants.

[I shall give Miss Jekyll's lists although I believe that she rather tends to exaggerate in her yearly and two-yearly divisions. Most of these good garden plants continue to flourish and flower for up to three years or more. She speaks of the ideal and therefore people think of her teaching as unfitted to modern-day gardening, when the paid gardener seldom exists, and the owner is part-time gardener and handyman. In the great National Trust borders, largely consisting of hardy herbaceous plants, many of them favourites of Miss Jekyll, lifting and dividing is nothing like so frequent (*see* plans of Cliveden borders and details of maintenance there on pp. 278–82).]

[Michaelmas Daisies, Munstead Wood.] 'Where space can be given, it is well to set apart a separate border for these fine plants alone. Here the Starworts occupy a double border ... planted and regulated with the two-fold aim of both form and colour beauty. In these borders of Michaelmas Daisies one other flowering plant is admitted, and well deserves its place, namely that fine white Daisy, *Chrysanthemum uliginosum*. There is more than usual pleasure in such a Daisy garden, kept apart and by itself; because the time of its best beauty is just the time when the rest of the garden is looking tired and overworn ... the fresh, clear, lively colouring of the lilac, purple and white Daisies is like a sudden change from decrepit age to the brightness of youth, from the gloom of late autumn to the joy of full springtide.' GJ

Every year I divide Michaelmas daisies, golden rod, helianthus, phlox, *Chrysanthemum maximum* [the common Shasta daisy and some of its superb garden forms; their white long-flowering flowers mix well in any border], *Helenium pumilum* [a form of *H. autumnale*], *Pyrethrum uliginosum* [*Chrysanthemum serotinum*, the moon daisy, flowering in great branching sprays in October and November], *Anthemis tinctoria* [now generally superseded by its hybrid forms with cream, pale yellow and deep yellow flowers], monarda, lychnis, primula, except *P. denticulata, P. rosea* and *P. auriculata*, which stand two years.

Every two years, white pinks, cranesbills, spiraea [astilbe], aconitum, gaillardia, coreopsis, *Chrysanthemum indicum* [a close relative of *C. morifolium*, this is one of the parents of the autumn-flowering chrysanthemum; the true species has small yellow flowers and is tender], galega, doronicum, nepeta, *Geum aureum* [*G. montanum grandiflorum*], *Oenothera youngii* [*O. fruticosa youngii*] and *O. riparia* [*O. tetragona* 'Riparia']. Every three years, tritoma [kniphofia], megasea [bergenia], centranthus, vinca, iris, narcissus.

A plasterer's hammer is a tool that is very handy for dividing plants. It has a hammer on one side of the head, and a cutting blade like a small chopper on the other. With this and a cold chisel and a strong knife one can divide any roots in comfort. I never divide things by brutally chopping them across with a spade. Plants that have soft fleshy tubers like dahlias and paeonies want the cold chisel; it can be cleverly inserted among

---

[Orange lilies and larkspur.] 'Some of us gardeners, searching for ways of best displaying our flowers, have observed that whereas it is best, as a general rule, to mass the warm colours (reds and yellows) rather together, so it is best to treat the blues with contrasts, either of direct complementary colour, or at any rate with some kind of yellow, or with clear white. So that whereas it would be less pleasing to put scarlet flowers directly against bright blue, and whereas flowers of purple colouring can be otherwise much more suitably treated, the juxtaposition of the splendid blue of the perennial larkspurs with the rich colour of the orange herring lily (*L. croceum*) is a bold and grand assortment of colour of the most satisfactory effect. This fine lily is one of those easiest to grow in most gardens. It takes its name from the Dutch, because they bloom at the time of their herring harvest.' GJ

the crowns so that injury to the tubers is avoided, and it is equally useful in the case of some plants whose points of attachment are almost as hard as wire, like *Orobus vernus* [*Lathyrus vernus*], or as tough as a doormat like *Iris graminea*. The Michaelmas daisies of the *novae-angliae* section make root tufts too close and hard to be cut with a knife, and here the chopper of the plasterer's hammer comes in. Where the crowns are closely crowded, as in this aster, I find it best to chop at the bottom of the tuft, among the roots; when the chopper has cut about two-thirds through, the tuft can be separated with the hands, dividing naturally between the crowns, whereas if chopped from the top many crowns would have been spoilt.

Tritomas [kniphofias] want dividing with care; it always looks as if one could pull every crown apart, but there is a tender point at the 'collar', where they easily break off short; with these also it is best to chop from below or to use the chisel, making the cut well down in the yellow rooty region. Veratrums divide much in the same way, wanting a careful cut low down, the points of their crowns being also very easy to break off. The Christmas rose [*Helleborus niger*] is one of the most awkward plants to divide successfully. It cannot be done in a hurry. The only safe way is to wash the clumps well out and look carefully for the points of attachment, and cut them either with knife or chisel, according to their position. In this case the chisel should be narrower and sharper. Three-year-old tufts of St Bruno's lily [*Paradisea liliago*] puzzled me at first. The rather fleshy roots are so tightly interlaced that cutting is out of the question; but I found that if the tuft is held tight in the two hands, and the hands are worked opposite ways with a rotary motion of about a quarter of a circle, that they soon come apart without being hurt in the least. Delphiniums easily break off at the crown if they are broken up by hand, but the roots cut so easily that it ought not to be a difficulty.

There are some plants in whose case one can never be sure whether they will divide well or not, such as Oriental poppies [*Papaver orientale*] and *Eryngium oliverianum*. They behave in nearly the same way. Sometimes a poppy or an eryngium comes up with one thick root, impossible to divide, while the next door plant has a number of roots that are ready to drop apart like a

226

bunch of salsify. Everlasting peas [*Lathyrus latifolius*] do nearly the same. One may dig up two plants – own brothers of say seven years old – and a rare job it is for they go straight down into the earth nearly a yard deep. One of them will have a black post of a root two and a half inches thick without a break of any sort till it forks a foot underground, while the other will be a sort of loose rope of separate roots from half to three-quarters of an inch thick, that if carefully followed down and cleverly dissected where they join, will make strong plants at once. But the usual way to get young plants of everlasting pea is to look out in earliest spring for the many young growths that will be shooting, for these if taken off with a good bit of the white underground stem will root under a handlight. Most of the primrose tribe divide pleasantly and easily: the worst are the auricula section; with these, for outdoor planting, one often has to slice a main root down to give a share of root to the offset.

When one is digging up plants with running roots, such as gaultheria, honeysuckle [lonicera], polygonum, Scotch briars [*R. pimpinellifolia*], and many of the rubus tribe, or what is better if one person is digging while another pulls up, it never does for the one who is pulling to give a steady haul; this is sure to end in breakage, whereas a root comes up willingly and unharmed in loosened ground to a succession of firm but gentle tugs, and one soon learns to suit the weight of the pulls to the strength of the plant, and to learn its breaking strain.

Toward the end of October outdoor flowers in anything like quantity cannot be expected, and yet there are patches of bloom here and there in nearly every corner of the garden. The pretty Mediterranean periwinkle (*Vinca acutiflora* [*V. difformis*]) is in full bloom. As with many another southern plant that in its own home likes a cool and shady place, it prefers a sunny one in our latitude. The flowers are of a pale and delicate grey-blue colour, nearly as large as those of the common *Vinca major*, but they are borne more generously as to numbers on radical shoots that form thick, healthy-looking tufts of polished green foliage. It is not very common in gardens, but distinctly desirable. [In fact here at Tintinhull it flowers very happily all autumn in deep and dry shade under an ilex tree where little else thrives.]

In the bulb beds the bright yellow *Sternbergia lutea* is in flower. At first sight it looks something like a crocus of unusually firm and solid substance; but it is an amaryllis, and its pure and even yellow colouring is quite unlike that of any of the crocuses. The numerous upright leaves are thick deep green and glossy. It flowers rather shyly in our poor soil, even in well-made beds, doing much better in chalky ground. [It often is difficult, yet in some gardens flowers magnificently.] Czar violets [a cultivated form of the ordinary hedgerow violet but with much bigger flowers – usually grown under glass] are giving their fine and fragrant flowers on stalks nine inches long . . . no plants answer better to good treatment, or spoil more quickly by neglect.

[The fashion for cultivating these fine violets has rather lapsed but Miss Jekyll goes on to emphasize the need of regular division, feeding and control. It is still lovely to grow different viola species at the base of hedges, under roses and other deciduous shrubs and a liberal dose of liquid manure will make them do twice as well as if allowed simply to exist. They can be grown as a carpet under a spring-flowering magnolia where bulbs such as martagon lily or alliums can succeed them, pushing through the violet foliage, and enjoying the slight protection given to emergent leaves.]

In such a simple matter as the culture of this good hardy violet, my garden, though it is full of limitations, and in all ways falls short of any worthy ideal, enables me here and there to point out something that is worth doing, and to lay stress on the fact that the things worth doing are worth taking trouble about. But it is a curious thing that many people, even among those who profess to know something about gardening, when I show them something fairly successful – the crowning reward of much care and labour – refuse to believe that any pains have been taken about it. They will ascribe it to chance, to the goodness of my soil, and even more commonly to some supposed occult influence of my own – to anything rather than to the plain fact that I love it well enough to give it plenty of care and labour. They assume a tone of complimentary banter, kindly meant no doubt, but to me rather distasteful, to this effect: 'Oh yes, of course it will grow for you; anything will grow for you; you have only to look at a thing and it will grow.' I have to pump up a laboured smile and accept the remark with what grace I can, as a necessary civility to the stranger that is within my gates, but it seems to me evident that those who say these things do not understand the love of a garden. I could not help rejoicing when such a visitor came to me one October. I had been saying how necessary good and deep cultivation was, especially in so very poor and shallow a soil as mine. Passing up through the copse where there were some tall stems of *Lilium giganteum* [*Cardiocrinum giganteum*] bearing the great upturned pods of seed, my visitor stopped and said, 'I don't believe a word about your poor soil – look at the growth of that lily. Nothing could make that great stem ten feet high in a poor soil, and there it is, just stuck into the wood!' I said nothing, knowing that presently I could show a better answer than I could frame in words.

A little farther up in the copse we came upon an excavation about twelve feet across and four deep, and by its side a formidable mound of sand, when my friend said, 'Why are you making all this mess in your pretty wood? are you quarrying stone, or is it for the cellar of a building? and what on earth are you going to do with that great heap of sand? why, there must be a dozen loads of it.' That was my moment of secret triumph, but I hope I bore it meekly as I answered, 'I only wanted to plant a few more of those big lilies, and you see in my soil they would not have a chance unless the ground was thoroughly prepared; look at the edge of the scarp and see how the solid yellow sand comes to within four inches of the top; so I have a big wide hole dug; and look, there is the donkey-cart coming with the first load of dahlia-tops and soft plants that have been for the summer in the south border. There will be several of those little cartloads, each holding three barrowfuls. As it comes into the hole, the men will chop it with the spade and tread it down close, mixing in a little sand. This will make a nice cool, moist bottom of slowly-rotting vegetable matter. Some more of the same kind of waste will come from the kitchen garden – cabbage-stumps, bean-haulm, soft weeds that have been hoed up, and all the greenest stuff from the rubbish-heap. Every layer will be chopped and pounded, and tramped down so that there should be as little sinking as possible afterwards. By this time the hole will be filled to within a foot of the top; and now we must get together some better stuff – road-scrapings and trimmings mixed with some older rubbish-heap mould, and for the top of all, some of our precious loam, and the soil of an old hotbed and some well-decayed manure, all well mixed, and then we are ready for the lilies. They are planted only just underground, and then the whole bed has a surfacing of dead leaves, which helps to keep down weeds, and also looks right with the surrounding wild ground. The remains of the heap of sand we must deal with how we can; but there are hollows here and there in the roadway and paths, and a place that can be levelled up in the rubbish-yard, and some kitchen-garden paths that will bear raising, and so by degrees it is disposed of.'

NOVEMBER

'There is nothing like true gardening for training the eye and Elgood,
mind to the habit of close observation; that precious acquirement p. 27
that invests every country object both within and without the
garden's bounds with a living interest, and that insensibly builds
up that bulk of mentally noted storehouse the brain, seems there
to sort itself, to distribute, to arrange, to classify, to reduce into
order, in such a way as to increase the knowledge of something
of which there was at first only a mental glimpse; so to build up
in orderly structure a well-founded knowledge of many of those
things of every-day outdoor life that adds so greatly to its present
enjoyment and later usefulness.'

Giant Christmas roses — Hardy chrysanthemums — Sheltering tender shrubs — Turfing by inoculation — Transplanting large trees — Sir Henry Steuart's experience early in the century — Collecting fallen leaves — Preparing grubbing tools — Butcher's Broom — Alexandrian laurel — Hollies and birches — A lesson in planting.

THE GIANT Christmas rose (*Helleborus maximus* [*H. niger macranthus*] is in full flower; it is earlier than the true Christmas rose [*H. niger*], being at its best by the middle of November. It is a large and massive flower, but compared with the later kinds has a rather coarse look. The bud and the back of the flower are rather heavily tinged with a dull pink, and it never has the pure-white colouring throughout of the later ones.

I have taken some pains to get together some really hardy November-blooming chrysanthemums. The best of all is a kind frequent in neighbouring cottage gardens, and known hereabouts as 'Cottage Pink'. I believe it is identical with 'Emperor of China', a very old sort that used to be frequent in greenhouse cultivation before it was supplanted by the many good kinds now grown. But its place is not indoors, but in the open garden; if against a south or west wall, so much the better. Perhaps one year in seven the bloom may be spoilt by such a severe frost as that of October 1895, but it will bear unharmed several degrees of frost and much rain. I know of no chrysanthemum of so true a pink colour, the colour deepening to almost crimson in the centre. After the first frost the foliage of this kind turns to a splendid colour, the green of the leaves giving place to a rich crimson that sometimes clouds the outer portion of the leaf, and often covers its whole expanse. The stiff wholesome foliage adds much to the beauty of the outdoor kinds, contrasting most agreeably with the limp mildewed leafage of those indoors. Following 'Cottage Pink' is a fine pompone called 'Soleil d'Or', in colour the richest deep orange, with a still deeper and richer coloured centre. The beautiful crimson 'Julie Lagravère' flowers at the same time. Both are nearly frost-proof, and true hardy November flowers.

The first really frosty day we go to the upper part of the wood and cut out from among the many young Scotch firs as many as we think will be wanted for sheltering plants and shrubs of doubtful hardiness. One section of the high wall at the back of the flower border is planted with rather tender things, so that the whole is covered with sheltering fir-boughs. Here are loquat, fuchsia, pomegranate, edwardsia [*Sophora macrocarpa*], piptanthus and choisya, and in the narrow border at the foot of the wall, crinum, nandina, clerodendron and hydrangea. In the broad border in front of the wall nothing needs protection except tritomas [kniphofias]; these have cones of coal-ashes heaped over each plant or clump. The crinums also have a few inches of ashes heaped over them.

Some large hydrangeas in tubs are moved to a sheltered place and put close together, a mound of sand being shovelled up all round to nearly the depth of the tubs; then a wall is made of thatched hurdles, and dry fern is packed well in among the heads of the plants. They would be better in a frost-proof shed but we have no such place to spare.

The making of a lawn is a difficulty in our very poor sandy soil. In this rather thickly populated country the lords of the manor had been so much pestered for grants of road-side turf, and the privilege when formerly given had been so much abused, that they have agreed together to refuse all applications. Opportunities of buying good turf do not often occur, and sowing is slow, and not satisfactory. I am told by a seedsman of the highest character that it is almost impossible to get grass seed clean and true to name from the ordinary sources; the leading men therefore have to grow their own.

In my own case, having some acres of rough heath and copse where the wild grasses are of fine-leaved kinds, I made the lawn by inoculation. The ground was trenched and levelled, then well trodden and raked, and the surface stones collected. Tufts of the wild grass were then forked up, and were pulled into pieces about the size of the palm of one's hand, and laid down eight inches apart and well rolled in. During the following summer we collected seed of the same grasses to sow early in spring in any patchy or bare places. One year after planting the patches had spread to double their size, and by the second year had nearly joined together. The grasses were of two kinds only, namely, sheep's fescue (*Festuca ovina*) and crested dog's-tail (*Cynosurus cristatus*). They make a lawn of a quiet, low-toned colour, never of the bright green of the rather coarser grasses; but in this case I much prefer it; it goes better with the heath and fir and bracken that belong to the place. In point of labour, a lawn made of these fine grasses has the great merit of only wanting mowing once in three weeks.

[The ideal conditions for a lawn are good drainage, rich preparation of the top spit, a fairly acid soil and not too much shade. There are today lawn-seed mixtures available to suit all types of soil and conditions, and, before sowing, you can make arrangements to have your lawn soil tested by the local Horticultural Institute. This will establish its degree of acidity, and a recommended mixture can then be used. A general purpose ornamental lawn usually has seed mixed in roughly these proportions: 30 per cent Chewings' fescue (*Festuca rubra* ssp. *mutata*), 25 per cent creeping red fescue (*F. rubra* ssp. *rubra*), 10 per cent browntop bent (*Agrostis tenuis*), 35 per cent smooth-stalked meadow grass (*Poa pratensis*). Miss Jekyll's *Festuca ovina* is still very often included in mixtures but tends to grow more quickly than the fescues recommended above. The crested dog's tail, *Cynosurus cristatus*, cannot be very closely mowed but is ideal for the wilder area where mowing is kept to once every three weeks. For the ornamental lawn rye grass is generally a mistake, although it is very hard-wearing, perhaps useful in an area around garden sheds and greenhouses. Mixtures can be treated with a bird repellent before sowing. Suitable fertilizers and weed killers should be applied, strictly as recommended for the type of grass, and the above mixture should be adapted for shady areas, damp places, hot dry sandy soils (such as Miss Jekyll had) and for calcareous clay. It will certainly be worth getting the very best, so economy on seed purchase would be a grave mistake. Most gardeners spend more time looking after their lawns than in any other more amusing garden occupation, but technical aftercare is not included in this book.]

[Miss Jekyll employed an old country woman to weed her lawn by hand, one who knew no plant distinctions except that of desirable flowers, which she called 'lilies', and the weeds which she called 'docks'.] An old woman that we had some years ago to weed the lawn was one of those who held to this broad and simple distinction in botanical nomenclature, for though there was not a dock in the grass, and her work was to fork up daisies and dandelions, plantains and hawkweed; yet whenever one asked how she was getting on, and of what kinds of weeds she found the greater number, her broad brown face would beam her appreciation of the interest shown in her work and her stout figure would make a sudden subsidence in the good old country bob-curtsey, as she gave the inevitable answer 'Docks, m'm.'

Home and Garden

I have never undertaken the transplanting of large trees, but there is no doubt that it may be done with success, and in laying out a new place where the site is bare, if suitable trees are to be had, it is a plan much to be recommended. It has often been done of late years, but until a friend drew my attention to an article in the *Quarterly Review*, dated March 1828, I had no idea that it had been practised on a large scale so early in the century. The article in question was a review of *The Planter's Guide*, by Sir Henry Steuart, Bart, LL.D. (Edinburgh 1828). It quoted the opinion and observation of a committee of gentlemen, among whom was Sir Walter Scott, who visited Allanton (Sir Henry Steuart's place) in September 1828, when the trees had been some years planted. They found them growing 'with vigour and luxuriance, and in the most exposed situations making shoots of eighteen inches...' From the facts which they witnessed the committee reported it as their unanimous opinion that the art of transplantation, as practised by Sir Henry Steuart, is calculated to accelerate in an extraordinary degree the power of raising wood, whether for beauty or shelter.

The reviewer then quotes the method of transplantation,

[Lutyens provided an architectural background of pavements, steps and walls for Miss Jekyll's sensitive planting schemes, but she knew too when not to embellish the pure lines of stonework.] 'Broad, easy steps in flights never too long, and spacious landings and resting places.' ['The idea of a garden', *Edinburgh Review*, July 1896.]

describing the extreme care with which the roots are preserved, men with picks carefully trying round the ground beneath the outer circumference of the branches for the most outlying root-lets, and then gradually approaching the bole. The greatest care was taken not to injure any root or fibre, these as they were released from the earth being tied up, and finally the transplant-ing machine, consisting of a strong pole mounted on high wheels, was brought close to the trunk and attached to it, and the tree when lowered, carefully transported to its new home. Every layer of roots was then replanted with the utmost care, with delicate fingering and just sufficient ramming, and in the end the tree stood without any artificial support whatever, and in positions exposed to the fiercest gales.

The average size of tree dealt with seems to have had a trunk about a foot in diameter, but some were removed with complete success whose trunks were two feet thick. In order that his trees might be the better balanced in shape, Sir Henry boldly departed from the older custom of replanting a tree in its original aspect, for he reversed the aspect, so that the more stunted and shorter-twigged weather side now became the lee side, and could grow more freely.

He insists strongly on the wisdom of transplanting only well-weathered trees, and not those of tender constitution that had been sheltered by standing among other close growths, pointing out that these have a tenderer bark and taller top and roots less well able to bear the strain of wind and weather in the open.

He reckons that a transplanted tree is in full new growth by the fourth or fifth year, and that an advantage equal to from thirty to forty years' growth is gained by the system. As for the expense of the work, Sir Henry estimated that his largest trees each cost from ten to thirteen shillings to take up, remove half a mile, and replant. In the case of large trees the ground that was to receive them was prepared a twelvemonth beforehand.

Now, in the third week of November, the most pressing work is the collecting of leaves for mulching and leaf-mould. The oaks have been late in shedding their leaves and we have been waiting till they are down. Oak-leaves are the best, then hazel, elm, and Spanish chestnut. Birch and beech are not so good; beech-leaves especially take much too long to decay. This is, no doubt, the reason why nothing grows willingly under beeches. Horse and cart and three hands go out into the lanes for two or three days, and the loads that come home go three feet deep into the bottom of a range of pits. The leaves are trodden down close and covered with a layer of mould, in which winter salad stuff is immediately planted. The mass of leaves will soon begin to heat, and will give a pleasant bottom-heat throughout the winter. Other loads of leaves go into an open pen about ten feet square and five feet deep. Two such pens, made of stout oak post and rail and upright slabs, stand side by side in the garden yard. The one newly filled has just been emptied of its two-year-old leaf-mould, which has gone as a nourishing and protecting mulch over beds of daffodils and choice bulbs and alströmerias, some being put aside in reserve for potting and various uses. The other pen remains full of the leaves of last year, slowly rotting into wholesome plant-food.

With works of wood-cutting and stump-grubbing near at hand, we look over the tools and see that all are in readiness for winter work. Axes and hand-bills are ground, fag-hooks sharpened, picks and mattocks sent to the smithy to be drawn out, the big cross-cut saw fresh sharpened and set, and the hand-saws got ready. The rings of the bittle are tightened and wedged up, so that its heavy head may not split when the mighty blows, flung into the tool with a man's full strength, fall on the heads of the great iron wedges.

Some thinning of birch-trees has to be done in the lowest part of the copse, not far from the house. They are rather evenly distributed on the ground, and I wish to get them into groups by cutting away superfluous trees. On the neighbouring moorland and heathy uplands they are apt to grow naturally in groups, the individual trees generally bending outward towards the free, open space, the whole group taking a form that is graceful and highly pictorial. I hope to be able to cut out trees so as to leave the remainder standing in some such way. But as a tree once cut cannot be put up again, the condemned ones are marked with bands of white paper right round the trunks, so that they can be observed from all sides, thus to give a chance of reprieve to any tree that from any point of view may have pictorial value.

Frequent in some woody districts in the south of England,

though local, is the Butcher's Broom (*Ruscus aculeatus*). Its stiff green branches that rise straight from the root bear small, hard leaves, armed with a sharp spine at the end. The flower, which comes in early summer, is seated without stalk in the middle of the leaf, and is followed by a large red berry. In country places where it abounds, butchers use the twigs tied in bunches to brush the little chips of meat off their great chopping-blocks, that are made of solid sections of elm trees, standing three and a half feet high and about two and a half feet across. Its beautiful garden relative the Alexandrian or Victory laurel (*R. racemosus – [Danaë racemosa]*), is also now just at its best. Nothing makes a more beautiful wreath than two of its branches, suitably arched and simply bound together near the butts and free ends. It is not a laurel, but a *Ruscus* [now a *Danaë*], the name laurel having probably grown on to it by old association with any evergreen suitable for a victor's wreath. It is a slow-growing plant, but in time makes handsome tufts of its graceful branches. Few plants are more exquisitely modelled, to use a term familiar to the world of fine art, or give an effect of more delicate and perfect finish. It is a valuable plant in a shady place in good, cool soil. Early in summer, when the young growths appear, the old, then turning rusty, should be cut away.

No trees group together more beautifully than hollies and birches. One such happy mixture in one part of the copse suggested further plantings of holly, birches being already in abundance. Every year some more hollies are planted; those put in nine years ago are now fifteen feet high, and are increasing fast. They are slow to begin growth after transplanting, perhaps because in our very light soil they cannot be moved with a 'ball'; all the soil shakes away, and leaves the roots naked; but after about three years, when the roots have got good hold and begun to ramble, they grow away well. The trunk of an old holly has a smooth pale-grey bark, and sometimes a slight twist, that makes it look like the gigantic bone of some old-world monster. The leaves of some old trees, especially if growing in shade, change their shape, losing the side prickles and becoming longer and nearly flat and more of a dark bottle-green colour, while the lower branches and twigs, leafless except towards their ends, droop down in a graceful line that rises again a little at the tip.

The leaves are all down by the last week of November, and woodland assumes its winter aspect; perhaps one ought rather to say, some one of its infinite variety of aspects, for those who live in such country know how many are the winter moods of forest land, and how endless are its variations of atmospheric effect and pictorial beauty – variations much greater and more numerous than are possible in summer.

With the wind in the south-west and soft rain about, the twigs of the birches look almost crimson, while the dead bracken at their foot, half-draggled and sodden with wet, is of a strong, dark rust colour. Now one sees the full value of the good evergreens, and, rambling through woodland, more especially of the holly, whether in bush or tree form, with its masses of strong green colour, dark and yet never gloomy. Whether it is the high polish of the leaves, or the lively look of their wavy edges, with the short prickles set alternately up and down, or the brave way the tree has of shooting up among other thick growth, or its massive sturdiness on a bare hillside, one cannot say, but a holly in early winter, even without berries, is always a cheering sight. John Evelyn is eloquent in his praise of this grand evergreen, and lays special emphasis on this quality of cheerfulness.

Near my home is a little wild valley, whose planting, wholly done by nature, I have all my life regarded with the most reverent admiration.

The arable fields of an upland farm give place to hazel copses as the ground rises. Through one of these a deep narrow lane, cool and dusky in summer from its high steep banks and over-arching foliage, leads by a rather sudden turn into the lower end of the little valley. Its grassy bottom is only a few yards wide, and its sides rise steeply right and left. Looking upward through groups of wild bushes and small trees, one sees thickly-wooded ground on the higher levels. The soil is of the very poorest; ridges of pure yellow sand are at the mouths of the many rabbit-burrows. The grass is of the short fine kinds of the heathy uplands. Bracken grows low, only from one to two feet high, giving evidence of the poverty of the soil, and yet it seems able to grow in perfect beauty clumps of juniper and thorn and holly, and Scotch fir on the higher ground.

On the steeply-rising banks are large groups of juniper, some

tall, some spreading, some laced and wreathed about with
tangles of honeysuckle, now in brown winter dress, and there
are a few bushes of spindle-tree, whose green stems and twigs
look strangely green in winter. The thorns stand some singly,
some in close companionship, impenetrable masses of short-
twigged prickly growth, with here and there a wild rose shooting
straight up through the crowded branches. One thinks how
lovely it will be in early June, when the pink rose-wreaths are
tossing out of the foamy sea of white thorn blossom. The hollies
are towering masses of health and vigour. Some of the groups of
thorn and holly are intermingled; all show beautiful arrangements of form and colour, such as are never seen in planted
places.

The track in the narrow valley trends steadily upwards and
bears a little to the right. High up on the left-hand side is an old
wood of Scotch fir. A few detached trees come half-way down
the valley bank to meet the gnarled, moss-grown thorns and the
silver-green junipers. As the way rises some birches come in
sight, also at home in the sandy soil. Their graceful, lissome spray
moving to the wind looks active among the stiffer trees, and their
white stems shine out in startling contrast to the other dusky
foliage. So the narrow track leads on, showing the same kinds
of tree and bush in endless variety of beautiful grouping, under
the sombre half-light of the winter day. It is afternoon, and as
one mounts higher a pale bar of yellow light gleams between the
farther tree-stems, but all above is grey, with angry, blackish
drifts of ragged wrack. Now the valley opens out to a nearly
level space of rough grass, with grey tufts that will be pink bell-
heather in summer, and upstanding clumps of sedge that tell of
boggy places. In front and to the right are dense fir-woods. To
the left is broken ground and a steep-sided hill, towards whose
shoulder the track rises. Here are still the same kinds of trees,
but on the open hillside they have quite a different effect. Now
I look into the ruddy heads of the thorns, bark and fruit both of
rich warm colouring, and into the upper masses of the hollies,
also reddening into a wealth of berry.

Throughout the walk, pacing slowly but steadily for nearly an
hour, only these few kinds of trees have been seen, juniper,
holly, thorn, Scotch fir, and birch (a few small oaks excepted),

and yet there has not been once the least feeling of monotony, nor, returning downward by the same path, could one wish anything to be altered or suppressed or differently grouped. And I have always had the same feeling about any quite wild stretch of forest land. Such a bit of wild forest as this small valley and the hilly land beyond are precious lessons in the best way of tree and shrub planting. No artificial planting can ever equal that of nature, but one may learn from it the great lesson of the importance of moderation and reserve, of simplicity of intention, and directness of purpose, and the inestimable value of the quality called 'breadth' in painting. For planting ground is painting a landscape with living things; and as I hold that good gardening takes rank within the bounds of the fine arts, so I hold that to plant well needs an artist of no mean capacity. And his difficulties are not slight ones, for his living picture must be right from all points, and in all lights.

No doubt the planting of a large space with a limited number of kinds of trees cannot be trusted to all hands, for in those of a person without taste or the more finely-trained perceptions the result would be very likely dull or even absurd. It is not the paint that makes the picture, but the brain and heart and hand of the man who uses it.

DECEMBER

'It is just in the way it is done that lies the whole difference between commonplace gardening and gardening that may rightly claim to rank as a fine art. Given the same space of ground and the same material, they may either be fashioned into a dream of beauty, a place of perfect rest and refreshment of mind and body – a series of soul-satisfying pictures – a treasure of well-set jewels; or they may be so misused that everything is jarring and displeasing. To learn how to perceive the difference and how to do right is to apprehend gardening as a fine art. In practice it is to place every plant or group of plants with such thoughtful care and definite intention that they shall form a part of a harmonious whole, and that successive portions, or in some cases even single details, shall show a series of pictures. It is to regulate the trees and undergrowth of the wood that their lines and masses come into beautiful form and harmonious proportion; it is to be always watching, noting and doing, and putting oneself meanwhile into closest acquaintance and sympathy with growing things. In this spirit the garden and woodland, such as they are, have been formed. There have been many failures, but, every now and then, I am encouraged and rewarded by a certain measure of success. Yet, as the critical faculty becomes keener, so does the standard of aim rise higher; and year by year, the desired point seems always to elude attainment.'

Colour Schemes, viii

The woodman at work — Tree-cutting in frosty weather —
Preparing sticks and stakes — Winter jasmine — Ferns in
the wood-walk — Winter colour of evergreen shrubs —
Copse-cutting — Hoop-making — Tools used — Sizes of
hoops — Men camping out — Thatching with hoop-chips
— The old thatcher's bill.

IT IS GOOD to watch a clever woodman and see how much he can
do with his simple tools, and how easily one man alone can deal
with heavy pieces of timber. An oak trunk, two feet or more
thick, and weighing perhaps a ton, lies on the ground, the
branches being already cut off. He has to cleave it into four, and
to remove it to the side of a lane one hundred feet away. His
tools are an axe and one iron wedge. The first step is the most
difficult – to cut such a nick in the sawn surface of the butt of
the trunk as will enable the wedge to stick in. He holds the wedge
to the cut and hammers it gently with the back of the axe till it
just holds, then he tries a moderate blow, and is quite prepared
for what is almost sure to happen – the wedge springs out backwards; very likely it springs out for three or four trials, but at
last the wedge bites and he can give it the dexterous, rightly-
placed blows that slowly drive it in. Before the wedge is in half
its length a creaking sound is heard; the fibres are beginning to
tear, and a narrow rift shows on each side of the iron. A few
more strokes and the sound of the rending fibres is louder and
more continuous, with sudden cracking noises, that tell of the
parting of larger bundles of fibres, that had held together till the
tremendous rending power of the wedge at last burst them
asunder.

Now the man looks out a bit of strong branch about four
inches thick, and with the tree-trunk as a block and the axe held
short in one hand as a chopper, he makes a wooden wedge about
twice the size of the iron one, and drives it into one of the

247

openings at its side. For if you have only one iron wedge, and you drive it tight into your work, you can neither send it farther nor get it out, and you feel and look foolish. The wooden wedge driven in releases the iron one, which is sent in afresh against the side of the wedge of oak, the trunk meanwhile rending slowly apart with much grieving and complaining of the tearing fibres. As the rent opens the axe cuts across diagonal bundles of fibres that still hold tightly across the widening rift. And so the work goes on, the man unconsciously exercising his knowledge of his craft in placing and driving the wedges, the helpless wood groaning and creaking and finally falling apart as the last holding fibres are severed by the axe. Meanwhile the raw green wood give off a delicious scent, sweet and sharp and refreshing, not unlike the smell of apples crushing in the cider-press.

The woodman has still to rend the two halves of the trunk, but the work is not so heavy and goes more quickly. Now he has to shift them to the side of the rough track that serves as a road through the wood. They are so heavy that two men could barely lift them, and he is alone. He could move them with a lever, that he could cut out of a straight young tree, a foot or so at a time at each end, but it is a slow and clumsy way; besides, the wood is too much encumbered with undergrowth. So he cuts two short pieces from a straight bit of branch four inches or five inches thick, levers one of his heavy pieces so that one end points to the roadway, prises up this end and kicks one of his short pieces under it close to the end, settling it at right angles with gentle kicks. The other short piece is arranged in the same way, a little way beyond the middle of the length of quartered trunk. Now, standing behind it, he can run the length easily along on the two rollers, till the one nearest him is left behind; this one is then put under the front end of the weight, and so on till the road is reached.

Trees that stand where paths are to come, or that for any reason have to be removed, root and all, are not felled with axe or saw, but are grubbed down. The earth is dug away next to the tree, gradually exposing the roots; these are cut through with axe or mattock close to the butt, and again about eighteen inches away, so that by degrees a deep trench, eighteen inches wide, is excavated round the butt. A rope is fastened at the right distance up the trunk, when, if the tree does not hold by a very strong tap-root, a succession of steady pulls will bring it down; the weight of the top thus helping to prise the heavy butt out of the ground. We come upon many old stumps of Scotch fir, the remains of the original wood; they make capital firewood, though some burn rather too fiercely, being full of turpentine. Many are still quite sound, though it must be six-and-twenty years since they were felled. They are very hard to grub, with their thick tap-roots and far-reaching laterals, and still tougher to split up, their fibres are so much twisted, and the dark-red heart-wood has become hardened till it rings to a blow almost like metal. But some, whose roots have rotted, come up more easily, and with very little digging may be levered out of the ground with a long iron stone-bar, such as they use in the neighbouring quarries, putting the point of the bar under the 'stam', and having a log of wood for a hard fulcrum. Or a stout young stem of oak or chestnut is used for a lever, passing a chain under the stump and over the middle of the bar and prising upwards with the lever. 'Stam' is the word always used by the men for any stump of a tree left in the ground.

A spell of frosty days at the end of December puts a stop to all planting and ground work. Now we go into the copse and cut the trees that have been provisionally marked, judged, and condemned, with the object of leaving the remainder standing in graceful groups. The men wonder why I cut some of the trees that are best and straightest and have good tops, and leave those with leaning stems. Anything of seven inches or less diameter is felled with the axe, but thicker trees with the cross-cut saw. For these our most active fellow climbs up the tree with a rope, and makes it fast to the trunk a good way up, then two of them, kneeling, work the saw. When it has cut a third of the way through, the rope is pulled on the side opposite the cut to keep it open and let the saw work free. When still larger trees are sawn down this is done by driving in a wedge behind the saw, when the width of the saw-blade is rather more than buried in the tree. When the trunk is nearly sawn through, it wants care and judgement to see that the saw does not get pinched by the weight of the tree; the clumsy workman who fails to clear his saw gets laughed at, and probably damages his tool. Good straight trunks of oak and chestnut are put aside for special uses; the rest of the larger stuff is cut into cordwood lengths of four feet. The heaviest of these are split up into four pieces to make them easier to load and carry away, and eventually to saw up into firewood.

The best of the birch tops are cut into peasticks, a clever, slanting cut with the hand-bill leaving them pointed and ready for use. Throughout the copse are 'stools' of Spanish chestnut, cut about once in five years. From this we get good straight stakes for dahlias and hollyhocks, also bean-poles; while the rather straight-branched boughs are cut into branching sticks for Michaelmas daisies, and special lengths are got ready for various kinds of plants – chrysanthemums, lilies, paeonies, and so on. To provide all this in winter, when other work is slack or impossible, is an important matter in the economy of a garden, for all gardeners know how distressing and harassing it is to find themselves without the right sort of sticks or stakes in summer, and what a long job it then seems to have to look them up and cut them, of indifferent quality, out of dry faggots.

By the plan of preparing all in winter no precious time is lost, and a tidy withe-bound bundle of the right sort is always at hand. The rest of the rough spray and small branching stuff is made up into faggots to be chopped up for fire-lighting; the country folk still use the old word 'bavin' for faggots. The middle-sized branches – anything between two inches and six inches in diameter – are what the woodmen call 'top and lop'; these are also cut into convenient lengths, and are stacked in the barn, to be cut into billets for next year's fires in any wet or frosty weather, when outdoor work is at a standstill.

What a precious winter flower is the yellow jasmine (*J. nudiflorum*). Though hard frost spoils the flowers then expanded, as soon as milder days come the hosts of buds that are awaiting them burst into bloom. Its growth is so free and rapid that one has no scruple about cutting it freely and great branching sprays, cut a yard or more long, arranged with branches of Alexandrian laurel [*Danae racemosa*] or other suitable foliage – such as andromeda or gaultheria – are beautiful as room decoration.

[Winter-flowering viburnums such as *V. farreri* (introduced in 1910) start flowering in November. Its hybrid *V. × bodnantense* and its clone 'Dawn' have particularly fragrant and frost-resistant flowers, carried over a long winter period. The evergreen *Buddleia auriculata* is a little tender but if a space on a warm wall can be found for it its small creamy-white flowers will scent the garden for yards around. By the end of December the male form of the evergreen *Garrya elliptica* will start to show its long greyish-green tassels. ('James Roof' is particularly vigorous with large leaves and very long tassels.) A well-established plant of winter-sweet, *Chimonanthus praecox* (syn. *fragrans*), starts to produce its strange highly scented pale yellow and purple flowers, after its leaves have fallen. It seems to be capricious, flowering well in some gardens and poorly or perhaps never in another. Its branches are lovely to bring into the house. It prefers a chalk soil and would not have been happy in the Surrey sand at Munstead Wood, but apart from needing a warm wall to ripen its summer growth, and some pruning after flowering, it demands little attention.]

Christmas roses keep on flowering bravely, in spite of our light soil and frequent summer drought, both unfavourable conditions; but bravest of all is the blue Algerian iris (*I. stylosa* [*I. unguicularis*]), flowering freely as it does, at the foot of a west wall, in all open weather from November till April. In the rock-garden at the edge of the copse the creeping evergreen *Polygala chamaebuxus* is quite at home in beds of peat among mossy boulders. [This alpine milkwort is suitable for acid soils only, with hard, box-like leaves and cream-coloured flowers. In the rather superior garden form *P. chamaebuxus* 'Grandiflora' the little pea-flowers are carmine and yellow.] Where it has the ground to itself, this neat little shrub makes close tufts only four inches or five inches high, its wiry branches being closely set with neat, dark-green, box-like leaves; though where it has to struggle for life among other low shrubs, as may often be seen in the Alps, the branches elongate, and will run bare for two or three feet to get the leafy end to the light. Even now it is thickly set with buds and has a few expanded flowers. This bit of rock-garden is mostly planted with dwarf shrubs – skimmia, bog-myrtle [*Myrica gale*], alpine rhododendrons, gaultheria and andromeda, with drifts of hardy ferns between and only a few 'soft' plants. But of these, only two are now conspicuously noticeable for foliage – the hardy cyclamens and the blue Himalayan poppy (*Meconopsis wallichi* – [*M. nepaulensis*]).

[It is now generally recognized that the blue and yellow meconopsis introduced in the early years of the twentieth century are supreme, although it is true that Miss Jekyll's species is still very desirable for its winter rosettes of fine-cut silvery foliage. Probably the best are the species *M. betonicifolia* (syn. *M. baileyi*), flowering in early summer with intense blue; *M. grandis* flowers earlier, and the various forms introduced from different areas of the Far East differ in flower colour and quality. All thrive only in moist lime-free soil, need feeding and shelter in woodland conditions.

Elsewhere Miss Jekyll suggests that to grow meconopsis successfully, watering twice a day in dry periods is essential.] Every winter I notice how bravely the pale woolly foliage of this plant bears up against the early winter's frost and wet.

The wood-walk, whose sloping banks are planted with hardy ferns in large groups, shows how many of our common kinds are good plants for the first half of the winter. Now, only a week before Christmas, the male fern [*Dryopteris filix-mas*] is still in handsome green masses; blechnum [*B. spicant*], is still good, and common polypody [*P. vulgare*] at its best. [Although evergreen the fronds should be cut down to the ground in late winter; this also applies to the hartstongue (*Asplenium scolopendrium*) and its very pretty form 'Crispum' with undulate goffered leaf-edges.] The noble fronds of the dilated shield fern [*Dryopteris dilatata*] are still in fairly good order and ceterach [*Asplenium ceterach* or *Ceterach officinalis*] in rocky chinks is in fullest beauty. Beyond, in large groups, are prosperous-looking tufts of the wood-rush (*Luzula sylvatica*); then there is wood as far as one can see, here mostly of the silver-stemmed birch and rich green holly, with the woodland carpet of dusky low-toned bramble and quiet dead leaf and brilliant moss.

By the middle of December many of the evergreen shrubs that

thrive in peat are in full beauty of foliage. *Andromeda catesbaei*
[*Leucothoe fortanesiana*] is richly coloured with crimson clouds
and splashes; skimmias are at their best and freshest, their bright,
light green leathery foliage defying all rigours of temperature or
weather. Pernettyas are clad in their strongest and deepest green
leafage and show a richness and depth of colour only surpassed
by that of the yew hedges. [In lime soils the leaves of the trailing
evergreen shrub, *Euonymus fortunei* 'Coloratus' turn reddish
purple in winter, and return to green in spring.]

Copse-cutting is one of the harvests of the year for labouring
men, and all the more profitable that it can go on through frosty
weather. A handy man can earn good wages at piece-work, and
better still if he can cleave and shave hoops. Hoop-making is
quite a large industry in these parts, employing many men from
Michaelmas to March. They are barrel-hoops, made of straight
poles of six years' growth. The wood used is birch, ash, hazel and
Spanish chestnut. Hazel is the best, or as my friend in the business
says, 'Hazel, that's the master!' The growths of the copses are
sold by auction in some near county town, as they stand, the
buyer clearing them during the winter. They are cut every six
years, and a good copse of chestnut has been known to fetch £54
an acre.

A good hoop-maker can earn from twenty to twenty-five
shillings a week. He sets up his brake, while his mate, who will
cleave the rods, cuts a post about three inches thick, and fixes it
into the ground so that it stands about three feet high. To steady
it he drives in another of rather curly shape by its side, so that
the tops of the two are nearly even, but the foot of the curved
spur is some nine inches away at the bottom, with its top pressing
hard against the upright. To stiffen it still more he makes a long
withe of a straight hazel rod, which he twists into a rope by
holding the butt tightly under his left foot and twisting with
both hands till the fibres are wrenched open and the withe is
ready to spring back and wind upon itself. With this he binds
his two posts together, so that they stand perfectly rigid. On
this he cleaves the poles, beginning at the top. The tool is a small
one-handled adze with a handle like a hammer. A rod is usually
cleft in two, so that it is only shaved on one side; but sometimes
a pole of chestnut, a very quick-growing wood, is large enough

to cleave into eight, and when the wood is very clean and straight they can sometimes get two lengths of fourteen feet out of a pole.

The brake is a strong flat-shaped post of oak set up in the ground to lean a little away from the workman. It stands five and a half feet out of the ground. A few inches from its upper end it has a shoulder cut in it which acts as the fulcrum for the cross-bar that supports the pole to be shaved, and that leans down towards the man. The relative position of the two parts of the brake reminds one of the mast and yard of a lateen-rigged boat. The bar is nicely balanced by having a hazel withe bound round a groove at its upper short end, about a foot beyond the fulcrum, while the other end of the withe is tied round a heavy bit of log or stump that hangs clear of the ground and just balances the bar, so that it see-saws easily. The cleft rod that is to be shaved lies along the bar, and an iron pin that passes through the head of the brake just above the point where the bar rides over its shoulder, nips the hoop as the weight of the stroke comes upon it; the least lifting of the bar releases the hoop, which is quickly shifted onwards for a new stroke. The shaving tool is a strong two-handled draw-knife, much like the tool used by wheel-wrights. It is hard work, 'wunnerful tryin' across the chest'.

The hoops are in several standard lengths, from fourteen to two and a half feet. The longest go the West Indies for sugar hogsheads, and some of the next are for tacking round pipes of wine. The wine is in well-made iron-hooped barrels, but the wooden hoops are added to protect them from the jarring and bumping when rolled on board ship, and generally to save them during storage and transit. These hoops are in two sizes, called large and small pipes. A thirteen-foot size goes to foreign countries for training vines. A large quantity that measure five feet six inches, and called 'long pinks', are for cement barrels, and for tacking round packing-cases and tea-chests.

The men want to make all the time they can in the short winter daylight, and often the work is some miles from home, so if the weather is not very cold they make huts of the bundles of rods and chips, and sleep out on the job. I always admire the neatness with which the bundles are fastened up, and the strength of the withe-rope that binds them, for sixty hoops, or thirty pairs, as they call them, of fourteen feet, are a great weight to be kept together by four slight hazel bands.

In this industry there is a useful by-product in the shavings, or chips as they call them. They are eighteen inches to two feet long, and are made up into small faggots or bundles and stacked up for six months to a year to dry, and then sell readily at two-pence a bundle to cut up for fire-lighting. They also make a capital thatch for sheds, a thatch nearly a foot thick, warm in winter, and cool in summer, and durable, for if well made it will last for forty years. I got a clever old thatcher to make me a hoop-chip roof for the garden shed; it was a long job, and he took his time (although it was piece-work), preparing and placing each handful of chips as carefully as if he was making a wedding bouquet. He was one of the old sort – no scamping of work for him; his work was as good as he could make it, and it was his pride and delight. The roof was prepared with strong laths nailed horizontally across the rafters as if for tiling, but farther apart; and the chips, after a number of handfuls had been duly placed and carefully poked and patted into shape, were bound down to the laths with soft tarred cord guided by an immense iron needle. The thatching, as in all cases of roof-covering, begins at the eaves, so that each following layer laps over the last. Only the ridge has to be of straw, because straw can be bent over; the chips are too rigid. When the thatch is all in place the whole is 'drove', that is, beaten up close with a wooden bat that strikes against the ends of the chips and drives them up close, jamming them tight into the fastening. After six months of drying summer weather he came and drove it all over again.

Thatching is done by piece-work, and paid at so much a 'square' of ten by ten feet. When I asked for his bill, the old man brought it made out on a hazel stick, in a manner either traditional, or of his own devising. This is how it runs, in notches about half an inch long, and dots dug with the point of the knife. It means, 'To so much work done, £4. 5s. 0d.'

COLOUR

[Describing Gertrude Jekyll's border:] 'Where such grouping as this, carefully designed and carried out, plays its part for some central third of the length of a 200-feet-long border, whose breadth is 14 feet, here is space to show the merit of the arrangement and the value that masses of strong colour so arranged can acquire, especially when the ends of the same border are treated to a corresponding way in large groupings of cool pale colouring ... such a border is the delight in autumn of Miss Jekyll's garden at Munstead. The colouring is gorgeous, and in such a border as described, the cool coloured ends have a ground-work of quiet low-toned bluish-green, as of yucca and iris; of bright glaucous blue-green as of crambe and elymus, both valuable for such use; and of grey and silvery tones in large masses represented by santolina and *Cineraria maritima*, with white and palest pink and pale yellow flowers only. Groups of colour so arranged not only give the fullest strength value of which flowers are capable, but they give it in a way that strikes the beholder with an impression as of boldness tempered by refinement, whereas the same numbers of plants mixed up would only have conveyed a feeling of garish vulgarity, mingled with an uncomfortable sensation as of an undisciplined, crowded jumble of coloured material ...'

E. T. Cook,
Gardens of England,
1908

IT IS A SIGN of distinct advance in the practice of horticulture that Gertrude Jekyll's Introduction to *Colour Planning of the Garden*, 1924 there is now so strong an interest in the subject of colour, and so general a desire for instruction or guidance in its best use. For colour, in gardening as in painting, does not mean a garish or startling effect, such as may be provided by a bed of scarlet geranium [pelargonium] in a setting of green turf; but it means the arrangement of colour with the deliberate intention of producing beautiful pictorial effect, whether by means of harmony or of contrast. In the old days of sixty years ago, it was simply the most garish effects that were sought for; the brightest colourings that could be obtained in red, blue and yellow were put close together, often in rings like a target, and there would be meandering lines, wriggling along for no reason, of Golden Feverfew [*Chrysanthemum parthenium* 'Aureum'], edged with a companion wriggle of lobelia [*L. erinus*] and an inner line of scarlet geranium, the only excuse being that such a ribbon border was then in fashion.

[The pelargonium is a genus of mainly tender sub-shrubs which are still frequently used for containers and summer bedding, and are nothing to do with the hardy cranesbill geranium. Many good colour forms exist, from scarlet to deep reds, pale pinks and whites. There are interesting leaf forms, some with good shapes, others with fragrance. The lobelia, a half-hardy South African perennial, is invariably grown here as an annual with two distinct forms, a compact bushy plant to nine inches and a trailing bedder useful for containers. Flower colours vary from pale to dark blue, usually with a conspicuous white eye.]

It was at a time when endless invention and ingenuity, time and labour, were wasted in what was known as carpet bedding; elaborate and intricate patterns worked out in succulents and a variety of dwarf plants. When the ingenious monstrosity was completed, the chief impression it gave was that it must have

259

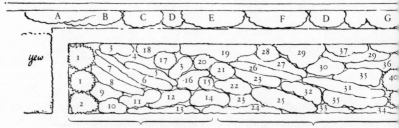

Grey foliage, white, pale blue
and pink move toward stronger
vivid blue and primrose yellow

Feathery cream plumes link
brighter yellows to orange,
flame and scarlet

MISS JEKYLL'S COLOUR BORDER

A *Rosa* 'Crimson Rambler'
B *Robinia* [*R. hispida*]
C *Laurustinus* [*Vibernum tinus*]
D *Nandina* [*N. domestica*]
E *Abutilon vitifolium*
F Loquat [*Eriobotrya japonica*]
G Bay [*Laurus nobilis*]
H Pomegranate [*Punica granata*]
I Japan privet [*Ligustrum
   japonicum*]
J *Pyrus* hybrid
K *Chimonanthus* [*C. praecox*]
L Fuchsia
M Claret vine [*Vitis vinifera
   'Purpurea'*]
N *Magnolia* [*M. conspicua*]
O *Choisya* [*C. ternata*]
P *Cistus* [*C. cyprius*]
Q *Piptanthus* [*P. laburnifolius*]
R *Carpentaria* [*C. californica*]

1 *Yucca recurvifolia*
2 *Yucca filamentosa*
3 White pea [*Lathyrus latifolius
   'Albus'*]
4 Pale blue *delphinium*
5 *Spiraea venusta* [*Filipendula rubra*]
6 *Elymus arenarius*
7 White snapdragon
8 *Campanula lactiflora*
9 *Lilium longiflorum*
10 *Crambe maritima*

11 *Clematis davidiana (heracleifolia)*
12 *Iris pallida dalmatica*
13 *Iberis sempervirens*
14 *Ruta graveolens*
15 White lily
16 *Salvia patens*
17 *Ligustrum ovalifolium* 'Aureum'
18 *Verbascum chaixii*
19 *Thalictrum flavum* and *Rudbeckia*
   'Golden Glow'
20 *Miscanthus sinensis* 'Zebrinus'
21 *Aruncus sylvester*
22 *Iris pallida dalmatica*
23 Yellow snapdragon
24 *Bergenia cordifolia*
25 *Tagetes erecta* (primrose yellow
   African marigold)
26 *Filipendula ulmaria* 'Flore Pleno'
27 *Digitalis grandiflora* and
   Verbascum phlomoides
28 Tall yellow dahlia
29 *Helianthus salicifolius*
30 *Achillea filipendulina*
31 *Senecio artemisae folia*
32 *Eryngium oliverianum*
33 *Helenium pumilum magnificum*
34 *Rudbeckia speciosa newmanii*
35 *Coreopsis lanceolata*
36 *Helenium striatum*
37 Helianthus (tall single hybrid)
38 Dark red hollyhock
39 *Kniphofia galpinii* (dwarf variety)

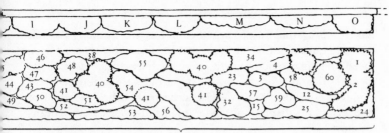

Dark red fades to warm yellow, white and cream with blocks of
blue-green foliage

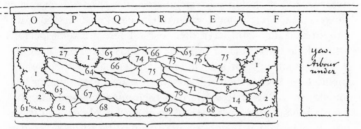

Foliage separates sulphur yellow, blue and pink ending in
lavender, mauve and darker mauve, blue and white

40 *Kniphofia uvaria*
41 *Gypsophila paniculata*
42 Scarlet *salvia*, perhaps *S.
    farinacea* 'Superba'
43 *Lilium tigrinum*
44 *Canna indica* (scarlet)
45 Dahlia 'Cochineal'
46 Dahlia 'Lady Ardilaun'
47 Dahlia 'Fire King'
48 Dahlia 'Orange Fire King'
49 *Lychnis chalcedonica*
50 Orange hemerocallis
51 *Phlox paniculata* 'Coquilot'
52 *Gladiolus brenchleyensis*
53 *Celosia thomsonii* (red)
54 *Tagetes erecta* (orange African
    marigold)
55 *Canna indica* (tall red)
56 *Tropaeolum majus* (dwarf
    yellow variety)
57 *Eryngium giganteum*
58 *Clematis recta*

59 Peony unspecified but certainly
    yellow
60 *Euphorbia wulfenii*
61 *Stachys lanata*
62 *Crambe maritima*
63 Blue hydrangeas
64 *Saponaria officinalis*
65 Sulphur yellow hollyhock
66 *Echinops ritro*
67 *Dictamnus fraxinella* 'Alba'
68 *Cineraria maritima*
69 *Santolina chamaecyparissus*
70 *Geranium ibericum*
71 *Aster acris (sedifolius)*
    (lavender-blue)
72 *Aster shortii* (pale mauve)
73 *Aster umbellatus* (tall,
    late flowering)
74 *Clematis jackmanii*
75 White dahlia
76 *Campanula latifolia*

taken a long time to do; whether it was worth doing did not come in question, for this again was the fashion. This must have been the time when general taste in horticulture was in its deepest degradation, when the sweet old garden flowers were thought not worth notice, and had been abolished in favour of the elaborate display of tender plants for some few months at most.

Happily we know better now, and as the new knowledge advances we are learning how to use our plants in the ways they deserve. But it should be remembered that the tender summer flowers that were almost exclusively employed in those un-enlightened days still have their uses. There are some persons with whom the revulsion from the methods of the old 'Bedding' days is so strong that it includes a condemnation of the plants themselves, so that they will not admit scarlet geranium, or blue lobelia, or yellow calceolaria into their pleasure-grounds. But, properly employed, these are all good garden plants, and it was not their fault that they were used in uninteresting ways. The sun-loving geranium is, and always will be, the best thing for vases [that is, outdoor flower-pots not indoor vases for flowers in the house]; and now that there are so many good varieties, there is ample choice for the exact shade of colour that may best suit the position. The clear pale yellow of *Calceolaria amplexi-caulis* is almost unmatched for purity, and is indispensable in some such arrangement as will be later described. The blue lobelia – the bluer the better – is of value for jewels of pure colour in the right setting. In fact there is hardly any garden plant, only excepting some that have flowers of a rank magenta colouring, that cannot be worthily employed in some well-considered connection or combination.

It may save confusion to consider some colour arrangements or our garden plants according to their seasons. It is usual that the earliest flowers to appear are the winter aconite (*Eranthis hyemalis*) and the Christmas roses, varieties of *Helleborus niger*. Though they bloom nearly at the same time, it is better to treat them separately. The little winter aconite is best planted under some deciduous tree in thin woodland, when this comes near the garden; perhaps for preference under the outer branches of a beech [*Fagus sylvatica*], as the yellow blooms and the carpet of rusty blooms come so well together.

[In my experience the little aconites flower much better if all fallen leaves are carefully raked away in the last months of the year. In small gardens they thrive in any corner under deciduous shrubs, either in a flowerbed or in lawn grass. The rather untidy leaves are already dying back by March and can then be mowed with the lawn. For some reason the aconite is difficult to establish and it is thought best to move it when still in flower, thus preventing it from drying out.]

The Christmas roses enjoy a cool place in rich loam where they are never droughted; a quiet dell of their own in a fern garden is a good place. They look well in a setting of some wintergreen fern, such as polypody [*P. vulgare*] or hartstongue [*Asplenium scolopendrium*] whose foliage is a little more lively than that of their own. [Where space is limited the ferns can thrive in the lower courses of a stone wall leaving a very narrow border for the hellebores. The latter genus provides us with some of the most attractive winter flowers and are easy to grow in any reasonably fertile soil to which good farmyard manure can be added when the flowers are just coming into bloom. *Helleborus niger* has evergreen broad leathery leaves from which the flower stems spring stiffly upwards, bearing white blooms faintly tinged with pink on the back of the petals.

The form *H. niger macranthus* (later referred to by Miss Jekyll as *H. altifolius*) flowers as early as the previous November and is flushed pink all over. Modern selected seedlings of the Christmas rose such as 'Potter's Wheel' (1958) and 'Lewis Cobbett' (1962) are particularly choice and have sumptuous flowers, all the more perfect if given some protective covering of glass as flowering time approaches.]

[In an earlier writing, *Colour Schemes for the Flower Garden*, Miss Jekyll includes a chapter on planting for winter colour, with special emphasis on coloured barks of deciduous trees and shrubs, and the value of evergreens in dispelling wintry discomfort.]

[Among small trees with eye-catching barks the] most useful are the red dogwood [forms of *Cornus alba*] and some of the willows . . . The Cardinal willow [*Salix fragilis decipiens*] has bright red bark, *S. britzensis* [*S. alba* 'Chermesina'] orange, and the golden osier [*S. alba* 'Vitellina'] bright yellow. The yearly growth has the best coloured bark, so that when they are employed for giving colour it is usual to cut them every winter; moreover, the large quantity of young shoots that the cutting induces naturally increases the density of the colour effect.

[Perhaps the best of the red dogwoods for bark colour is *Cornus alba* 'Sibirica', known as the Westonbirt dogwood, with bright crimson winter shoots. The suckering American *C. stolonifera* 'Flaviramea' likes moist situations and has young yellow to olive-green shoots, while our native *C. sanguinea* has rich flushed red stems. Most of these also have splendid autumn colour. *Salix fargesii* (1911) has polished brown bark. Of course Miss Jekyll means that all these shrubs should be cut after the winter, in early spring. They can be cut right to the ground or given more gentle pruning.]

Early in February comes the bloom of the different kinds of the Lent hellebores. They are the species and garden varieties of *H. olympicus*, *H. orientalis*, *H. abschasicus* and *H. atrorubens*. [Most of these are now classified under *H. orientalis*, except for *H. atrorubens*, which is probably a parent of the original *H. orientalis* hybrids.] They are mainly in shades of quiet purplish-red with a darker spotting, and as they intercross freely the variation of tint and marking seems to be infinite. Of several there are white varieties, the patches of white-flowered plants serving as a pleasant break in the general purple colouring. With many may well be grown the little shrub *Daphne mezereum*, whose bloom of a low-toned pink tones well with the colour of the hellebores. There are still some flowering plants that may join into the same harmony and that can with advantage be intergrouped with the hellebores, or be planted on their outskirts. The best of these will be the fine form of *Megasea ligulata*, known as *M.l. speciosa* [now *Bergenia × schmidtii*; *see* p. 45

for description of Miss Jekyll's favourite bergenias and some good modern hybrids]. Its flowering time is nearly that of the hellebores; its colour, a pleasant, tender pink, is not too clear to interfere with its lower-toned companions, though it is best when massed with the white Lenten flowers. The roundish leathery leaves are in pleasant contrast to the other palmate foliage. A place that is partly shaded in summer is best for the hellebores and also suits the megasea; such as a border on each side of a path backed by nuts, for the hellebores are in flower before the leaves of the nuts come, and so get the benefit of the late winter sunshine, while for the rest of the year they are glad of the shade.

[At Tintinhull the Lent hellebores have been planted in the shade of a north-facing wall, with an edging of *Bergenia cordifolia* and the modern *B.* 'Silberlicht', *Philadelphus* 'Belle Etoile', and a magnificent oak-leaved hydrangea, *H. quercifolia*, gives flowers later in the year, and of course the hydrangea leaves have a fine autumn colour. More recently, *Aster divaricatus* (Miss Jekyll's *A. corymbosus*) has been placed behind the bergenias, as shown in an illustration in *Colour Schemes for the Flower Garden*. In September the clouds of starry flowers fall gracefully over the leathery leaves in front.]

The nuts, which will be of some of the good kinds, cobnuts or filberts [*Corylus avellana* or *C. maxima*], will in time arch over the path, so making a pleasant shady way from one part of the garden to another [*see* JANUARY, pp. 31–3].

Crocuses will be in flower in February. Besides their use in garden ground proper, they are still better in open woodland or any half-shaded grassy places. For the best colour effects it will be found advisable to plant the purples and whites in the shadier or quieter places – though shade in February is barely more than nominal – and the strong yellows in the open, and not to have the three colourings in view at the same time. As in many matters connected with wild gardening this requires more care in the doing than many more regular garden operations. It is certainly best to plant the crocuses in long-shaped drifts rather than in patches, and, above all, never, as has sometimes been seen, in concentric rings round a tree. The drifts, a little wider in the middle and narrowing into nothing at the ends, may be of any length, according to the space of ground that has to be planted, and they had better be more or less parallel to the path or most usual point of view; each drift or adjoining group of drifts being of one kind only. In a large space two or three of the purple shades may find a place, with a stream of white here and there, but the white had better be less in quantity than the purple.

[One of Miss Jekyll's characteristic tenets was the use of drifts of plants rather than symmetrical patches of threes, fives, sevens etc. as so often recommended.]

Colour Schemes   Many years ago I came to the conclusion that in all flower borders it is better to plant in long rather than block-shaped patches. It not only has a more pictorial effect, but a thin long planting does not leave an unsightly empty space when the flowers are done and the leaves have perhaps died down. The word 'drift' conveniently describes the shape I have in mind, and I commonly use it in speaking of these long-shaped plantings.

[Such drifts are shown clearly in the plan of the grey border at Hestercombe (*see* pp. 144–5) and there they are so developed as to spread up walls behind the border as well as to spill out on the wide warm paving in the front. Thus colours merge like an embroidery rather than having sharply defined edges, and good foliage serves as a background for differing plants.]

Daffodils will be beginning in March, and will go on through April and into May. These also, and many other woodland plants, should be in drifts rather than in patches. It is both interesting and instructive as well as being best for colour effect, to plant them in this woodland in a kind of natural sequence; beginning with the pale *Narcissus pallidus praecox* [*N. pallidiflorus*], then passing to other trumpets of fuller yellow and then to the bicolor trumpets, and from these to the hybrids of trumpets with *incomparabilis* [now classified as large-cupped narcissi]. The next to follow will be the true *incomparabilis* and then the hybrids of these with *N. poeticus* [the poet's or pheasant's-eye narcissus] – the *poeticus* influence making the colour paler; and ending with the type *poeticus* and its better variety *N.p. ornatus* [*N. exsertus ornatus*]. This is the white pheasant-eye of gardens, with a strong sweet scent. It is, with a few exceptions that need not concern wild planting, the latest of the daffodils, its blooming time being in May when the sweetbriar [*R. rubiginosa*] is making its fragrant young foliage. The fine double *poeticus* [*N. majalis patellaris*] should also be planted, and in suitable soil will show as a sheet of white. *N. poeticus* is a plant of the limestone Alps and is not happy in light soils. The greater number of the narcissi do quite well in sandy ground, though they may scarcely have the size and vigour of those grown on a good loam.

April and May is the time of primroses. The wild primrose [*Primula vulgaris*], with its rare colouring of a pale yellow that may well be called cool, for it has a greenish quality, is much the best for wild planting, for not only does it look more suitable, but the garden kinds of stouter build and stronger colouring demand regular garden cultivation. It is best to have these in a place of their own – some place that is partly shaded, such as a spacious clearing in a grove of oaks, where they can be grown in thousands, and where they can have a further irregular shading of hazel or garden nuts [*see* pp. 31–3]. When space allows, a sort of sequence of primrose gardens would be desirable, for the true primroses, with all radical stems, are the first to flower, to be followed by the larger growing bunch kinds. Even these, for the sake of colour effect, should be divided into two or even three sections; one for the rich and dark colours, red-crimson, and brownish, with a few only of the deeper yellows; one for the yellows and whites, robust plants of fine effect; and a smaller section for those whose colour is a tender mauve or pinkish or light purple shade, with whites. This might include the fine old double mauve and double white, now comparatively rare, but these only do well on a strong loam or a chalky soil.

[We owe a great debt to Miss Jekyll for her skill and taste in developing the Munstead strain of bunch primroses. Handsome leaves, elegant flower stems, a cluster of loose flowers at their summit, and a continuous selection process to obtain the best and purest colours, have made the modern polyanthus a desirable plant, even if few of us can afford to devote a separate garden area to its spring display, or, indeed, would be willing to devote the annual attention to moving and dividing which is essential for maintaining strong healthy plants. Miss Jekyll had plenty of gardeners and her primrose garden was in a place by itself,] a clearing half-shaded by oak, chestnut and hazel. I always think of hazel as a kind nurse to primroses; in the copses they generally grow together, and the finest primrose plants are often nestled close into the base of the nut-stool.

[The polyanthus, probably a chance cross between the primrose and the cowslip (*Primula officinalis*), was developed by Miss Jekyll, who picked out the best yellow and white varieties and over a long period continued to select seedlings which had some special characteristic, such as bloom with wavy edges, or almost flat and even edges; some with deep shades of yellow] with the eye so brightly coloured as almost to approach a red. Some of the most refined are of a pure canary colour all over . . . The object of the continued selection is the production of a type of primrose that shall be a well-doing and handsome garden plant. [From these white and yellow varieties raisers have obtained other desirable shades of colour which have greatly enhanced the value of polyanthus as a garden plant.]

THE SPRING GARDEN AT MUNSTEAD
[Miss Jekyll liked to plant perennials with striking spring foliage amongst her spring bulbs. The M and V symbols in the spring border represent *Myrrhis odorata* and *Veratrum nigrum*, making architectural groups behind colourful foreground flowers. Pale yellow and creamy primroses, *tiarella*, daffodils, lemon wallflowers are interplanted with long drifts of pale tulip, and darker, purple wallflowers and tulips towards the back. Approaching E on the plan, from bottom right, strong colours predominate – orange and brown wallflowers, Crown Imperials and scarlet tulips. The corner is accentuated by plantings of grey-green *Yucca gloriosa*, *Euphorbia wulfenii* and glossy *acanthus* in front of a yew hedge. At G hollies form a background to a sloping flower bed of strong reds and browns, with accompanying bronze-red foliage of *Heuchera americana*. *Iberis sempervirens* and the blue *Lithospernum prostratum* carpet the ground next the path; white tulips and pale yellow *Alyssum sulphureum* join the harsher colours.

At the lower end of the garden (marked 'Near Rock') the plants reflect the pale colouring of the main border opposite, but are white and pink in place of primrose and yellow. Nut trees and oaks shade beds for woodland *dentarias* and *uvularias*. *Clematis montana* and pink tree paeonies in beds edged with grey *Stachys lanata* are followed in flowering season by Rose 'Madame Alfred Carrière'. The long tree paeony border is backed by rich clumps of *Cardiocrinum giganteum*; berberis and *Rosa virginiana* flourish beyond. Dwarf irises in clumps do well under the paeonies, and honesty and wallflowers in appropriate colours fill any bare space. The red primroses are grouped with reddish-leaved *heuchera* in front of a low wall.]

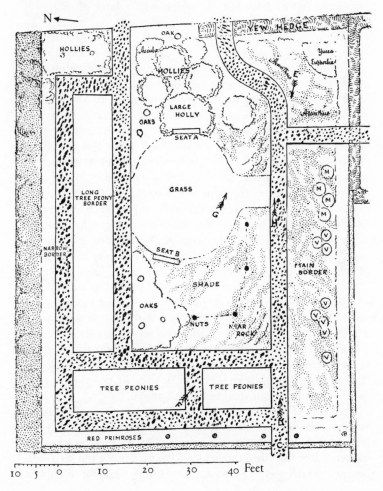

There are a number of small bulbous plants, such as scilla and chionodoxas, that are best used in a place by themselves; they look well carpeted with low-growing things, such as the mossy or encrusted saxifrages. The front of a flower border with a rocky edge is a good place for them; they can be planted just behind the stones, with the saxifrages creeping between the stones and partly between the little flowers; or if there is a bank or border for hardy ferns, the small plants may well run up in streams or drifts between the ferns, whose later growth will completely cover them and fill the border.

With April the spring flowers come crowding in. Planted dry walls and rock gardens this month and next are full of bloom, and hosts of bulbous plants are in flower. Iberis, aubrietia, arabis, alyssum and myosotis are some of the most conspicuous of the lower-growing plants. They are often placed all together, but it is better to avoid the garish contrast of purple aubrietia and yellow alyssum, keeping the aubrietia only in company with the white flowers. Aubrietia is one of the flowers that has of late suffered by the perversion of its proper colouring in the direction of reddish tones. These are bad reds at the best, with the sole exception of a rather pretty one of a pale pinkish tint. The proper colour of aubrietia is a clear, rather light purple, such as one may get by choosing the best of the produce of a packet of seed of *A. graeca*. [This is the wild form of *A. deltoidea* and seldom now available.] There are some fine things of deeper colouring of which the best is a well-known kind named from its raiser Dr Mules. The finest effect of a group of aubrietia is when it is composed of more than three-quarters of the normal pale colour, with a few plants only of *Dr Mules* in a setting of the pure white bloom and deep green foliage of *Iberis sempervirens*. There is a beautiful garden cultivar called 'Lavender' in which the bloom is large and of a good colour [a modern equivalent might be 'Godstone' or 'Gurgedyke'], but the flowers are not so numerous as in those that are nearer the typical *graeca*.

Myosotis is delightful with anything white or pale yellow, such as primroses or white tulips, the clear yellow *T. retroflexa* [this is probably not a true species but belongs to the group of garden tulips introduced from Turkish gardens in the sixteenth century which gave rise to an astonishing variation of plants

270

with different shapes and colours. *T. retroflexa* flowers in May with bright yellow three-inch-long petals, *see* p. 98], pale daffodils, and the palest wallflowers. Such an arrangement may well have a back planting of the purple-leaved sage [*Salvia officinalis* 'Purpurescens']. There are several varieties of myosotis, and many may be tempted by the stronger blue of some of the newer kinds, but the best for general use is *M. dissitiflora* [mostly grown as a biennial; a white form is attractive]. The dark wallflowers, known as blood red, are fine with the tall scarlet *Tulipa gesneriana* [similar origin as above] and the colour effect is all the better for a groundwork of the satin-leaf, *Heuchera richardsonii* [*H. americana*], with foliage tinted reddish-brown and a satin-like lustre. [Introduced in 1656, this valuable garden plant has broad ivy-like leaves of glistening quality, dark green, flushed and veined with coppery brown. The flowers are small and greenish]. Shorter red tulips come in front of this and quite at the edge the reddish-leaved Ajuga [*A. reptans* 'Atropurpurea']. Such a groundwork of related but quieter colour with brilliant flowers is a most important matter in good gardening; and in spring and summer effects this heuchera, with its ruddy tinted satin-lustred leaves, and the purple-leaved sage above mentioned, are of the greatest use. The sage, whose leaves have a soft suffusion of pinkish purple, is an excellent setting to anything pink, such as the fine tulip 'Clara Butt'.

'Between Plants for the Spring Border', *Gardening Illustrated,* 13 June 1925

May brings a wealth of bloom not only on hardy shrubs but on a number of good garden flowers. The old paeony (*P. officinalis*) should have a special place, in its three varieties of crimson, rosy red and white. They are best in good masses accompanied by white flowers only – Solomon's Seal [*Polygonatum multiflorum*], white columbine [*Aquilegia alpina*, white form], and little bushes of *Deutzia gracilis* and *Olearia stellulata* [*O. phlogopappa*, the white form in the Splendens group. At Hestercombe they have substituted *O.* × *scilloniensis*, a free-flowering garden hybrid from Tresco], and they may well be backed by the white Portugal broom [*Cytisus multiflorus*] which flowers at the same time. [It prefers an acid loam; for a lime soil the hybrid *C.* × *praecox*, with tumbling masses of creamy flowers, or its white form, 'Albus', would be best.] A separate portion of bank or border would be beautiful with purple pansies, the pink

Dicentra eximia [there are several good new garden forms with exceptional foliage, *D. e.* 'Langtrees' and *D. e.* 'Boothmans', which should be obtained if possible] and the taller *Dieltra spectabilis* [now *Dicentra spectabilis*] and St Bruno's lily (Anthericum) [now *Paradisea liliastrum*, a fragrant white-flowered perennial for a shady corner, *see* SEPTEMBER, p. 204], with a goodly planting of some of the earlier flag irises of white and purple colouring; the dwarf, dark 'Purple King', the grey-white *florentina*, the stately purple 'Kharput', with white fox-glove to follow at the back. Some of the common pink China rose would come in well with this grouping.

[The bedding pansy as distinct from the true violas are usually described under the heading of *Viola × wittrockiana*, one of the parents being the old heartsease (*V. tricolor*). They have large flowers and are more robust in growth. Summer-flowering hybrids are in flower from May to

---

THE HIDDEN GARDEN AT MUNSTEAD

1 *Myrrhis odorata* [Sweet Cicely]
2 *Polygonatum multiflorum* [Solomon's Seal]
3 Purple iris and blue Florentine iris
4 Pink tree paeonies
5 Lady fern [*Athyrium felix-femina*] and male fern [*Dryopteris felix-mas*]
6 Lilies
7 Pale lilac iris
8 *Camassia esculenta*
9 *Phlox divaricata*
10 Yellow iris
11 *Corydalis ochroleuca* [cream-coloured fumitory]
12 *Olearia phlogopappa* [*gunniana*] [Tasmanian daisy bush]
13 Blue iris
14 *Paradisea liliastrum* [St Bruno's lily]
15 *Achillea umbellata*
16 Pink *Rosa pimpinellifolia*
17 *Aquilegias* [columbine] – pale yellow, warm white with touch of purple
18 *Arenaria montana*
19 *Asphodelus luteus*
20 *Cerastium columnae*
21 *Muscari comosum*
22 *Nepeta mussinii* [faassenii]
23 *Sedum telephium*
24 *Anemone sylvestris*
25 *Saxifraga umbrosa* [London Pride]
26 *Phyllitis scolopendrium* [Hartstongue fern]
27 *Rhododendron ferrugineum, pieris* and *leucothoe*
28 *Iris cristata*
29 *Iberis sempervirens* [Candytuft]
30 *Geranium ibericum*
31 Pale lilac pansy
32 *Onoclea sensibilis*
33 *Uvularia grandifolia*
34 *Hosta sieboldiana*
35 *Asarum europeum*

[Miss Jekyll made a rock garden in a hollow, protected from the north by beech, yews and *Quercus ilex* and from the south shaded by young bushes of holly and more ilex. Here 'natural' woodland plants are mixed with sun-loving irises, tree paeonies and lilies. Drifts of blue-lilac *Phlox divaricata* are grouped with pale pink Scotch brier, pale yellow *corydalis* and creeping, white-flowered *Arenaria montana*; in shade, ferns and *epimedium* make a quiet background of green leaves for the elegant Solomon's Seal and the feathery flowers of London Pride.

As years passed this little garden became entirely shaded by evergreen trees and so is mainly a collection of favourite ferns.]

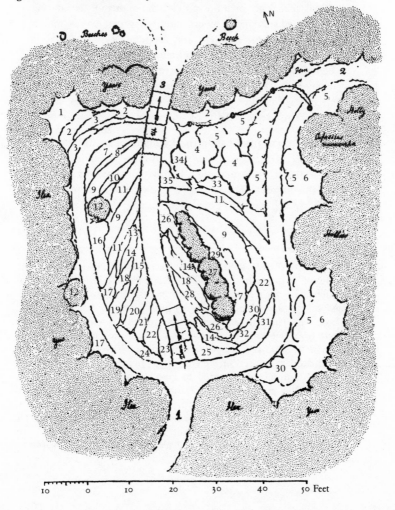

September, and winter-flowering forms can be sown in June to flower during the late winter. Old-fashioned named varieties need to be grown from cuttings taken from non-flowering basal shoots in July. Miss Jekyll refers elsewhere to *V. gracilis* and its rich purple flowers in early spring borders. Probably this is a hybrid with the tufted viola, *V. cornuta.*

The common monthly rose, *R. chinensis* 'Old Blush', which flowers so lavishly through the summer and even to Christmas, may be a bit tall for this planting. 'Hermosa', with cupped soft pink flowers and grey-green leaves, makes a rounded three-foot bush and 'Natalie Nypels' (used in the Hestercombe replanting scheme) is smaller with darker green glossy leaves, admirable for a mixed border. The darker pink, almost pale crimson, flowers of the taller 'Fellemberg' could be a great feature here, perhaps at the back surrounded by drifts of self-sown white foxgloves.]

June brings the later paeonies, the many beautiful varieties of *P. albiflora* [*P. lactiflora*]. The great number now in commerce present a difficulty in making a choice without some guidance. This is the more to be desired because numbers of the rose-coloured kinds have a taint of rank colouring that is best avoided.

THE JUNE GARDEN ROUND THE HUT, MUNSTEAD
[Miss Jekyll's cottage in the wood just beyond the Hidden Garden was approached through a screen of fine Spanish chestnuts and was her home while the house itself was being built. Later she had a studio and workshop in The Hut and its garden remained self-contained and separate from her main borders and woodland. Box-edged beds were filled with traditional cottage garden plants: flowers of pale shades predominated, roses grew on curving hoops and evergreen shrubs, such as Portugal laurel, were planted to give privacy round much of the perimeter. The giant hemlock, *Heracleum mantegazzianum*, seeded freely, giving an exotic air in contrast to traditional paeonies, irises, lupins and catmint. The colour schemes of white with lilac and purple changed to vivid blue and orange as the season advanced. The plan is shown as she drew it and might well serve as a pattern for a sophisticated cottage garden today.]

10 5 0   10   20   30   40   50   60   70 Feet

N

THE HUT

cold

[From among the whites some Miss Jekyll recommended are still the best: 'Duchesse de Nemours', 'Festiva maxima', 'Marie Lemoine'. To these we might add 'James Kelway', an early pure white, and 'Kelway's Glorious', a white double. Those of yellowish colours are 'Solange', which is double-scented cream-buff fading to white-buff, and a pure white imperial 'Jan Van Leeuwen', which has firm cupped petals surrounding a golden centre. For flesh colours there are 'President Wilson' and 'Lady Alexander Duff' with conspicuous yellow stamens. Fuller pink and rosy are 'Madame Calot', 'Bowl of Beauty' and, for dark red, 'Peter Brand'.]

These grand paeonies are worthy of an entire garden space to themselves, though they are also in place as either single plants or as groups of two or three in flower borders. One good way of having them is intergrouped with the roses in a rose garden, where the beds are apt to look thin and unfurnished; a weakness that the large foliage of the paeonies tends to correct.

Another great family of June-flowering plants contains the most useful of the irises, namely the flag-leaved kinds. [Few of the named varieties of Miss Jekyll's day are now available but the lavender-coloured *I. pallida dalmatica* is still one of the most attractive with excellent grey leaves which last all the year. Personally I dislike the bearded irises with a two-colour effect, and those with frilly petals, and feel that Miss Jekyll would have preferred those with a single tone. Unfortunately none of the old names seem to be available now so we can only guess at equivalent colours. 'White Witch' and 'White City' are white with a trace of lavender or grey. 'Gay Trip' is a rich mahogany red, 'Bronze Bird' is buff to copper, and 'St Crispin' and 'Canary Bird' are pure lemon-yellow. All have flower stems of three feet of less, so should only require individual staking in a very wind-torn situation.]

A whole iris garden is no doubt desirable, but it would have to be carefully interplanted with something of which the foliage would overspread the irises because, except in the case of the *pallidas* or varieties with near *pallida* parentage, the leaves wither up and become unsightly. But this does not matter if a

One of Graham Thomas's borders at Cliveden where drifts of colour interweave like a complicated tapestry.
'Each portion now becomes a picture in itself and everyone is of such a colouring that it best prepares the eye, in accordance with natural law, for what is to follow, *Colour Schemes*, p. 55.

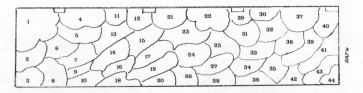

1 *Aruncus sylvester*, interplant
  Fritillaria imperialis
2 *Helenium* 'Butterpat'
3 *Euphorbia epithymoides*,
  interplant *Lilium* 'Destiny'
4 *Verbascum vernale*
5 *Artemisia lactiflora*
6 Phlox four-foot scarlet with
  Lilium tigrinum 'Fortunei'
7 *Anthemis tinctoria* 'Buxton'
8 *Salvia* 'East Friesland'
9 *Crocosmia masonorum*
10 *Geranium sylvaticum* 'Mayflower'
11 *Delphinium* six-foot purple
12 *Helenium* 'Riverton Beauty'
13 *Polygonum* 'Firetail'
14 *Hemerocallis* 'Dorothy McDade'
15 *Lychnis chalcedonica*
16 *Rudbeckia maxima*
17 *Helenium* 'Moerheim Beauty'
18 *Bergenia cordifolia purpurea*
19 *Hemerocallis flava*
20 *Sedum* 'Autumn Joy'
21 *Thalictrum speciosissimum*
22 *Rudbeckia* 'Herbstsonne',
  interplant *Fritillaria imperialis*
23 *Curtonus paniculatus*
24 *Helenium* 'Wyndley'
25 *Achillea* 'Gold Plate'
26 *Euphorbia epithymoides*
27 *Salvia superba*
28 *Buphthalmum salicifolium*
29 *Delphinium* six-foot purple
30 *Verbascum vernale*
31 *Artemisia lactiflora*
32 *Hemerocallis* 'Stafford'
33 *Hemerocallis* 'Spanish Gold'
34 *Solidago* 'Golden Gates'

35 *Crocosmia* yellow
36 *Geranium* 'Johnson's Blue',
  interplant *Lilium hollandicum*
  orange-red
37 *Crambe cordifolia*
38 *Heliopsis* 'Summer Sun'
39 *Phlox* four-foot scarlet
40 *Achillea* 'Gold Plate'
41 *Rudbeckia* 'Goldquelle'
42 *Rudbeckia deamii*
43 *Phlomis russeliana*
44 *Bergenia cordifolia purpurea*
45 *Hemerocallis* 'Dorothy McDade'
46 *Aruncus sylvester*, interplant
  Fritillaria imperialis
47 *Iris ochraurea*
48 *Lychnis chalcedonica*
49 *Sedum* 'Autumn Joy'
50 *Solidago* 'Goldenmosa'
51 *Bergenia cordifolia purpurea*
52 *Thalictrum speciosissimum*
53 *Curtonus paniculatus*
54 *Phlox* 'Border Gem'
55 *Buphthalmum salicifolium*
56 *Macleaya* 'Coral Plume'
57 *Phlox* four-foot scarlet
58 *Solidago* 'Golden Gates'
59 *Rudbeckia* 'Goldsturm'
60 *Helenium* 'Bandirector Linne'
61 *Crambe cordifolia*
62 *Hemerocallis* 'Spanish Gold'
63 *Rudbeckia* 'Goldquelle'
64 *Crocosmia masonorum*
65 *Geranium* 'Johnson's Blue',
  interplant *Lilium hollandicum*
  orange-red
66 *Delphinium* six-foot purple
67 *Kniphofia* 'Royal Standard',
  interplant *Lilium* 'Maxwill'

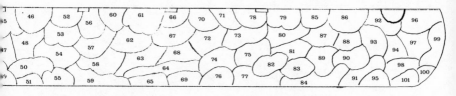

68 *Helenium* 'Golden Youth'
69 *Euphorbia epithymoides,*
    interplant *Lilium* 'Destiny'
70 *Helenium* 'Riverton Gem'
71 *Helenium* 'Riverton Beauty'
72 *Inula magnifica*
73 *Curtonus paniculatus*
74 *Hemerocallis* 'Dorothy McDade'
75 *Phlox* 'Border Gem'
76 *Sedum* 'Autumn Joy'
77 *Phlox* 'Mia Ruys' with
    Pulmonaria
78 *Verbascum vernale*
79 *Aruncus sylvester,* interplant
    Fritillaria imperialis
80 *Helenium* 'Butterpat'
81 *Phlox* four-foot scarlet
82 *Solidago* 'Goldenmosa'
83 *Helenium* 'Moerheim Beauty'
84 *Buphthalmum salicifolium*

85 *Rudbeckia* 'Herbstsonne'
86 *Macleaya* 'Coral Plume'
87 *Hemerocallis* 'Stafford'
88 *Kniphofia* 'Royal Standard'
89 *Salvia superba*
90 *Achillea* 'Gold Plate'
91 *Hemerocallis flava*
92 *Geranium sylvatica* 'Mayflower'
93 *Hemerocallis fulva*
94 *Euphorbia epithymoides,*
    interplant *Lilium* 'Destiny'
95 *Euphorbia palustris*
96 *Hemerocallis fulva*
97 *Rudbeckia deamii*
98 *Salvia nemerosa* 'East Friesland'
99 *Bergenia cordifolia purpurea*
100 *Platycodon grandiflorum*
    purpureum
101 *Bergenia cordifolia purpurea*

CLIVEDEN BORDERS

[Few gardens today can boast herbaceous borders on the same scale as Miss Jekyll's own at Munstead Wood. The exceptions are found mainly in properties of the National Trust where the standards of design (often rather rigidly controlled inside an historical context) and superb upkeep set an example of twentieth-century gardening for all to follow. The writings of William Robinson and Miss Jekyll were read by the comparatively few educated gardeners. Today the gardens of the National Trust are seen by hundreds of thousands every year and the impressions and notes carried away serve as guides to each aspiring gardener and influence taste and fashion more emphatically and thoroughly than any written message.

As adviser to the Trust for most of the period since 1955, Graham Stuart Thomas has had more opportunity to influence current private gardening practice than any other contemporary landscape designer.

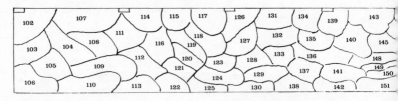

102 *Aruncus sylvester*, interplant
    Fritillaria imperialis

103 *Astilbe* 'Amethyst'

104 *Monarda* 'Croftway Pink'

105 *Lunaria rediviva*

106 *Euphorbia epithymoides*,
    interplant *Lilium* 'Destiny'

107 *Polygonum amplexicaule*
    'Firetail'

108 *Phlox* 'Caroline Vandenburg'

109 *Astilbe* 'Ostrich Plume'

110 *Bergenia cordifolia purpurea*

111 *Aster frikartii* 'Wonder of Staffa'

112 *Anemone tomentosa*

113 *Phlox* 'Mia Ruys'

114 *Artemisia lactiflora*

115 *Delphinium* six-foot bright blue

116 *Geranium psilostemon*

117 *Crambe cordifolia*

118 *Phlox* four-foot pink

119 *Veronica virginiana*

120 *Lythrum* 'Brightness'

121 *Nepeta gigantea*

122 *Sedum* 'Autumn Joy'

123 *Chrysanthemum maximum*

124 *Scabiosa rumelica*

125 *Ruta* 'Jackman's Blue'

126 *Lavatera olbia rosea*

127 *Echinops ritro*

128 *Sidalcea candida*

129 *Scabiosa* 'Clive Greaves'

130 *Anaphalis triplinervis*

131 *Eupatorium purpureum*,
    interplant *Fritillaria imperialis*

132 *Aconitum bicolor*

133 *Hemerocallis* 'Pink Damask'

134 *Macleaya cordata*

135 *Sidalcea* 'Sussex Beauty'

136 *Anthemis tinctoria* 'Buxton'

137 *Nepeta gigantea*, interplant
    Lilium 'Regale'

138 *Salvia nemerosa* 'East Friesland'

139 *Delphinium* six-foot bright blue

140 *Aster frikartii* 'Wonder of Staffa'

141 *Hemerocallis flava*

142 *Filipendula hexapetalplena*

143 *Galega* 'Lady Wilson'

144 *Polygonum* 'Firetail'

145 *Phlox* four-foot mauve

146 *Monarda* 'Croftway Pink'

147 *Geranium sylvatica* 'Mayflower',
    interplant *Galtonia candicans*

148 *Anemone* 'Queen Charlotte'

149 *Lilium* 'Regale'

150 *Kniphofia* 'Maid of Orleans'

151 *Geranium* 'Johnson's Blue'

152 *Bergenia cordifolia purpurea*

153 *Lavatera olbia Rosea*

154 *Echinops* 'Taplow Blue'

155 *Chrysanthemum maximum*
    'Wirral Pride'

156 *Limonium* 'Blue Cloud'

157 *Lysimachia ephemerum*

158 *Euphorbia epithymoides*,
    interplant *Lilium* 'Destiny'

159 *Geranium* 'Johnson's Blue'

160 *Eupatorium purpureum*,
    interplant *Fritillaria
    imperialis*

161 *Sidalcea* 'Sussex Beauty'

162 *Anemone hybrida* 'Honorine
    Jobert'

163 *Kniphofia* 'Maid of Orleans'

164 *Artemisia lactiflora*

165 *Geranium psilostemon*

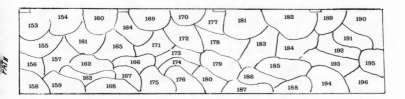

166 *Campanula latiloba* 'Alba'
167 *Phlox* 'Mia Ruys'
168 *Centaurea dealbata* 'John Coutts'
169 *Crambe cordifolia*
170 *Delphinium* six-foot bright blue
171 *Monarda didyma* 'Adam'
172 *Phlox* four-foot pink
173 *Campanula latiloba* 'Highcliffe'
174 *Eryngium tripartitum*
175 *Nepeta gigantea*, interplant *Lilium* 'Regale'
176 *Phlomis russeliana*
177 *Campanula lactiflora*
178 *Aconitum bicolor*
179 *Aster frikartii* 'Wonder of Staffa'
180 *Sedum* 'Autumn Joy'
181 *Lavatera olbia rosea*

182 *Aruncus sylvester*, interplant *Fritillaria imperialis*
183 *Chrysanthemum maximum*
184 *Echinops ritro*
185 *Baptisia australis*
186 *Geranium sylvatica* 'Mayflower', interplant *Galtonia candicans*
187 *Bergenia cordifolia purpurea*
188 *Euphorbia epithymoides*, interplant *Lilium* 'Destiny'
189 *Macleaya cordata*
190 *Echinops nivens*
191 *Lythrum* 'Brightness'
192 *Phlox* four-foot mauve
193 *Monarda* 'Croftway Pink'
194 *Geranium* 'Johnson's Blue'
195 *Hemerocallis flava*
196 *Nepeta mussinii*

A painter himself, he is clearly influenced by the Jekyllian vision of colour, and understands and executes the subtleties of her art, which lie not only in the gradual build up of related shades and tones of colour but in a sure sense of what ancillary plants should be used as links to unite a whole scheme. Just as she knew, for instance, that clumps of white lilies in a blue garden intensified the effects of pure blue and of grey foliage, so Mr Thomas uses white and cream flowered groups as a background to his borders of hot strong colours as well as in those of misty pinks and purples.

By chance the herbaceous borders at Cliveden (for labour-saving reasons entirely planted with hardy perennials) are almost identical in length and width to Miss Jekyll's own (*see* pp. 260–1) approx. two hundred feet by eighteen, and similarly are backed by high walls, which provide a frame for climbers and wall-shrubs which play a part in the whole design. Miss Jekyll chose to emphasize the archway in her wall and framed the path and doorway with strong architectural evergreens including yucca, *Choisya ternata* and the inevitable bergenia and grey stachys, while at Cliveden Mr Thomas treats the borders, also broken by a path and entrance, as a continuing scheme.

The Cliveden west-facing bed is planted predominantly with heavy hot colours, the east-facing bed with pink, purplish blue and low-toned grey foliage. The former glows with colour in strong sunlight while in the quieter border the pale flowers stand out in the evening light.

Although giving such distinctly different impressions some of the most important plant groups are repeated in both borders. *Crambe cordifolia*, from whose large heart-shaped leaves six-foot stems carry sprays of white star-flowers (a giant version of Miss Jekyll's favoured *Gypsophila paniculata*), *Aruncus sylvester* syn. *diocus* with tall feathery plumes (much used too by Miss Jekyll, then as *Spiraea aruncus*), and the creamy-white mugwort, *Artemisia lactiflora*, are all used repeatedly towards the back but adjacent to plants with different flower colour. Facing west *Kniphofia* 'Royal Standard' with scarlet buds opening to bright yellow, is planted next to the vivid vermilion of *Lychnis chalcedonica*. Facing east the pale *Kniphofia* 'Maid of Orleans' has mauve phlox and pale *Monarda* 'Croftway Pink' as later flowering companions. *Euphorbia epithymoides* (syn. *polychroma*), *Sedum* 'Autumn Joy' and one of Miss Jekyll's preferred plants, *Bergenia cordifolia* 'Purpurea' are planted freely as edging groups flowering at different seasons, but linking the two borders across the smooth lawn.]

Mr Graham Stuart Thomas writes: 'These borders were designed to give maximum colour during July and August. To provide a little interest in spring groups of *Fritillaria imperialis* were planted at the back, to show before the general mass of foliage obscures them. In addition, here and there, along the fronts of the borders a few June-flowering plants were included, but only those whose foliage remains respectable for the rest of the summer – such as *Hemerocallis flava* and *Geranium* "Johnson's Blue".

'The colour schemes are augmented by rich purple clematises and yellow roses on the west-facing wall; lavender and pink clematises and pink roses on the east-facing wall. Besides these there are other long-established shrubs trained on the walls, such as *Magnolia grandiflora* "Exmouth variety" and "Goliath".'

Mr Philip Cotton, the head gardener at Cliveden writes: 'The borders are situated on very poor gravelly soil, so they require mulching with manure and leaf soil. This helps to improve fertility, but also aids moisture retention on this too well-drained site. Although our annual rainfall is approximately twenty-six inches we frequently have to irrigate in dry periods.

'These conditions make it difficult to grow some plants well, for example monarda and delphiniums, and even rudbeckias wilt sometimes. This has dictated minor changes in the plans over the years, using different plants to obtain the effect originally intended.

'Cliveden House stands on a hill, and although the high walls of its forecourt contain the borders, a "whirlwind effect" is apparent when the buildings deflect winds, so staking is necessary. We use twigs, usually beech pea-sticks available on the estate, though not long-lasting, for all but the tallest plants, which are surrounded by strings tied to stakes of wood or metal hidden among the clumps.

'We have not found it necessary to lift and divide all the plants annually. The front groups of sedum, geranium, bupthalmum, bergenia, etc. are left undisturbed for three or four years, whereas other subjects such as phlox, rudbeckia, some heleniums, and curtonus require attention at least every two years, or their flowering will suffer. But this is not the case with groups of campanula, verbascum, crambe, and hemerocallis which, if not restrained annually, will squeeze out their neighbours, even on these large-scale eighteen-foot deep borders. The amount of maintenance outlined is not a great price to pay for so historically interesting and attractive a feature of this varied garden.

---

special bit of garden can be given to the irises and a few other flowers of June, and treated carefully for colour effect. It would begin with one end with irises purple and white, purple perennial lupins, pink China rose and the beautiful little shrub *Olearia stellulata*, which is covered in June with its myriad of little starry white flowers. Then irises of a lighter purple, the kinds that are nearest to blue, and the fine white Oriental poppy [*Papaver orientale*], 'Perry's White', and white lupins. All this region has a plentiful planting of white foxglove at the back. Then comes the pale yellow *Iris flavescens* [flowers lemon-yellow almost white] with one of the shorter yellow irises in front, and a goodly planting of yellow tree lupin [*L. arboreus*], followed by the deeper yellow *Iris variegata aurea* [a sort of yellow to chestnut colour]; all this with a front and middle underplanting of the reddish satin-leaf *Heuchera richardsonii*.

This underplanting is continued as the irises darken in colour to those that have claret falls and smoky yellow standards. After this the colour again passes to yellow, with a good deal of interplanting of a most useful plant, *Peltaria alliacea*, about a foot high, with a cloud of tiny cruciferous bloom of a warm white colour. [This seldom seen plant is a spreading perennial with a strong smell of garlic, growing well in light soil.] Then there are again white irises and China roses and the pretty rosy tall iris

'Queen of the May', one of the latest of the *pallidas*; for the fine
I. pallida dalmatica is a little too early for the iris border, its
bloom being over before the greatest number of the more
numerous kinds are in flower. The end of the border has some
white tree lupins, the tall warm white spires of asphodel
[*A. ramosus*] and the creamy plumes of *Spiraea aruncus* [*Aruncus
dioicus*, syn. *A. sylvester*].

The colouring of roses has been so much altered and extended
of late that in planning a rose garden the separate needs of the
newer shades should be kept in mind. For though roses pink
and white, and red and white and pink and red are fine in
company, the whites and some of the cooler pinks do not agree
with the salmon and orange shades, although the whites and
pure pale yellows inclining to a canary tint go charmingly
together.

[Miss Jekyll gives suggestions for colour combinations.
The selection today is even more bewilderingly large and
in a short space it would be impossible to do justice to the
range of plants and colours.]

Of late years we have learnt better ways of arranging flower
borders for colour effect. Formerly a border was planted
according to the heights of plants only; tall at the back, short in
the front, and those of intermediate height in the middle, and
they were placed, not only without regard to colour combinations, but in single plants, so that the whole effect was like a
patchwork of small pieces indiscriminately dotted about. It is a
good plan, before planting, to settle on a definite scheme; and
one that can be recommended is to keep flowers of tender
colouring at the ends of a border and to work gradually towards
a grand effect of gorgeous colouring in the middle of the length.
There is one thing to be noted, that whereas all the strong, warm
colours, deep yellow, orange, scarlet, crimson, and any deeper
kinds of rich colouring are best suited for a gradual progression
of intermingling shades, the cool colours, and pure blue especially, demand a contrast. This being so, it is convenient, in
arranging a long border, to have the blues at one end and the
purples at the other. When in these notes blue is mentioned it is
to be understood that a true pure blue is meant, not any of the

cool purple or violet colourings such as are so frequent in, for instance, asters and campanulas, and that are so often miscalled blue.

[She defines the colours:] I am always surprised at the vague, *Wood and* not to say reckless, fashion in which garden folk set to work to *Garden* describe the colours of flowers, and at the way quite wrong colours are attributed to them . . . some of these errors are so old that they have acquired a kind of respectability, and are accepted without challenge . . . when we hear of golden buttercups, we know that it means bright-yellow buttercups; but in the case of a new flower, or one not generally known, surely it is better and more accurate to say bright yellow at once . . . the irrelevance of comparison seems to run through all the colours. Flowers of a full bright blue are often described as of a 'brilliant amethystine blue'; what . . . is the sense of likening a flower, such as a delphinium, which is really of a splendid pure-blue colour, to the duller and totally different colour of a third-rate gem? Another example of the same slip-shod is the term 'flame-coloured', and it is often preceded by the word 'gorgeous'. This contradictory mixture of terms is generally used to mean bright scarlet. When I look at a flame . . . I see that the colour is a rather pale yellow, with a reddish tinge about its upper forks, and side wings often of a bluish white – no scarlet anywhere . . . It seems most reasonable in describing the colour of flowers to look out for substances whose normal colour shows but little variation – such, for example, as sulphur . . . citron, lemon and canary are useful colour names indicating different strengths of pure pale yellow, inclining towards a tinge of palest green. Gentian-blue is a useful word . . . crimson is a word to beware of; it covers such a wide extent of ground and is used so carelessly in plant catalogues, that one cannot know whether it stands for a rich blood colour or for a malignant magenta. But often in describing a flower a reference to texture much helps and strengthens the colour word. I have often described the modest little *Iris tuberosa* [*Hermodactylus tuberosus*] as a flower mass of green satin and black velvet. The green portion is only slightly green, but it is entirely green satin, and the black of the velvet is barely black, but it is quite black-velvet-like . . . Indeed texture plays so important a part in the appearance of colour-surface, that one can hardly think of colour without also thinking of texture.

[The Royal Horticultural Society has made some attempt at defining different colours, and have produced a string of coloured panels which they hoped would eliminate much confusion, particularly among the descriptions given in nurserymen's catalogues. This scheme has hardly been a success, although I daresay it is some help – and is adhered to – for registering new plant names. By 1966, in order to avoid confusion, it was decided not to use colour names, but instead to consider hue, brightness and saturation

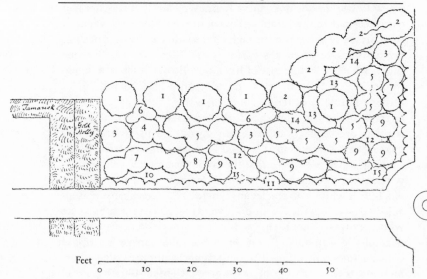

THE GOLD GARDEN

1 Holly

2 Golden plane [probably
  Platamus × hispanica
  'Suttneri']

3 Elaeagnus [probably E. pungens
  'Maculata']

4 Gold elder [either Sambucus
  nigra 'Aurea' or S. racemosa
  'plumosa Aurea']

5 Gold privet [Ligustrum
  ovalifolium 'Aureum']

6 Spanish broom [Spartium
  junceum]

7 Cassinia fulvida

8 Canna

9 Euonymus

10 Primrose, African marigold
   [Tagetes]

11 Small golden box, euonymus
   [Buxus sempervirens, golden
   form, and dwarf evergreen
   euonymus]

12 Coreopsis lanceolata

13 Helianthus lactiflorus
   [H. decapetalus]

14 Helianthus 'Miss Mellish'

15 Yellow snapdragon

[If there is an area rather separate from the rest of a garden and perhaps an approach through a dark shrubbery] 'the shade and solidity of this would rest and refresh the eye and mind, making them more ready to enjoy the colour garden. Suddenly entering the gold garden, even on the dullest day, will be like coming into sunshine.' [For the gold garden there is no formal hedge but] 'A planting of unclipped larger golden hollies, and the beautiful golden plane [can she intend the variegated *Platanus* × *hispanica* 'Suttneri'?] so cut back and regulated as to keep within the desired bounds.'

[This gold garden will be filled with shrubs with plain golden leaves and with leaves splashed with cream and gold. Yellow-flowered herbaceous plants can be used not only to fill in between shrubs while they are growing but it is important to use only pale and primrose colours and not orange which would appear harsh with the subtle leaf colours. Miss Jekyll uses golden elder (*Sambucus nigra* 'Aurea' and *S. racemosa* 'Plumosa Aurea'), golden privet (*Ligustrum ovalifolium* 'Aureum'), *Cassinia fulvida* (*Olearia solandri* is very similar but ultimately a larger shrub), elaeagnus (probably *E. pungens* 'Maculata'; there are now clones with more distinctive splashed leaves), euonymus (*E. japonicus* has several good coloured cultivars) and an edging of dwarf gold-variegated box about two feet high, possibly interplanted with bushes of euonymus which are kept tightly clipped.

Between the shrubs she used pale yellow helianthus, *Coreopsis lanceolata* (now *C. verticiliata*), yellow snapdragons, *Spartium junceum*, the quick-growing Spanish broom, and pale primrose African marigolds. In a scheme she did for Pyford Court she planted Dickson's Golden Elm (*Ulmus* × *sarniensis*) 'Dicksonii' amongst the columnar variegated hollies and we might add some more deciduous shrubs: the golden variegated *Cornus alba* 'Spaethii', *Physocarpus opulifolius* 'Luteus', the golden-leaved scented *Philadelphus coronarius* 'Aureus', a golden berberis, *B. thunbergii* 'Aurea' and *Spiraea bumalda* 'Goldflame' (disliked by some for the pinkish-red tinge to the leaves). Herbaceous plants which are more permanent than some of Miss Jekyll's might be: creeping jenny (*Lysimachia nummularia*, a low-growing evergreen), the golden feverfew (*Chrysanthemum parthenium* 'Aureum'), pale hosta leaves and Bowles' Golden Grass (*Milium effusum* 'Aureum' and golden-leaved margoram (*Origanum vulgare* 'Aureum').]

---

giving each an appropriate numerical reference. The duller colours of brown and grey are the most difficult to analyse.]

[In an article written in 1929 Gertrude Jekyll says:] Fifty years ago, when the bedding out of tender plants for a summer display

Journal of the Royal Horticultural Society, Vol. LIV, 1929

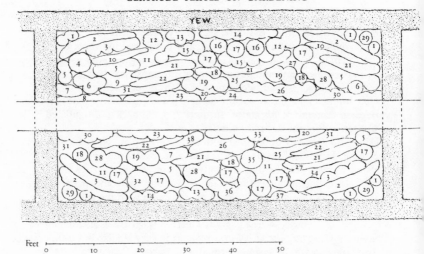

THE BLUE GARDEN

1 White pea [Lathyrus latifolia 'Albus']
2 Delphinium
3 Variegated maize [Zea mays 'Variegata']
4 White tree lupin
5 Rue [Ruta graveolens]
6 Yucca [Y. filamentosa]
7 Eryngium giganteum
8 Lithspernum prostratum [L. diffusum]
9 Eryngium oliveranum
10 Lilium szovitzianum
11 Plumbago capensis
12 Yucca [Y. recurvifolia]
13 White hollyhock
14 Thalictrum flavum
15 Maize
16 White lupin
17 Anchusa
18 LC [Lilium candidum]
19 Clematis davidiana [C. heracleifolia davidiana]
20 Phaecilia

21 Delphinium belladonna
22 Lilium longifolium
23 Plumbago larpentae [Ceratostigma plumbaginoides]
24 Variegated coltsfoot [Tussilago farfara 'Variegata']
25 White snapdragon
26 Salvia patens
27 Palest yellow snapdragon
28 Clematis recta
29 Eulalia japonica [Miscanthis sinensis]
30 Funkia sieboldi [Hosta sieboldiana]
31 Delphinium grandiflora
32 Spiraea aruncus [Aruncus dioicus syn. sylvester]
33 Funkia grandiflora [Hosta plantaginea grandiflora]
34 White foxglove [Digitalis purpurea 'Alba']
35 Lupin 'Somerset'
36 White perennial lupin
37 Verbascum phlomoides
38 Glyceria aquatica 'Variegata'

'It is a curious thing that people will sometimes spoil some garden project for the sake of a word. For instance, a blue garden, for beauty's sake may be hungering for a group of white lilies, or for something of palest lemon-yellow, but it is not allowed to have it because it is called the blue garden, and there must be no flowers in it but blue flowers. I can see no sense in this; it seems to me like fetters foolishly self-imposed. Surely the business of the blue garden is to be beautiful as well as blue as may be consistent with its best possible beauty. Moreover, any experienced colourist knows that the blues will be more telling – more purely blue – by the juxtaposition of rightly placed complementary colour.'

Colour Schemes, p. 98

[Describing the blue garden:] 'The brilliancy and purity of colour are almost incredible. Surely no blue flowers were ever so blue before. That is the impression received. For one thing all the blue flowers used, with the exception of eryngium and *Clematis davidiana* [*C. heracleifolia davidiana*] are quite pure blues; these two are grey-blues. There are no purple-blues, such as the bluest of the campanulas and the perennial lupines; they would not be admissible. With the blues area few white and palest yellow flowers; the foam-white *Clematis recta*, a delightful foil to *Delphinium belladonna*; white perennial lupine with an almond-like softness of white; *Spiraea aruncus* [*Aruncus dioicus* syn *A. sylvester*], another foam-coloured flower. Then milk-white lupin, in its carefully decreed place near the bluish foliage of rue and yucca. Then there is the tender citron of Lupine "Somerset" and the full canary of the tall yellow snapdragon, the diffused pale yellow of the soft plumy thalictrum and the strong canary of *Lilium szovitzianum*, with white everlasting pea and white hollyhock at the back. White-striped maize [*Zea mays* 'Variegata'] grows up to cover the space left empty by the delphiniums when their bloom is over, and pots of *Plumbago capenseare* [*P. capensis*] dropped in to fill empty places. One group of this is trained over the bluish-leaved Clematis recta which goes out of flower with the third week of July.'

Colour Schemes, p. 112

[Miss Jekyll used yuccas and hostas too for glaucous and pale foliage, which admirably set off the pure blues. The blues are represented by delphiniums, *Lithospernum prostratum*, *Ceratostigma plumbaginoides* (*Plumbago larpenate*), phacelia, anchusa and the exquisite *Salvia patens*. Today we might add *Salvia guaranitica* (syn. *ambigens*), a cultivar of *Salvia farinacea* 'Victoria', and the tall pale blue *Salvia uliginosa*. None of these salvias is reliably hardy but their vivid flowers and attractive habits make them worth growing; cuttings should be taken each autumn, or they can be grown from seed. The variegated coltsfoot (*Tussilago farfara* 'Variegata' and *Glyceria maxima* (*Glyceria aquatica* 'Variegata') are chosen for the front of the borders, matching up with the tall variegated miscanthus and maize towards the back. A hedge of yew runs behind the borders, a sombre contrast to the glowing colours.]

was the general garden practice, if any thought was given to arranging them for colour it was to produce the crudest and most garish effects; such as a round bed of vivid scarlet geranium with a border of blue lobelia, or a wavy ribbon border of scarlet, blue and yellow. Now that all that concerns the planning of our gardens is engaging the attention of our best designers, the better use of colour is being carefully considered, and is already being gloriously practised. For when colour is rightly used the various portions of the garden will have the highest pictorial value as living pictures of plant beauty.

[Returning to Miss Jekyll's description of the long border:] At the blue end, the border will begin with delphinium and anchusa, enough of each to make a good show, for the true blues are not too many. Farther forward there will be the shorter hybrid delphiniums and the beautiful still dwarfer *D. belladonna* and *Commelina coelestis*, with *Salvia patens* dropped in for the summer. At the front will be the pretty Cape daisy, *Agathea coelestis* [*Felicia amelloides*], and the bright little *Lobelia erinus*. A strong plant of *Clematis flammula* is at the back of the delphiniums; when their bloom is over, the fast-growing seed-pods are cut away and the white-flowered clematis is trained over the delphinium stems which now stand between four and five feet high. Here at the back are also white dahlias and creamy spiraeas [probably *Aruncus dioicus*, syn. *A. sylvester*] and tall snapdragons [antirrhinums] of palest yellow, half-way between yellow and white. Pure pale yellow snapdragons are *Colour Schemes* delightful with the blue flowers. Between the clumps of *belladonna* are bushes of white lavender [*L. angustifolia* 'Nana'] and the whole is carpeted and edges with the white foliage of *Artemisia stelleriana*, the quite hardy plant that is such a good substitute for the tenderer *Cineraria maritima* [now correctly *Senecio bicolor*, but still generally known by the older name].

[Since 1924 there have been many new hybrid delphiniums which cover a huge colour range. Almost certainly by delphiniums Miss Jekyll means the species *D. elatum*, from which most hybrids are descended, as it tends to be tall. Hybridizing began at Kelways as early as 1875,

290

the Belladonna hybrids being selected from forms of
D. elatum crossed with the Siberian species *D. grandiflorum*
(and *D. cheilanthum*). Miss Jekyll certainly used *D. grandiflorum* and its rarer double form, which gave her a pure
blue shade not always to be found among modern hybrids.
Commelina coelestis has sky-blue flowers rather similar to
pale forms of its relative tradescantia, but is not reliably
hardy; the true spiderwort might be a useful alternative.
Salvia patens and *Felicia amelloides* will only survive mild
winters and the little lobelia is virtually an annual. *Stokesia
laevis* (with blue flowers similar to the common annual
China aster) is a late-flowering summer perennial about
one foot high. Forms of *Campanula carpatica* have clear
blue flowers and make small mounds, suitable for the
front of the border. *C. latiloba* grows to three feet with
cup-shaped rich lavender-blue flowers springing with
stiff stems from handsome green rosettes, and a form of
C. lactiflora, 'Pouffe', makes a dense eighteen-inch hum-
mock covered for many weeks in late summer with pale blue
flowers. The shrubby *Ceratostigma willmottianum* (introduced in 1908) is reliable (although often cut to the ground
in cold districts) and bears its clear cobalt-blue flowers for
many weeks from late July, and has attractive small leaves.
C. griffithii, of later introduction, seems to be hardier than
originally thought, and has the perfect flower colouring of
true blue; it might well be planted instead of felicia. The
platycodons flower in late summer and cover a wide range
from deep Wedgwood-blue to white.

Instead of dahlias, which need storing each winter, and
snapdragons, which must be grown from seed each year,
hardy perennials can be used, such as cimicifuga and the
white *Sanguisorba canadensis* which have white and cream
bottle-brush flowers and attractive leaves. *Cimicifuga
racemosa* grows to five feet and the sanguisorba to six feet,
but should not need staking. Many of the mainly biennial
verbascums have yellow to white flowers varying from
three to six feet and can be allowed to seed freely (or
cuttings taken from named hybrids). The single-flowered
fragrant *Philadelphus* 'Innocence' has leaves with a pale

variegation which gives this free flowerer an all-over cream effect which could be useful in this colour scheme, and the leaf interest extends the season from the flowering period in July into the autumn. The white forms of *Buddleia davidii* and the more tender *B. fallowiana* could also be used; both continue to flower into the autumn.]

[Continuing Miss Jekyll's description:] Following this comes a beautiful combination some yards in length, near and at the front of the old garden plant, *Mentha rotundifolia*, whose leaves are variegated with warm white, with the cream-striped grass *Glyceria aquatica* [*G. maxima*]; and at the back of these the fine old pure canary-yellow *Calceolaria amplexicaulis*. Now there are yellow hollyhocks and yellow dahlias at the back and the tall yellow *Thalictrum flavum* [probably not *T. flavum*, which has green leaves, but *T. speciosissimum*, syn. *T. flavum glaucum*]; even a bush of the brightly-gold variegated privet [*Ligustrum ovalifolium* 'Aureum'] is not out of place.

Next we come to the region of the strong yellows: *Helenium pumilum* [*H. autumnale* 'Pumilum'] in a large important drift and oenothera of the *fruticosa* section [a good one is *O. fruticosa* 'Youngii'], leading to the orange colourings of helianthus and *Coreopsis lanceolata*, and the still deeper orange African marigold [forms of *Tagetes erecta*], dwarf tropaeolums and orange pot marigold [*Calendula officinalis*] and gazania [*G. rigens* or its hybrids] are now in front, with tritomas [kniphofias] in the middle spaces and towards the back, and dahlias of deepest orange colour approaching scarlet. Then we come to actual scarlet and rich blood-red of dahlia and hollyhock, with a softening setting of the annual *Atriplex hortensis*. Here are also the brightest scarlet phloxes, penstemons and gladioli, and in front a dozen or so of the grand bedding geranium 'Paul Crampel'. The whole of this region of gorgeous colouring is softened and tempered by an interplanting of deep reddish foliage – iresine [*I. herbstii*], the atriplex just mentioned, and among the red dahlias at the back, the red-leaved *Ricinus gibsonii*, and some bushes of *Prunus pissardii*, yearly pruned so that the deep reddish shoots may accompany the dahlias and provide something that tones well with the whole gorgeous mass, and that is better than the dull green of the dahlia foliage. At the back of the dahlias is a tall old kind of a blackish crimson colour, and the blood-red hollyhocks also have a companion of the same claret tint.

[Miss Jekyll suggests subduing the most vivid and striking of the rich colourings in the centre of the border by interplanting with] the cloudy masses of *Gypsophila paniculata*. Five-year-old plants of this form masses of the pretty mist-like bloom four feet across and as much high. This bold introduction of grey among the colour masses has considerable pictorial value.

The strong colour then passes again through orange and full yellow to white, with palest green foliage. Here are white dahlias and white everlasting pea [*Lathyrus latifolia* 'Albus'] and foliage of striped maize [*Zea mays* 'Variegata'], and then a group of pink hollyhocks. After this the accompanying foliage is mostly grey – *Cineraria maritima* [*Senecio bicolor*], santolina, and stachys; the colour passes from pink to mauve and on to the strong light purple of *Aster acris*.

Echinops and erigeron are grouped with the white of *Chrysanthemum maximum* [this type species is usually now superseded by named varieties such as 'Esther Read', 'Wirral Supreme' etc.] and Paris daisy [*Chrysanthemum frutescens*], and white and pink gladioli, and these are backed by taller purple asters, white dahlias, white hollyhocks, and the creamy white of *Aster umbellatus*. Here also, at the end, are some tall yuccas, *Y. gloriosa*, and *Y. recurva* [*Y. recurvifolia*] with the lower-growing *Y. filamentosa*; all with a dusky background of yew [*Taxus baccata*] which comes forward from the high wall that is at the back of the whole border. The flowers on the wall agree in colour with those in the border. The grey-blue of *Ceanothus* 'Gloire de Versailles' tones in with the flowers at the blue end; then comes the white of *Laurustinus lucidus* [*Viburnum tinus lucidum*] and of Japan privet [*Ligustrum japonicum*], with dark foliage of bay [*Laurus nobilis*] backing the yellow group.

Where the mass of strong colour comes in the middle there is a *Fuchsia riccartonii* with the orange-scarlet trumpets of *Bignonia radicans* [*Campsis radicans*], while the pink and purple at the farther end are accompanied by the pink of *Robinia hispida* and *Clerodendron foetidum* [*C. bungei*], and the purple of *Buddleia veitchii* [*B. davidii veitchiana*].

[If we wish to design an equivalent colour border without bedding out we must look for plants to take the place of the yellow dahlias and hollyhocks (the latter can well be perennial but are very liable to rust disease) as a background to the variegated apple mint and striped grass. With these plants Miss Jekyll moves from clear blues and whites into pale then darker yellows as she skilfully builds up her colour crescendo. The thalictrum has finished flowering by the end of July so that although *Cephalaria gigantea*, *Lilium monadelphum szovitsianum* and pale citron-coloured day-lilies (such as *Hemerocallis* 'Marian Vaughan' or 'Citrinum') are excellent colour complements to it they do not cover the more difficult periods of August into September and even later. *Oenothera biennis*, the biennial evening primrose, may be allowed to seed and its pale yellow flowers are borne from June to October. Most perennial hybrid verbascums bear yellow flowers from mid to late summer, and species verbascums such as *V. olympicum* have attractive grey felted foliage which softens the border picture.

The Spanish broom, *Spartium junceum*, and the taller elegant Mount Etna broom, *Genista aetnensis*, flower through July. The wall behind may be enriched by the pineapple-scented flowers of the silver-leaved Moroccan broom, *Cytisus battandieri*, which is also July flowering. The hypericums make a good solid background to a flowering border, mixing well with herbaceous plants, and flowering from July into October. The taller ones such as *H. patulum* 'Hidcote' and the tender but graceful 'Rowallane' grow to six feet, while *H. p.* 'Forrestii' makes a four-foot mound for the centre of the border. *H. p. uralum* has arching branches and grows to three feet with fragrant orange-scented foliage. The shrubby potentillas have a flowering season from June to October and their flowers can be pale lemon-coloured with attractive silver or pale green leaves. (Those with more vivid oranges can be useful in the stronger colour section which comes later.) *P. fruti-cosa* 'Primrose Beauty' and *P. vilmoriana* are particularly valuable.

Among the strong yellows leading on to orange the flower and foliage of *Coreopsis verticilliata* are exceptional, and some of the *C. grandiflora* varieties, with a taller habit useful for the back of the border, are plants with strong dark yellow to orange long-lasting flowers. Helianthus, as Miss Jekyll points out elsewhere, can be partly cut down long before flowering time so that shorter stems are covered with blooms and the coarse foliage is partly hidden. Low-growing orange flowers for the front edge to take the place of annual tagetes and half-hardy gazanias are difficult and the nearest might be orange-flowered helianthemums; particularly those with pale grey leaves.

Rudbeckias, short hybrid solidagos and the bigeneric × *Solidaster hybridus* (1910, an attractive hybrid between solidago and aster, with tiny canary-yellow daisy flowers carried over a long period) all flower in late summer, but need interplanting with good foliage plants to give body. The orange-flowered *Ligularia dentata* has large leathery heart-shaped leaves which are an asset to any border, but it needs moist and rich soil. *L. hodgsonii* grows only to two feet and there are forms from which to choose with yellow and orange daisy flowers.

Kniphofia flowers give pale cream to orange-red tones with strong architectural foliage, the best would blend as orange moves into reds and scarlets. *K. praecox* grows to six feet with scarlet flowers in late summer. *K. rooperi* is orange-red in bud, opening to greenish yellow, and smaller. Some of the new hybrids with grassy foliage are paler coloured and less assertive. *Crocosmia masonorum*, a relative of the ubiquitous montbretia, is splendid with brilliant orange to scarlet flowers, perfect with clashing copper or purple foliage and vivid deep red flowers, such as that of the bergamot *Monarda didyma*.

Some of the taller *Phlox paniculata* clones could be used at the back of the border in place of the rich deep colours of hollyhock and dahlia, but may not perhaps give such an impression of solid texture. It may be worth treating the dahlias as hardy perennials and taking a chance with wine-red hollyhocks, allowing them to behave like biennials as no other flower produces quite the same richness of colour. *Penstemon campanulatus* 'Garnet' has wine flowers, *P. hartwegii* and the taller (to three feet) *P. isophyllus* has scarlet flowers and rich green leaves. Most of these penstemons are reasonably hardy but cannot survive exceptionally cold springs; ideally, cuttings should be taken each autumn. *Phygelius capensis* has suckering stems bearing bright red tubular flowers from summer into late autumn. (The paler *P. aequalis* is a little tender but can be tried in the area where with light purple and pinks, the border fades away into the grey foliage at the furthest end.)]

[Miss Jekyll does not neglect the importance of fine foliage. At one end of a border mainly kept for tender plants] forming a background to the whole, there are raised banks of grey and glaucous foliage – yuccas, phormium, *Senecio greyii* [*S.* 'Sunshine'], *Cineraria maritima* [*Senecio bicolor*], euphorbia, othonnopsis and cerastium, with pink and purple flowers only. [Does Miss Jekyll mean that she cuts off, in season, the yellow flowers of senecio, euphorbia and othonnopsis? I think she does as she certainly recommends this elsewhere. The yucca and the little cerastium will be allowed to keep their white flowers.] This combination of grey foliage with pink and purple flowers is so important that a whole double border may well be given to it. Such a border is in existence and is every year a source of greater pleasure. Here are bold clumps of hollyhocks and tumbling masses of *Clematis jackmannii*, the shrubby pink-flowered *Lavatera olbia*, a lavender-coloured ceanothus trimmed to bush form, echinops, purple and white China asters, ageratum tall and dwarf, the mist-like gypsophila, a fine purple form of the annual *Delphinium consolida*, and another valuable annual, the double pink godetia, with tall white and palest pink snapdragons. All these, with the silvery *Eryngium giganteum* and a plentiful filling of *Cineraria maritima*, santolina, and *Stachys lanata*, form a most satisfactory picture of good garden colour in and about the month of August.

[In the smaller garden of today it may not be wise to embark on a full colour border on the grand scale Miss Jekyll has described. However, the National Trust and a few large private gardens do still have borders of sufficient dimensions. At Cliveden one border is planted with the 'hot' colours, and another with the cool misty tones which Miss Jekyll would have used at the further ends, while keeping vivid contrasts in the centre. A plan of the modern planting at Cliveden with plants and colours chosen by Graham Stuart Thomas is on pp. 278–82. In her *Colour Schemes for the Garden* Miss Jekyll gives suggestions for restful garden areas with individual colour schemes, where each garden compartment is backed by and divided from another by appropriate hedging. Orange, grey, gold, blue and green schemes are built up using leaves and flowers to make the desired impact. Texture and colour of leaf play as important a role as do the fleeting and seasonal flower colours. These gardens can equally well be adapted for the smaller areas of today, indeed a whole small garden may be based on just one of these colour plans. Each part of her carefully built up great border could be used as the basis for a whole garden design. The grey garden at Hestercombe, the gold garden at Pyrford Court, a scarlet and red border, such as still exists at Hidcote, the white and grey garden at Sissinghurst and the pale misty tones of one of the pool borders at Tintinhull are all examples of the use of separate colour areas inside a garden. In her own Munstead Wood she liked to have areas devoted to seasonal gardens and had her famous Michaelmas daisy border (painted by Elgood and Helen Allingham, *see* p. 224).]

The Michaelmas daisies are so important in September and October that it is well worth while to give them a separate place, in addition to their use with other flowers in the mixed border. And though their colouring is restricted to shades of purple and pinkish, yet whole borders of them, if rightly arranged, are full of beauty and interest. It will be found better to concentrate on a few good kinds and have them in bold masses, than to try to accommodate a larger number of varieties. A few other plants may well go with them, especially the September-blooming *Chrysanthemum uliginosum* [*C. serotinum*], a big white daisy that makes a better show among the asters than any white variety of their own kind. The large pink-flowered *Sedum spectabile*, beloved of butterflies, will also be welcome, and some of the latest China asters. The front edges may well be filled with the silvery stachys and purple ageratum both tall and dwarf. The tendency of growers who specialize in these excellent asters seems of late to incline to the production of more of the pinkish kinds, but the use of these had better not be overdone, for the true character and chief beauty of Michaelmas daisies must always be in those of the clear purple colourings.

[Choosing good and appropriate colours is difficult enough, but the choice of Michaelmas daisies is made difficult by the many poor kinds, so prone to mildew, that have been around. I find it hard to accept Miss Jekyll's thesis on the merit of the 'clear purple colourings', and prefer the beautiful mauve *Aster lateriflorus* 'Horizontalis' and the white *A. umbellatus*, a wiry bush covered with many small white daisies with yellow eyes.]

The practice of good colour arrangement in gardening is full of delightful potentialities. In the foregoing pages it has only been possible to put forward some general principles and their application in one or two more or less definite schemes. But to anyone who delights in the beauty of flowers, and has, either by natural endowment, or by the education of perception, acquired some knowledge of how to use colour, they may serve as an early guide or substructure on which to build further, according to their own desire or inclination. In any case, the study and practice of good use of colour in the garden cannot fail to be a source of abiding interest and unfailing inspiration.

WATER

'To have water . . . in a garden is the greatest possible gain, for it enables the ingenious garden owner not only to grow in perfection many beautiful plants, but to treat the watery places, according to their nature and capability, in various delightful ways.'

'Streamside Garden', *Country Life*, 13 February 1916

AMONG THE MORE modern developments of horticulture the water garden has taken an important place. It does not matter whether the site is of large extent, as of lake and river, or quite small as in such a place as may have only a trickle of water artificially supplied; either of these, and everything between, can be adapted for good use in the display of the many beautiful plants of the water and waterside.

'The Water Garden', Black's Gardening Dictionary

The diversity of circumstances and way of treatment may be as great as the nature and conditions of the place, but as in all good gardening the natural possibilities of the site have first to be considered and respected, for it is out of these that is formed, in the mind of the competent designer, the conception of the best form of treatment. The nature of the site will govern the main distinction, which is, whether the place is suitable for a free kind of planting on natural lines, or whether, in the case of a restricted area and where it will necessarily be near buildings, it will have to be of a purely formal character.

In the first case let us suppose that the water supply is a natural one of pond and stream on the extreme outskirts of garden ground. Here, if the water has a naturally good edge, that is, an edge that is easily accessible and not much above the water level, all that is needed will be to clear adequate spaces for planting, leaving the natural growth, especially when it has any suitable character as of sedge, or bur-reed [sparganium], undisturbed.

There are plants for all degrees of moisture. [In her description of moisture-loving plants Miss Jekyll adds to what she has said above:] It is well as a general rule, in planting wild places that are in connection with gardens, to keep exotics nearest to the home end, and to leave the native plants for the further part of the wild. Thus, there would be a bold planting of the Japanese *Iris laevigata* [and *I. kaempferi*] with the large-leaved *Saxifraga peltatum* [*Peltiphyllum peltatum*, the handsome leaves only appear after spring flowering is over; the flowers are pink stars set in wide round heads above a red-tinted three-foot stalk] and the handsome rodgersia.

Country Life, 13 May 1911

[Miss Jekyll could only have known *R. podophylla* (then known as *R. japonica*, 1880) the only Japanese one. Strangely this plant grows almost equally well in a dry situation, although the leaves 'go off' early in late summer. The other very attractive and valuable Chinese rodgersias do need moisture. Perhaps the most ornamental is *R. pinnata* and its cultivar 'Superba'. The leaves are pinnate, rich green and rough, and the flowers pale and dark pink respectively. *R. tabularis* is very different, with large round green leaves rather similar to peltiphyllum, and long four-foot stems bearing tiny white flowers in a dense head. All species (there are a few others) make wonderful foliage plants for waterside and most colour well in autumn.] This would be quite enough of plant interest for some yards of ground. Then would come the irises of the *sibirica* class with their larger forms, and the tall yellow and white *I. ochroleuca*, and . . . a group of *Pieris floribunda* on a mound of peaty earth, just raised above bog-level . . . the long mound might well lead to one of larger size for a good group of kalmias, their roots just raised above the swamp and their heads in full sun.

At the foot of these would be groups of the pale pink *Spiraea venusta* [*Filipendula rubra* 'Venusta'] and of the double Meadow Sweet, the double form of our native *S. ulmaria* [*F. ulmaria*] . . . and the larger *S. aruncus* [*Aruncus dioicus*, syn. *A. sylvester*] of alpine torrents with its handsome foliage and beautiful plumes of cream-white flowers . . . The Water Forget-me-not [*Myosotis palustris*] should have a region nearly to itself, its only companion being the yellow mimulus [*M. guttatus*] and lady fern [*Athyrium filix-femina*]. After that, though before it in time of blooming, would come Marsh marigold [*Caltha palustris* and the double kind *C.p.* 'Flore Pleno'] . . . With this, and flowering at the same time, should be the double form of the common Lady's smock (*Cardamine pratensis*), loose-strife (*Lysimachia vulgaris*) and the tall yellow meadow rue (*Thalictrum flavum*).

[Although Miss Jekyll used hostas in her shady borders and in tubs near her own water tanks, and recommends them for formal water planting, she seldom suggests their use in the wilder areas. Planted in groups of three or five (or in much larger quantities for a great garden) these plants with their handsome leaves of green, grey-green and attractive variegation, and their upright flowers of pale mauve or white, are perfect foils to other water plants with more spiky outlines.]

[She describes] the glorious *Cypripedium spectabile*, the North American Mocassin-flower . . . for planting in black peaty mud, where . . . the roots will grow strong and interlace into a kind of vegetable rook's nest. Every year the tufts will become stronger and send up still nobler spikes of leaf and bloom. [Earlier she describes the plant] with its great pouched and winged flowers of rose and white, and its fine plaited leaves of bright fresh green, what a plant! Its beauty almost takes one's breath away. Anyone who had never seen it before, suddenly meeting it in such a place, with no distractions of other flower-forms near, would think it was some brilliant stove orchid escaped into the wild.

Wall and Water

[Many plants, although not exactly water plants, like ground that is moist and cool.] In the wettest of this would be a plantation of *Primula denticulata*, a grand plant indeed when grown in long stretches in damp ground at the edge of a hazel copse, when its luscious leaves and round heads of lilac flower are seen quite at their best. Several others of the Asiatic primroses are also happiest in such a place. Next to it, and only divided by some clumps of lady fern [*Athyrium filix-femina*], would be the equally wet-loving *Primula sikkimensis*, and then a further drift of *P. japonica*.

Wall and Water

[*P. sikkimensis* needs an acid loam but *P. florindae* (1924), from the same group, adapts easily and thrives in any moist soil. A most useful plant, it flowers in mid-summer, much later than most of the other primulas, and with its large handsome rounded leaves and yellow to orange flowers is most desirable. It spreads quickly by seed or by division. The best white form of *P. japonica* is 'Postford White', and it and others of what we call the Candelabra section (meaning flowers arranged in whorls around the stems) are more fussy about soil acidity. Many were introduced in the earlier years of this century, and of these a number of good species have played a part in producing modern hybrids of great garden value.]

[For water of some depth there are] the noble water lily [(nymphaea) and] fine things that thrive in quite shallow water . . . some belonging to our native flora. These are the yellow flag iris (*I. pseudocorus*) [and the startling variegated form], with showy flowers in June and upright sword-like leaves; the water plantain (*Alisma plantago*) with large ribbed leaves, something like those of veratrum, and a wide spreading, lace-like panicle of flower; then the beautiful rosy-pink flowering rush (*Butomus* [*umbellatus*]), looking like something tropical. For a grand plant of stately habit there is a great water dock (*Rumex hydrolapathum*), with very large leaves that, as the season advances, take on brilliant colourings of yellow and red . . . All these plants will bear occasional immersion by flooding . . .

Where spaces are large, good use can be made of the great cow parsnip, *Heracleum mantegazzianum*, with its very large leaves and branches of white bloom four feet across. The still larger foliage of the giant gunneras [*G. manicata*] require cautious placing as it is almost out of scale with ordinary vegetation. In waterside planting ferns should not be forgotten. The best for general use are the royal fern (*Osmunda* [*regalis*]), the graceful lady fern [*see* above] and the dilated shield fern [*Dryopteris dilatata*].

The shape of the bank next the water is well worth considering. It is often of a steep rounded form that seems to plunge suddenly into the water. Such a bank is far from pretty. It gives a sense of insecurity and does not admit of convenient planting. Where there are such banks it is well worthwhile to make a complete alteration and to shape the ground afresh, so as to leave a level grassy pathway some seven feet wide, only raised enough above the water to be sound and dry; thus providing easy access, security, and the best opportunity for good planting [this is shown in Miss Jekyll's drawing, p. 305].

A natural running stream, especially if it flows fast over a shallow pebbly bed, with sides either naturally near the water-level or purposely made so, is one of the very best settings for beautiful plants. It can often be so arranged that the path shall cross it from time to time, either by well-set stepping stones or by a simple plank or log bridge. But it is most desirable, especially in places that have a natural character . . . that a wise restraint should be observed about the numbers of different plants that are to be seen at a glance. If many different kinds are seen together, restful enjoyment of their beauty will be lost.

[This needs special emphasis for the smaller garden today. Often a water garden is constructed to look like a natural pool and it is planted up with too many plants in too many small groups. The whole aspect would be much improved by the discipline of using only a few groups of a few different plants. This point cannot be over-emphasized. There are more modern gardens ruined by the artificially created 'pond', with curving lines and a natural-looking water edge, when a strictly formal water tank or canal with stone edging in a strong geometric shape would be much more suitable.]

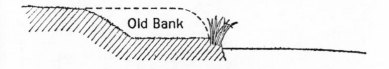

[As Miss Jekyll says:] When the water garden is in a more restricted space, or where, as is often the case, it is desired to have water plants near the house or in close connection with formal gardening, it will take the form of a built tank, symmetrical pool or miniature canal; or a series of tanks may be connected by a narrow rill [as at Hestercombe] that may be stepped over. The edges will either have a flat pavement or a raised curb of wrought stone. There is sometimes hesitation about having a tank deep enough for water-lilies on account of the danger to children, but there is a way of building the outer yard or two of the tank that minimizes the danger and is in any case desirable. This is to have the outer portions only a foot deep for a yard at least from the edge. This also provides a way of having plants in pots that thrive in shallow water; such as the noble water plantain and arrow-heads [see above], or if the wall to the deeper level is carried up so as to retain four to five inches of soil for the plants to root in, it will be all the better. In all, where water is

*Black's
Gardening
Dictionary*

305

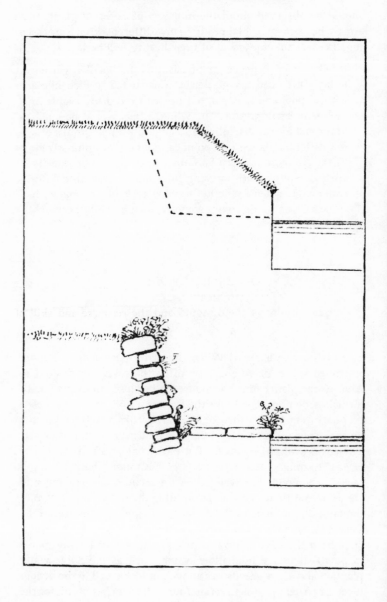

employed in conjunction with masonry, as in such tanks or rills or in fountain basins, it is important that the water level should be placed high and carefully maintained. Nothing is more common or has a more slovenly and uncared for appearance than a half-empty tank. If it is used for dipping, and the supply is not automatically continuous, it should be turned on at once.

[Another very attractive formal treatment often employed by Miss Jekyll was to let masonry steps continue down one or two steps into water. This may be almost too inviting for children but will not be as dangerous as a sudden drop.]

The gardens of the Italian Renaissance show some of the finest examples of the use of water in connection with garden architecture; but it rarely happens in our islands that there is an opportunity of using such vast masses of water; for there are in Italy examples where whole rivers were turned into the garden to form rushing cataracts, water stairs, water theatres and endless arrangements of fountain, rill and pool; lasting monuments to the inventions of the designer and the resource and skill of the hydrostatic engineer.

[Nowadays when PVC or butyl rubber sheeting, or a fibreglass mould, are used for retaining the water, and for making the shape of the pond, it is even more essential to keep the water level to its planned depth. Sadly, how often we see the rim of material or the edge of the artificial container showing above the water. When it is designed as a natural pond additional soil can quickly cover this eyesore, but in a formal tank water must be added and this is not always possible in winter when the normal supply is frozen (or turned off at the mains). How Miss Jekyll would have deplored any carelessness of this sort!]

PERGOLAS

'I much enjoy the pergola at the end of the sunny path. It is
pleasant while walking in full sunshine, and when that sunny
place feels just a little too hot, to look into its cool depth, and to
feel that one has only to go a few steps farther to be in shade, and
to feel that little air of wind that the moving summer clouds say
is not far off, and is only unfelt just here because it is stopped by
the wall. It feels wonderfully dark at first, this gallery of cool
greenery, passing into it with one's eyes full of light and colour,
and the open-sided summerhouse at the end looks like a black
cavern; but on going into it, and sitting down on one of its broad
low benches, one finds that it is a pleasant subdued light, just
right to read by.'

*Wood
and Garden
p. 212*

It is only of comparatively late years that we have borrowed the pergola from the gardens of Italy. Borrowed is perhaps, in its complete sense, not quite the right term to use, for borrowing implies returning or repaying, whereas, having borrowed the pergola, we have certainly kept it for our own.

Its main use in Italy is as a support for grape vines and at the same time to give shade to paths. Here we use it, not only for shade, but as an important feature in garden design and for the display of the best plants of rambling growth, whether for beauty of flower or foliage. In the old English gardens of Tudor times there was something that approached the uses of the pergola in the pleached alleys of Hornbeam or some such tree trained on a framework of laths. But these shaded alleys were slow of growth and wasteful of labour, and did nothing to display the beauty of flowers. Our adaptation of the pergola gives a much quicker and better addition to the delights of the garden, for we have our shady walk, and in addition some of the most charming pictures of flower beauty that the garden can be made to show. It is therefore no wonder that a pergola or something of the kind is now wanted in almost every garden.

Before considering how it is to be planted it may be well to give an idea of the different ways in which it is made. The simplest form of pergola in Italy is made of stout poles guiding and supporting the trunks of the vines, connected across the path by others of less diameter, with a roofing of any long rods laid lengthways along the top. This is repaired from time to time by putting in fresh uprights or other portions in the careless happy-go-lucky way that characterizes the methods of domestic and rural economy of the Italian peasant or small proprietor.

But often in Italy one sees solid piers of rubble masonry coarsely plastered, either round or square in plan, or even marble columns from ancient buildings. These have a more solid wooden beam connecting them in pairs across the path, and stouter stuff running along the length.

For our English gardens we have the choice of various materials

311

for the main structure. If the pergola is to be near enough to the house to be in any sort of designed relation to it, and especially if the house be of some importance, the piers should be of the same material as the house walls – brick or stone as the case may be. Fourteen-inch brick piers laid in cement are excellent and easily made. Such piers may be said to last for ever, and if it is desirable that they should not be red, or whatever may be the normal colour of the brick used, it is easy to colour them in lime-wash to suit any near building. For association with refined brick building bricks are sometimes moulded on purpose of thinner shape, either square or half-round in plan, the latter being for piers that are to show as round columns. Brick, stone or marble, or wooden columns are also used in refined designs.

Jekyll
and Weaver,
*Gardens for
Small Country
Houses*
In a very beautiful open pergola at Marsh Court, designed by Sir Edwin Lutyens, the piers are built of tiles with wide joints; they have stone plinths and moulded stone caps, the section being square and concave square alternately. This fine example also shows the value of the solid, slightly cambered beam. In some cases a good effect is gained by building the piers round and square alternately. It is not difficult to have bricks specially moulded for building in the circular form.

[At Hestercombe this alternate square and round pillar system was used with flowerbeds continuous along the southern side where there is a steep drop and views out into the Taunton vale beyond. At Marsh Court the masonry is more elaborate, the piers of flat tiles being set austerely in large stone flags, with central panels of herringbone brick patterns. The only planting is that of suitable roses and twining plants against the pillars and arching across the cambered beam above. Rectangular and circular pools for water-plants echo the alternating pillar shapes at the side and a high retaining wall of flint and stone is also connected to the pergola with similar beams.]

For more ordinary work the piers may be of oak trunks of a diameter of eight to ten inches. These if tarred or charred at the butts high enough up to show a charred space of a foot above the ground-line, and put into the ground like gate-posts, will last from fifteen to eighteen years, or have about the lifetime of

an ordinary field gate-post. A better and more enduring way is
to have the posts of oak eight inches square, set on squared
stones that stand a foot out of the ground, with a stout iron
dowel let into the foot of the post and the top of the stone. Unless
the appearance of the oak post is desired there is little if anything to choose in point of cost between this and the solid brick
pier, as the oak has to be squared and the plinth shaped and
bedded on a concrete foundation.

In most places local custom and convenience of obtaining
local material will be the best guide in choosing what the pergola
is to be made of. Larch posts are nearly as good as oak, and larch
tops are the best of all materials for the top roofing.

Whatever may be the kind of post or pier, it is important to
have them connected by good beams. The beam ties the opposite
pairs of posts or piers together across the path. In the case of
brick or stone piers it should be of oak or larch seven to eight
inches square, not quite horizontal, but slightly rising in the
middle. This is of some importance, as it satisfies the eye with the
feeling of strong structure, and is actually of structural utility.

It is of course possible to make a pergola of iron with very
flat arches, and supporting rods and wires or wire netting for
the top; but it is the material least recommended and the one
that is the least sympathetic to the plants; indeed in many cases
contact with the cold iron is actually harmful.

In some large gardens iron pergolas have been adapted for the *Gardens for*
growing of pears and apples trained as cordons. They are formed *Small Country*
of successive arches all in one piece, of thick iron rod, with *Houses*
wires fastened longitudinally. They form a pleasant as well as
interesting shady path, and, as the trees are necessarily pruned
to short spurs, the quantity of bloom is a wonderful sight in
proportion to the space. [Here Miss Jekyll, albeit unwittingly,
as she is talking about adaptations in large old gardens, makes a
useful suggestion for the small garden of today. When there is
no ground for a separate orchard for fruit, a pergola or arbour
of such a kind combines usefulness with beauty and, once the
pruning methods are understood, is very little trouble. The
blossom comes in May and low-growing plants for summer
fragrance and colour can be grown around the base of each fruit,
or in a continuous bed on one or both sides. If the pergola runs

east to west sun-loving plants thrive to the south; perhaps as at Hestercombe lavender, phlomis, rosemary, santolina and *Othonnopsis cheirifolia* could be interplanted with a pink China rose such as 'Natalie Nypels'. The shady side will have bergenias, one of Miss Jekyll's favourites, perhaps overhung in September by *Aster divaricatus* (*A. corymbosus*: I find it with megasea [bergenia], one of the most useful of these filling plants for edge spaces that just want some pretty trimming but are not wide enough for anything larger). Hostas also thrive in shade and can be the large-leaved *H. sieboldiana* for borders on a large scale, or the small tidy *tardiana* hybrids. Similarly London Pride (*Saxifraga umbrosa*) can be substituted for bergenia for smaller gardens.]

A modification of the continuous pergola is in many cases as good as, or even better than, the more complete kind. This is the series of posts and beams without any connection in the direction of the length of the path, making a succession of flowering arches; either standing quite clear or only connected by garlands swinging from one pair of piers to the next along the sides of the path, and perhaps light horizontal rails also running lengthwise from pier to pier. This is the best arrangement for roses, as they have plenty of air and light, and can be more conveniently trained as pillars and arches, while the most freegrowing of the Ayrshires and hybrid multiflora ramblers willingly make swinging garlands. Roses are not so good for the complete pergola.

To come to the plants, and to take first the cases in which most shade is desired, with beauty of flower and foliage, the best are certainly grape vines [cultivated forms of *Vitis vinifera*], aristolochia [*A. macrophylla*, the vigorous Dutchman's Pipe], Virginia creeper [correctly *Parthenocissus quinquefolia*, but the Boston Ivy, *P. tricuspidata* 'Veitchii', is often grown in its place and very similar] and wistaria.

[To these we may add the Chinese gooseberry, *Actinidia chinensis*, with large heart-shaped leaves and reddish hairy young stems and creamy-white scented flowers in late summer (the fruit seldom ripens in this country). A good example of this is on a west pergola at Mountstewart in Northern Ireland where the favourable mild climate, although with little hot sun, leads to fruiting.]

They are all, except Virginia creeper, slow at first, but in four years they will be growing strongly. Vines should be planted a fair size, as large as can be had in pots, or two or three years will be lost at the beginning. Aristolochia, and especially wistaria, though they grow fast when established, always make a long pause for reflection at the beginning of their new life's journey.

It is therefore a good plan, when a pergola is planted with these as the main things for its future clothing, to plant at intervals several *Clematis montana* or even the common but always beautiful *C. vitalba* [as on one of the pergolas at Bodnant]. These, especially *C. montana*, will make a fine show for some years, while the slower plants are making their first growth; and as *C. montana* has in many soils not a very long lifetime, the best it can do will be over by the time the permanent plants are maturing and wanting the whole space. The sweet-water vines of the Chasselas class, known in England as Royal Muscadine [a good open-air early grape with firm, juicy, sweet and pleasant fruit], have foliage of excellent form that is beautiful in autumn with its marbling of yellow. The parsley or cut-leaved vine [*Vitis vinifera* 'Apiifolia'] is another desirable kind. *V. cordata* [*Ampelopsis cordata*], the sweet-scented vine, has large wide leaves that give ample shade, and a strong habit of growth, and flowers that in hot sunshine freely give off their delicious scent; while for gorgeous autumn colouring of crimson and yellow the vine commonly known as *V. coignetiae* [this is its correct name] is quite unequalled. There is also the Claret vine [*V. vinifera* 'Purpurea'] whose leaves turn a low-toned red in late summer and autumn.

[Two other ampelopsis are worthy of a place: *A. aconiti-folia* and *A. brevipendunculata*. The former is a vigorous but comparatively unknown luxurious climber with deeply lobed leaflets, the latter has large three-lobed leaves; after a hot summer it bears a quantity of attractive and startling deep blue fruits.]

The height and width of the pergola and the width apart of the pairs of piers can only be rightly estimated by a consideration of the proportions of other near portions of the garden, so that it is only possible to suggest a kind of average size for general use. The posts or piers should stand from seven feet two inches to eight feet out of the ground when the piers stand from eight to nine feet apart across the path. In a garden where there is nothing very high close by, this kind of proportion, rather wider than high, will be likely to be the most suitable; but there may be circumstances, such as a walk through a kitchen garden, where economy of space is desired, or when the pergola has to pass between tall trees at a little distance to right and left, when the proportion that is rather taller than wide had best be used.

In a whole or covered pergola, the pairs of piers would be further apart in the length of the walk than between the individuals of each pair *across* the walk, but in the open pergola, where there is no roof and either no connection or only garlands and level side rails – or garlands alone – they may stand closer.

For the open pergola without top, roses are among the best of plants; on one post a pillar rose and on the other a rambler. A select list for this use would be: as pillars, 'Alister Stella Gray', nankeen yellow; 'Reine Marie Henriette', red; 'Climbing Aimée Vibert', white; 'Carmine Pillar' and 'Waltham Climber', No. 1, reds; and for ramblers, the 'Garland', 'Dundee Rambler', 'Bennett's Seedling', and 'Madame Alfred Carrière', all white or flesh white; 'Crimson Rambler', 'Reine Olga de Württemberg', 'Longworth Rambler', and 'Dawson', reds; as well as multiflora single and double, the large-flowered multiflora and *R. brunonii*. To keep the bases of the piers clothed, some strong young shoots of the current year should be shortened so as best to cover the space, when, instead of making the whole length they would otherwise have attained, they will stop growing at the tips and throw their strength into preparation for flowering shoots at the lower levels.

[Some of these roses are still available but others can have modern-day substitutes. For the pillars: 'Alister Stella Gray', a noisette with pale yellow clustered flowers, is a good autumn repeat flowerer. Instead of 'Reine Marie

Henriette', the double pink modern rose 'Aloha' might be excellent. It withstands wet weather, is disease free, robust and grows to ten feet, flowering off and on all summer. 'Climbing Aimée Vibert', a pure white late-flowerer with almost evergreen leaves is still worthwhile. 'Carmine Pillar', a hybrid rose of deep pink, and the red Waltham climber (or rambler) can have modern substitutes. 'Crimson Glory', a modern Hybrid Tea climber, has large double cupped flowers in deep velvety crimson with a strong pleasant summer fragrance (excellent at Tintinhull against a south wall). The popular 'Danse du Feu' has double, fragrant scarlet repeat flowers. The leaves are rich and glossy and it grows to ten feet. For the ramblers: 'The Garland', such a favourite of Miss Jekyll's, is still obtainable, with medium-size semi-double blush-pink flowers in large clusters. The colour contains a hint of creamy yellow and later fades to white. 'The Dundee Rambler' is more rampant (an Ayrshire rose); it has double white flowers edged with pink, and is suitable for an arbour.

'Bennett's seedling' is another Ayrshire, pure white and tough for a windy exposure. 'Madame Alfred Carrière' grows to twenty-five feet and is seldom without flowers throughout the summer. Turner's 'Crimson Rambler', closely related to the *multifloras* or *wichurianas*, was new and popular at the end of the nineteenth century. A 1909 hybrid (other parent unknown) is 'Veilchenblau', with small cupped semi-double violet-blue flowers, glossy leaves and almost thornless. 'Reine Olga de Württemberg', a climbing Hybrid Tea type, flowers only in summer: 'There is no red climber to equal it.' I do not know which modern crimson rose would adequately take its place, although 'Guinée' is suggested elsewhere. Possibly it is still available, very much one of Miss Jekyll's roses. 'Longworth Rambler', another crimson Hybrid Tea type, flowered freely in the autumn. 'Dawson' was rose-coloured. *R. brunonii* is usually seen as its cultivar 'La Mortala', a grey-leaved white-flowered summer rose.

At Hestercombe, where the original Jekyll plans for the pergola are missing, other more gentle pink colours have been used, chosen from among modern climbers and ramblers, as well as from contemporary lists. On the south side are R. 'Françoise Juranville', salmon-pink fading to pale pink, 'Climbing Cecile Brunner', massed thimble-sized soft-pink, very vigorous to twenty feet, 'Albertine', coppery-pink, lovely but subject to mildew, 'Madame Gregoire Staechlin', early double-pink flowers, not repeat, but most desirable (1927, so unlikely to have been known to Miss Jekyll), R. 'Madame Abel Chatenay'; 'Violetta', crimson-purple with yellow stamens, 'Aloha' (see above); 'The Garland'; 'New Dawn', blush-pink double flowers borne all summer with great freedom, an invaluable rose (1930, just too late for Miss Jekyll); R. 'Frances Lester', blush-white clusters of single small flowers followed by small orange heps. On the nothern side, with the addition of 'Little White Pet', these roses are repeated.

In all gardens I would have, if space permits, the magnificent 'Bobby James', with small semi-double cupped creamy-white flowers in large trusses, which is suitable for an arbour covering. The species R. longicuspis (R. mulliganii) and R. filipes 'Kiftsgate' are also good for the large space, both are once-flowering but magnificent, with creamy-white flowers of great fragrance.]

[Returning to the Pergola:] Among some others of the best plants for the open pergola are the free Japan honeysuckle [Lonicera japonica], the common but always delightful white jasmine [J. officinale], the new Polygonum baldschuanicum, Clematis flammula, the little known but quite excellent C. paniculata [C. maximowicziana, still little known, probably, as Christopher Lloyd says, because it flowers late and needs greater summer heat than we usually have in the British Isles. Still often called C. paniculata, it is more suitable for a warm south-facing wall than for a pergola], blooming in October; the large-flowered clematises; late Dutch honeysuckle [Lonicera periclymenum 'Serotina']; Crataegus pyracantha [Pyracantha coccinea, a good cultivar of which is 'Lalandei']; Rhodotypos kerrioides [R. scandens, grows only to three or four feet, suitable for clothing a bare pillar base], *Kerria japonica*, double-flowered brambles [*Rubus ulmifolius* 'Bellidiflorus'] and *Forsythia suspensa*.

[In a warm sheltered garden *Campsis radicans*, the trumpet vine, was included by Miss Jekyll. At Hestercombe *Polygonum aubertii*, very similar to *P. baldschuanicum*, is also grown. In *Gardens for Small Country Houses* more plants are recommended, for tying in to the pillars. Viburnums such as the Guelder rose (*V. opulus*) and the evergreen *V. tinus* [*Solanum crispum*:] Every season it is smothered with its pretty clusters of potato-shaped bloom of a good bluish-colour; [the cultivar 'Glasnevin' is to be recommended. She suggests also *Robinia hispida* to be grown as a wall-shrub or for the pergola pillar:] It is perfectly hardy, but the wood is so brittle that it breaks off short with the slightest weight of wind or snow or rain . . . but I do not regret having given it the space . . . so beautiful are its rosy flower-clusters and pale-green leaves. As it inclines to be leggy below, I have trained a 'Crimson Rambler' rose over the lower part, tying it in to any bare places in the robinia. *Wood and Garden*

[To return to the Pergola:] There is another class of shady covered way made of flowering trees that differs from the pergola in that when mature it has no adventitious supports whatever, the structure being formed by the trees themselves. It may be of shade trees only, when it comes near the pleached alleys of our ancestors. For this the best trees are plane, hornbeam, wych elm, and beech. The planes should be planted ten to twelve feet apart, and pollarded at eight feet from the ground; their after-growth is then trained down to a temporary roofing framework of poles. In the case of this tree the sides are open. Hornbeam, wych elm and beech are trained as they grow to form both walls and roof. But many of the small flowering trees do very well trained as flowering shady ways, though when they have arched over and form a complete roof the flowers are mostly on the outer sides. One of the best for this use is laburnum, but the beautiful Japanese flowering apple (*Pyrus malus floribunda* – [now *Malus floribunda*]), the snowy mespilus [amelanchier], the Guelder rose [*Viburnum opulus*], the Siberian and other fruiting crabs [*Malus* × *robusta*, or correctly *M. baccata*] are all amenable to the same treatment.

[In one of the gardens where Miss Jekyll contributed to
the design, at West Dean in Sussex, the ends of a laburnum
pergola have arches clothed with thick ivy, which gives
rich green colour to the whole effect, especially in winter
when the laburnums show only their bare stems. This
garden is in the process of being restored.]

This leads naturally to covered ways of other fruit trees, and
the delights of the fruit garden are much increased by the
presence of a naturally formed pergola of apple, pear, plum,
medlar and quince trees.

Gardens for
Small Country
Houses
The pleached alleys of our Tudor ancestors have much in
common with the pergola. Columns, arches and whole galleries
of shady verdure, trained on a foundation of wooden treillage,
are described by Bacon. They were commonly planted with
hornbeam or wych elm. Treillage was also used to a large extent
in French gardens in the eighteenth century [and much earlier]
but it is only now that it is being revived in England.

[Trellis-work walls and divisions have always been useful in town gardens, and now, eighty years later, it is
possible to buy interlocking ready-made trellis with
attractive architectural arches and pediments which can
be appropriately clothed in plants climbing and tangling
through the open lattice work.]

[Returning to the Pergola:] Some adaptation of the pergola,
of a temporary kind, is also extremely useful in the case of a
garden that is new and raw, or in some place that is held on a
short tenancy, when the tenant wishes to enjoy shade without
having to wait for the growth of long-lived and slow-growing
plants. Any poles, from the hop-pole to the bean-pole size, put
up as the framework of a covered way, can in one season be
clothed with a grand growth of Orange gourds, the Potiron
Rouge of our French neighbours. These with others of the
ornamental gourds and quick-growing climbers, such as Japanese
hop [*Humulus japonicum* is an annual hop with green and white
variegated leaves; *H. lupulus* 'Aureus', the golden hop, is a
quick-growing herbaceous perennial very effective in shade],
Major convolvulus [*Ipomaea purpurea*, the morning glory, a

320

half-hardy annual], *Mina lobata* [*Ipomaea vericolor*, with rosy crimson and yellow flowers], Canary creeper [*Tropaeolum aduncum*] and the trailing nasturtiums [*T. majus*], will give ample shade in the hottest months and a glory of autumn fruit and bloom. [To these I would add the splendid and vigorous *Cobaea scandens*, which may prove more than an annual in mild regions and the little *Thunbergia alata* and *T. gibsonii* which twine to ten feet or so among other climbers.]

Plants that are suitable for the open pergola are equally suitable for verandahs with the addition of some others of the tenderer kinds that will succeed in the shelter and warmth of the sunny house-front, especially in the southern counties. For here we may have, as in Devonshire, Cornwall and the Isle of Wight: fuchsia, myrtle, pomegranate, *Solanum jasminoides*, and *Solanum crispum*, and even a little further north the beautiful *Bignonia radicans* [*Campsis radicans*] and the blue passion-flower [*Passiflora caerulea*].

[In fact many or most of these plants survive an average winter in the south, in the home counties and in western coastal regions to the north of Scotland. In cold eastern and north-eastern counties if plants are given protection from biting frost-laden winds they may survive better than when in warmer districts they are lulled into premature growth at intervals throughout our very changeable winters.] Perhaps a well-grown wistaria is the best of all verandah plants, for not only does it yield its masses of bloom almost unfailingly year after year, but its foliage is both graceful and handsome, and always looks fresh and clean.

It is well to think out various combinations for verandah planting that will give a good succession of flower. Thus, as one example, the season of bloom might begin with wistaria, or *Robinia hispida*, a capital shrub for this use; then in full summer would come white jasmine [*J. officinale*, and possibly the cultivars with variegated leaves] and later *Bignonia radicans* [*Campsis radicans*]. Wistaria, if allowed to grow at will, covers a very large space, but if rather closely pruned it can be kept within bounds and flowers with astonishing freedom.

BIBLIOGRAPHY

Allan, Mea *E. A. Bowles and His Garden* Faber, 1973

Bean, W. J. *Trees and Shrubs Hardy in the British Isles* 8th ed.
John Murray, 1970–6

Bowles, E. A. *My Garden in Spring* Jack, 1914

Bowles, E. A. *My Garden in Summer* Jack, 1914

Cook, E. T., and Beatrice Parsons *Gardens of England*
Black, 1908

Earle, Mrs C. W. *Pot-Pourri from a Surrey Garden etc.*
Smith Elder and Co., 1903

Earle, Mrs C. W. and others *Garden Colour Illustrated by
Margaret Waterfield*

Ellacombe, Canon *In a Gloucestershire Garden*
Edward Arnold, 1895

Grounds, Roger *Ornamental Grasses* Pelham Books, 1979

Gathorne-Hardy, Robert *Wild Flowers in Britain*
Batsford, 1973

Gibson, Michael *The Book of the Rose* Macdonald, 1980

Hibberd, Shirley *Familiar Garden Flowers* Cassell, Peter,
Galpin and Co., approx mid-19th century or 1870

Hope, Frances *Gardens and Woodlands* Macmillan, 1881

Ingwersen's Manual of Alpine Plants Will Ingwersen and
Dunnsprint Ltd, 1978

Jekyll, Francis *Gertrude Jekyll: Memoir*
Jonathan Cape, 1934

Massing, Betty *Miss Jekyll* Country Life, 1966

King, Frances *The Well-Considered Garden* Scribners, 1915

Lloyd, Christopher *The Well-Tempered Garden* Collins, 1970

Lloyd, Christopher *Clematis* Collins, 1977

Le Lievre, Audrey *Miss Willmott of Warley Place*
Faber, 1980

Loudon, John Claudius *Encyclopaedia of Plants*
Spottiswoode, 1829

Lutyens, Edwin *Architectural Monograph*
Academy, London, 1979

Mathew, Brian *Dwarf Bulbs* Batsford, 1973

Nicholson, George (Ed.) *Illustrated Dictionary of Gardening*
L. Upcott Gill, 1896

O'Neill, Daniel *Lutyens's Country Houses*
Lund Humphries, 1980

The Readers Digest *Encyclopaedia of Garden Plants and
Flowers* 2nd ed., 1978

Robinson, William *The English Flower Garden*
John Murray, various eds, 1883–1933

The RHS Dictionary of Gardening Clarendon, 2nd ed., 1956

Sander's Encyclopaedia of Gardening Collingridge, 1950

Smith *A Gardener's Dictionary of Plant Names* Cassell, 1971

Stearn, William T. *Botanical Latin* David and Charles, 1973
revised ed.

Thomas, Graham Stuart *The Old Shrub Roses*
Phoenix House, 1971

Thomas, Graham Stuart *Plants for Groundcover* Dent, 1970

Thomas, Graham Stuart *Perennial Garden Plants* Dent, 1976

Tooley, M. J. *Gardens Designed by Miss Jekyll in the North*
GHS *Journal* Vol. viii 3

Books by Gertrude Jekyll

1899 *Wood and Garden* Longmans

1900 *Home and Garden* Longmans

1901 *Wall and Water Garden* Country Life, 2nd ed., 1913

1901 *Lilies for English Gardens* Country Life

1902 *Roses for English Gardens* (with Edward Mawley)
Country Life

1904 *Old West Surrey* Longmans

1904 *Some English Gardens* (With Elgood) Longmans

1907 *Flower Arrangement* Country Life

1908 *Colour for the Flower Garden* (later editions)
Colour Schemes for the Flower Garden Country Life

1908 *Children and Gardens* Country Life

1912 *Gardens for Small Country Houses* (with Sir Lawrence
Weaver) Country Life

1916   *Annuals and Biennials* (cultural notes by E. H. Jenkins)
        Country Life
1918   *Garden Ornament* (Folio with Christopher Hussey)
        Country Life, 2nd ed., 1927
1925   *Old English Household Life*   B. T. Batsford

Other publications include:
A number of articles in Black's *Encyclopaedia of Gardening* 1918
A pamphlet for the Civic Arts Association on Public Parks and
    Gardens 1918
Articles in *The Garden, Edinburgh Review, Empire Review,
    Journal* of the RHS, *Country Life, Gardening Illustrated,
    New Flora and Silva* and *Ladies Field*
Introduction to *Colour Planning of the Garden* by Tinley,
    Humphreys and Irving Jack, 1924
Extracts from many of these articles published in 1937 *A
    Gardener's Testament* (edited by Francis Jekyll and G. C.
    Taylor)
Extracts from some of her books published in 1964 (Charles
    Scribner), 1966 (Studio Vista) *On Gardening*
Gertrude Jekyll: a Memoir Francis Jekyll   Jonathan Cape, 1934
Miss Jekyll: Portrait of a Great Gardener Betty Massingham
    Country Life, 1966, and David and Charles, 1973
In 1907 *Wood and Garden* was translated into German by G. von
    Sarden and Gertrude Jekyll wrote the preface to an American
    publication *The Garden Day by Day* by Mrs Frances King

APPENDIX ON COLOUR THEORIES

M. E. Chevreul's *Principles of harmony and contrast of colours*, written in 1838, was first translated into English in 1854. Chevreul, recognizing that neighbouring colours alter (as perceived by the retina of the eye) when placed alongside each other, formulated rules demonstrating the effects of simultaneous contrast, successive contrast and mixed contrast. Using as his spectrum a colour wheel where the complement of each colour was directly opposite it, he developed his theories from the simple observation that the eye, after gazing at one colour for a short period, was then prepared for its complement. The 'after image' retained on the retina would therefore 'colour' and change the neighbouring colours or colours viewed in succession. Having established the rules of contrast Chevreul proceeded to suggest the principles of harmony of pairs or threes of colours. Those closely related in the spectrum (analogous) and those that were widely separated (contrasting) could be harmonious and much depended on the 'tone' of widely separated hues. (This meant the amount of black or white which was added to the hue; it would also depend on the light or shade (diffused light) in which the associated colours were viewed.) In 1878 an American physicist, Ogden Rood, in *Modern Chromatics*, drew heavily on Chevreul's conclusions but deduced from the arrangement of the colour spectrum a natural order of colours. Yellow is the lightest of colours and violet (its complement) the darkest. On the one hand the colours between yellow and violet, moving through orange, red and purple, were the 'warm' colours and those moving through green, green-blue and blue were 'cool'. Both Chevreul and Rood stressed that white and grey heighten and enhance neighbouring colours and could serve as links between pale insipid colours as well between strong contrasts. Miss Jekyll, already with a highly developed colour sense, partly from her early training in painting when she learnt to make copies of Turner's fiery and luminous visions of light, and partly through her friendship with the water-colourist Hercules Brabazon Brabazon, may well have been introduced to these works. Certainly she made use of the laws of simultaneous contrast and understood the effects of 'after images' on colours seen in sequence. In her monochromatic flower schemes pale flowers would merge gradually into blooms of progressively stronger tints of the same hue, accentuating their brightness by contrast. In her main colour borders Miss Jekyll used colours closely linked in the colour spectrum. In full sunlight luminous warm colours were beautiful together, seen in their natural order, and pale colours were separated and linked by white and grey. Contrasting complementary colours are harsh in full light but in shade blend and enhance each other as each colour is affected by the blue tones of darkness. Red becomes violet, green is yellowed and blue becomes deeper. In her woodland schemes tints, tones and shades of one colour, including green of different textures, could be enriched by strong complementary hues as the eye moved from sun to shade.

ACKNOWLEDGEMENTS

Felicity Bryan thought of this book and paid me the great compliment of suggesting I should write it. I would like to thank her warmly for this and for all her help and support throughout. I am grateful to her and to Robin Baird-Smith at Collins for believing that I understood sufficiently the genius of Miss Jekyll.

I am very grateful to all the owners of gardens where Miss Jekyll had contributed, who have allowed me to visit freely, in particular the Chief Fire Officer at Hestercombe (and the Somerset County Council's Architect's department].

I have had help and advice from Madeleine Pickthorne and Lorna McGroby, who helped to replant at Hestercombe, carefully following Miss Jekyll's original plans. Graham Stuart Thomas, Jim Marshall and Anthony Lord, the gardens advisers of the National Trust, have all given me assistance and Mr Thomas has allowed us to reproduce his own plans for the herbaceous borders at Cliveden as examples of modern Jekyll-type planting.

I am grateful to Richard Bisgrove for allowing me access to The Garden History Society's microfilm of Gertrude Jekyll's plans at Reading University (donated by The Beatrice Farrand Library at Berkeley, University of California). I must thank Juliet Cooper for retyping my untidy script and checking my typing errors and spelling mistakes. I am very grateful to Gill Gibbins of Collins and to Vera Brice, the designer, who have worked so hard to produce the book.

Jane Brown's excellent *Gardens of a Golden Afternoon* was published just as this book was approaching proof stage. I have found it most exciting and stimulating, and full of new information. Fortunately, I have been considering Miss Jekyll as a writer rather than as a designer, so there is still a place for my book. In two cases where our choice of plans has overlapped, we have adopted Jane Brown's successful system of numbering, placing figures where Miss Jekyll's writing is almost indecipherable – in the plan of the Colour Border and the plan of the Hidden Garden.

Finally I wish to acknowledge all the help given to me by John Malins, who checked and double-checked botanical names and terms. I could not have written the book without his ceaseless encouragement and forbearance.

326

INDEX

belia schumannii, 188
x grandiflora, 188
butilon vitifolium, 187
cers, 217
chillea 'The Pearl', 190, 210
argentea, 200
clavenae, 200
clyopeolata, 200
tomentosa, 200
umbellata, 122
x 'King Edward', 200
cidanthera murielae, 182
onite, winter see Eranthis
  hyemalis
onitum, 225
ctinidia chinensis (Chinese
  gooseberry), 314
diantum pedatum
  (A. nigrum), 202, 204
donis vernalis, 96
esculus parviflora
  (A. macrostachys), 175,
  177, 187
gathea coelestis [Felicia
  amelloides], 189, 290–1
eratum, 208, 296, 298
geratum houstonianum, 210
mexicanum, 210
grostis tenuis (browntop
  bent), 235
uga reptans
  'Astropurpurea', 271
ugas, 120
chemilla alpina, 103
isma plantago (water
  plantain), 304–5
lanton, 236
llingham, Helen, 297
iums, 227
strömeria aurantiaca, 35,
  156–7
hilensis, 157
aemantha, 157
x ligtu, 157
yssum saxatile (yellow
  alyssum), 206
manita muscaria (fly
  agaric), 191
aryllis, 227
elanchier (snowy
  mespilus), 319
melanchier canadensis, 95

laevis, 95
lamarckii, 95
Ampelopsis aconitifolia, 79,
  315
brevipedunculata, 79, 315
cordata [Vitis cordata], 315
Anaphalis nubigena
  (Gnaphalium orientale), 205
anchusa, 158, 189, 289–90
Anchusa 'Opal', 141
myosotidiflora [Brunnera
  macrophylla], 96
Andromeda catesbaei
  [Leucothoe fontanesiana],
  31, 56, 71, 253
floribunda [Pieris
  floribunda], 56, 91, 302
japonica [Pieris japonica], 91
andromedas, 45, 56, 67,
  173–6, 217, 250, 252
Anemone apennina, 64
blanda, 53
coronaria, 53
fulgens, 53, 100
hepatica [H. nobilis], 53
hupehensis, 209
japonica [A. hupehensis
  japonica], 163, 183, 209,
  224
nemorosa robinsoniana, 64
puisatilla [P. vulgaris], 54
x hybrida [A. hupehensis
  japonica], 163, 183, 209,
  224
Anthemis tinctoria, 165, 225
Anthericum liliago [Paradisea
  liliastrum; St Bernard's
  lily], 205, 272
antirrhinums see snapdragons
apple trees, 49, 320
Aquilegia alpina (columbine),
  69, 271
arabis, 270
Arenaria serpyllifolia
  (sandwort), 118
Aristolochia macrophylla
  [A. sipho], 79, 314–15
Arkwright, Rev. Edwyn, 36
Armeria maritima, 109, 115,
  118
plantaginea leucantha 'Alba'
  (A. cephalotes), 109
Arnebia echieides

(A. echioides longiflorum);
  [Prophet flower], 99
arrow-heads (Sagittaria
  sagittifolia), 305
Artemisia canescens, 200
lactiflora (creamy-white
  mugwort), 164, 280
ludoviciana, 211
pedemontana [A. lanata],
  200
schmidtiana 'Nana'
  [A. nana], 122, 200
sericea, 122
stelleriana, 176–7, 189, 200,
  211, 290
artemisias, 187, 200
artichoke, globe see Cynara
  scolymus
arum, wild, 101
Arum italicum 'Pictum', 101
Aruncus dioicus (A. sylvester;
  Spiraea aruncus;
  meadow sweet), 184, 186
  280, 283, 289–90, 302
Arundinaria japonica
  [Bambusa metake], 179
Asperula odorata (woodruff),
  105
Asphodelus albus, 142
ramosus, 283
Asplenium ceterach see
  Ceterach officinarum
rutamuraria, 202
scolopendrium (hartstongue),
  58, 202, 204, 252, 263
asters, 215, 293, 298
China, 296, 298
Aster acris, 223, 293
amellus, 216, 223
divaricatus [A. corymbosus],
  223, 265, 314
frikartii 'Mönch', 216, 223
lateriflorus 'Horizontalis',
  298
paniculatus shortii, 223
umbellatus, 293, 298
astilbe see spiraea
Athyrium filix-femina (lady
  fern), 71, 116, 179, 180,
  302–4
Atripex halimus, 57
Atriplex hortensis, 292
aubrietia, 118, 270

Aubrietia deltoidea (graeca),
  270
aucuba, 60
Aucuba japonica 'Variegata'
  (spotted aucuba), 37
auriculas, 97–8, 226
azaleas, 39, 41, 113–14
Azalea pontica [Rhododendron
  luteum], 113–14, 173, 217
azara, 58
Azara microphylla, 59
serrata, 59

Bacon, Francis (Lord
  Verulam), 98, 320
Bambusa metake [Arundinaria
  japonica], 179
ragamowski [Sasa tessellata],
  174–5
Banks, Sir Joseph, 78
barberry, 46
common see Berberis
  vulgaris
Barr, Mr, 123
bay see Laurus nobilis
Bean, W. J., 113
bedstraw, 81
beech see Fagus sylvatica
cut-leaved see Fagus
  sylvatica heterophylla
bent, browntop see Agrostis
  tenuis
Bentham, George, 50
berberis see mahonia
Berberis aquifolium [Mahonia
  aquifolium], 37, 39, 45–6,
  57, 60
candidula, 57
thunbergii 'Aurea', 287
verruculosa, 57
vulgaris (common barberry),
  120, 203
bergenias [megaseas], 22, 38,
  45, 56, 65, 120, 223, 225,
  279, 281, 314
Bergenia 'Silberlicht', 265
ciliata ligulata (Megasea
  ligulata), 45, 64, 175, 264
cordifolia (Megasea
  cordifolia), 45, 265, 280
crassifolia (Megasea
  crassifolia), 45
x schmidtii (Megasea

ligulata speciosa), 45, 64, 177, 265
Betula albosinensis 'Septentrionalis', 31
jacquemontii, 31
papyrifera, 31
pendula (birch), 30–1, 142, 221, 239–42; bark, 106; leaf-mould, 238; timber, 250; hoops, 253
Bignonia radicans (*Campsis radicans*; trumpet-vine), 183, 293, 319, 321
birch *see Betula pendula*
bittervetch *see Lathyrus vernus*
blackberry *see Rubus fruticosus*
Black's Gardening Dictionary, cit., 301, 304–5
Blechnum spicant (hard fern), 180, 202, 252
bluebell *see Endymion non-scriptus*
Californian *see* nemophila
blue-eyed Mary *see Omphalodes verna*
Boletus fungus, 191–2
Bowles, E. A., 100, 109
Bowles' Golden Grass *see Milium effusum* 'Aureum'
box, 34; *see also* Buxus
Christmas *see Sarcococca*
bracken *see Pteris aquilina*
New Zealand dwarf *see Hypolepsis millifolia*
Bramley (near Godalming, Surrey), 16
Bramley seedling apples, 34
briars *see Rosa pimpinellifolia*
bridal wreath *see Spiraea x arguta*
broom, butcher's *see Ruscus aculeatus*
Moroccan *see Cytisus battandieri*
Mount Etna *see Genista aetnensis*
Spanish *see Spartium junceum*
white *see Cytisus multiflorus*
Brunnera macrophylla see Anchusa myosotidiflora
bryony, black *see Tamus communis*
Bryonia dioica (white bryony], 81
buckthorn, grey-leaved sea *see Hippophae rhamnoides*
Buddleia auriculata, 251
davidii, 165, 292, 294

davidii veitchiana (*B. veitchii*), 294
fallowiana, 292
x 'Loch Inch', 165
Bupleurum fruticosum, 188
bupthalmum, 281
Butomus umbellatus (flowering rush), 304
buttercup bush *see Kerria japonica*
Buxus balearica, 59
sempervirens (gold, green or variegated box), 37, 68–9
sempervirens 'Prostrata', 176

Calceolaria amplexicaulis, 262, 292
Calcot nursery (near Reading), 33
calendula (pot marigold), 195, 207
Calendula arvensis (orange marigold), 36
officinalis (orange pot marigold), 292
Californian bluebell *see* nemophila
Calluna vulgaris (ling), 179
Caltha palustris (marsh marigold), 96, 302
palustris 'Flore Pleno', 302
Camassia leichtlinii, 86
campanula, 115, 281, 289
Campanula caespitosa, 205
carpatica, 122, 291
cochlearifolia (or *pulsilla*), 205
fragilis, 122
garganica, 122
glomerata, 163
griffithii, 291
isophylla, 122
lactiflora, 189, 291
latiloba, 282, 291
macrantha, 163
macrocarpa, 163
persicifolia, 163
portenschlagiana [*C. muralis*], 122
poscharskyana, 122
pyramidalis (chimney campanula), 80
Campsis radicans [*Bignonia radicans*; trumpet vine], 183, 293, 319, 321
cannas, 158, 166, 181
Canterbury bells, 139
Cantherallus cibarius (chanterelle), 192
Cardamine pratensis (lady's smock), 302

trifolia (*trifoliata*), 93
Cardiocrinum giganteum (*Lilium giganteum*), 161, 229
cardoon *see Cynara cardunculus*
carnations, 158–60, 168–9, 171
carpet bedding, 259
Caryopteris incana [*C. mastacanthus*], 175, 187
x *clandonensis*, 175
Cassinia fulvida, 60, 286
cassiope, 45
Castle Drogo (Dartmoor), 20
catchfly, Alpine *see Silene alpestris*
catmint *see Nepeta x faassinii*
ceanothus, 296
Ceanothus 'Gloire de Versailles', 46, 190, 293
prostratus, 120
thyrsiflorus repens, 120
Celastrus orbiculatus, 216
Centaurea montana (cornflower), 110
centranthus, 225
Cephalaria gigantea, 294
cerastium, 118, 122, 296
Cerastium tomentosum, 115
ceratostigma, 217
Ceratostigma plumbaginoides (*Plumbago larpentae*), 35, 289
Ceterach officinarum, 212, 252
Chaenomeles japonica [*Pyrus mauleii*], 91
speciosa (Japan quinces), 91, 120
Chamaecyparis lawsoniana (Lawson's cypress), 220
chanterelle *see Cantharellus cibarius*
Chasselas, 78
Cheiranthus alpinus, 108
marshallii, 108
mutabilis, 108–9
cherry, wild *see Prunus avium*
chestnut, 250, 254
Spanish, 238, 250, 253
Chevreul, M. E., 16
Chiastophyllum oppositifolium, 57
Chimonanthus praecox (*fragrans*), 40, 251
chionodoxas, 64, 270
Chionodoxa gigantea, 63
luciliae, 63
choisya, 139, 187, 206, 234
Choisya ternata (Mexican

orange flower), 39, 60, 101, 110, 115, 139, 184, 279
Christmas rose *see Helleborus niger*
chrysanthemums, 233–4, 2█
Chrysanthemum frutescens (Paris daisy), 183, 221, 2█
indicum, 225
maximum (Shasta daisy), 163–4, 224, 293
morifolium, 225
parthenium 'Aureum' (golden feverfew), 259, 2█
serotinum (*Pyrethrum uliginosum*; moon daisy)█ 224, 298
Cimicifuga racemosa, 291
Cineraria maritima (*Senecio bicolor*), 140, 176, 189, 211, 257, 290, 293, 296
cistus, 119, 139
Cistus cyprius, 58, 69, 187
halimifolius (*hamilifolium*█ 175
ladanifer (*ladaniferus*), 17█
laurifolius, 69, 71
monspeliensis, 174
salviifolius, 174
x *corbariensis*, 174
x *florentinus*, 174
x *skanbergii*, 165
clematis, 164, 186, 190, 21█ 282
wild *see Clematis vitalba*
Clematis cirrhosa balearica, 36
flammula, 22, 48–9, 74, 1█ 290, 318
heracleifolia davidiana (*C. davidiana*), 135, 145█ 160, 189, 289
integrifolia, 160
jackmanii, 166, 190, 208, 296
maximowicziana (*C. paniculata*), 318
montana, 74, 114, 139–4█ 315
orientalis, 49
recta, 140, 145, 163, 289
rehderiana, 49
tangutica, 49
vitalba (wild clematis), 7█ 80, 315
viticella, 49
x *durandii*, 160
x *jackmanii*, 49, 160, 189█
x *jouiniana*, 160
clerodendron, 234
Clerodendron bungei (*C. foetidum*), 183, 293

Cleyera fortunei (variegated eurya), 37
Cliveden, 21, 277; borders, 278–81, 297
Cobaea scandens, 321
Cobbett, William, 142
cob-nuts, 177
 Kent see Corylus avellana
Collinsia verna, 195
coltsfoot, variegated see Tussilago farfara 'Variegata'
columbine see Aquilegia alpina
Commelina coelestis, 291
Convallaria majalis (lily-of-the-valley), 41, 107–8
Cook, E. T.: Gardens of England, 257
coreopsis, 225
Coreopsis grandiflora, 295
 verticiliata [C. lanceolata], 158, 287, 292, 295
cornflower see Centaurea montana
Cornus alba (red dogwood), 264, 287
 sanguinea (Thelycrania sanguinea; dogwood), 68, 264
 stolonifera 'Flaviramea', 264
corydalis, 115, 118
Corydalis bulbosa (Fumaria bulbosa; fumaria), 64, 67, 87, 93
 marshalliana (capnoides), 93
 solida, 87
Corylopsis glabrescens, 93
 pauciflora, 91
 spicata, 93
Corylus avellana (hazel or Kent cob-nut), 31–3, 241, 265, 268; leaf-mould, 238; hoops, 253
 maxima (filbert), 265
cotoneasters, 60, 110, 176
Cotton, Philip, 280
Cotyledon umbilicus [Umbilicus pendulinum; wall-pennywort], 204
Country Life (journal), 16, 52, 53, 54, 58, 67, 141, 146, 163, 184, 299, 301
Court Farm (Broadway), 73
cowslips see Primula veris (officinalis)
 Virginian see Mertensia virginica
crambe, 257, 281
Crambe cordifolia, 280
 maritima (sea-kale), 140,

184
cranesbills, 139, 141, 163, 224
Crataegus monogyna (oxyacantha; white thorn), 46, 68
 pyracantha [P. coccinea], 318
 coccinea], 318
creeper, canary see Tropaeolum aduncum
creeping Jenny see Lysimachia nummularia
creeping lady's tresses see Goodyera repens
crinum, 234
Crinum x powellii, 183, 203
crocus, 64, 227, 265–6
Crocosmia masonorum, 166, 295
crown imperial see Fritillaria imperialis
Cupressus sempervirens (Italian cypress), 50
curtonus, 281
Curtonus paniculatus, 166
cyclamens, 68
Cyclamen coum, 52
 repandum (vernum), 53
cydonia, 219
Cydonia oblonga (quinces), 217–18, 320
Cymbaleria aequitriloba, 201
 hepaticifolia, 201
Cynara cardunculus (cardoon), 155
 scolymus (globe artichoke), 155
Cynosurus cristatus (crested dog's tail), 235
cypress, 173
 Italian see Cupressus sempervirens
 Lawson's see Chamaecyparis lawsoniana
Cypripedium spectabile (N. American mocassin flower), 303
Cytisus battandieri (Moroccan broom), 294
 multiflorus (white broom), 70, 271
 x praecox, 271

daffodils, 41, 65, 88, 100–1, 266, 271
 dwarf see Narcissus nanus
 Pyrenean see Narcissus pallidiflorus
dahlias, 166, 181, 197–8, 206, 209, 216, 221–2, 250, 291–5; dividing, 225
Dahlia 'Cochineal', 182

'Fire King', 182
'Lady Ardilaun', 182
 coccinea, 182
daisy, blue Cape see Felicia ameloides
 moon see Chrysanthemum serotinum
 Paris see Chrysanthemum frutescens
 Shasta see Chrysanthemum maximum
Danae racemosa (Ruscus racemosus; Alexandrian or victory laurel), 37, 56, 240, 250
Daphne mezereum, 87, 264
 pontica, 60, 100
day-lily see Hemerocallis fulva 'Flore Pleno'
Deanery Garden, 15
delphiniums, 22, 93, 153, 155–6, 163–4, 184, 186–7, 189, 226, 280–1, 284–5, 289–90
Delphinium belladonna, 156, 289–91
 consolida (larkspur), 195, 296
 elatum, 290–1
 grandiflorum (D. cheilanthum), 291
Dennstaedtia punctiloba see Dicksonia punctilobulata
Dentaria diphylla, 69
 pinnata, 93
Desmodium penduliflorum [Lespedeza thunbergii], 80, 120
deutzias, 39
Deutzia amurensis (D. parvifolia), 175
 gracilis, 39, 271
 setchuenensis, 188
Dianthus 'Mrs Sinkins', 141
 caesius (Cheddar pink), 159
 caryophyllus, 159
 deltoides, 160
 fragrans, 118
 petraeus (rock pink), 115, 118, 206
 plumarius, 159
 x allwoodii, 159
Dicentra eximia, 86, 272
 spectabilis, 272
Dicksonia punctilobulata (Dennstaedtia punctilobula), 108
Dictamnus fraxinella, 139
Dingley Park, 73
dock, great water see Rumex hydrolapathum

dog-rose, 76, 81
dog's tail, crested see Cynosurus cristatus
dogwood see Thelycrania sanguinea
 red see Cornus alba
doronicum, 225
Doronicum austriacum, 96
 plantagineum, 96
Downe, Lady, 73
Dryopteris dilatata (Lastraea dilatata; dilated shield fern; broad buckler fern), 180, 252, 304
 filix-mas (male fern), 58, 64, 252
Dutchman's pipe see Aristolochia macrophylla

Earle, Mrs C. W., 37, 40
echinops (globe thistle), 135, 163–4, 187, 189–90, 208, 293, 296
Echinops ritro (E. ruthenicus), 209
Eden, Lady, 72
edwardsia see Sophora macrocarpa
Edgeler, Mrs, 130
Edinburgh Review, 237
Elaeagnus macrophylla, 59
 pungens 'Maculata', 59, 286
 x ebbingei, 59
 x reflexa, 59
elder see Sambucus nigra
Elgood, George S., 171, 213, 231, 297
Elgood, George S. and Jekyll, G.: Some English Gardens, 125, 193
elm, 238
 Dickson's golden see Ulmus x sarniensis 'Dicksonii'
 wych, 319–20
elymus, 257
Elymus arenarius (lyme grass), 140, 184, 210
Endymion hispanicus (Scilla campanulata; Spanish squill), 64
 non-scripta (bluebell), 63, 106
Epilobium angustifolium (French willow, or rose bay willow herb), 69, 138
epimediums, 120
Epimedium pinnatum colchicum, 37, 69, 85
 perralderianum, 85
 x rubrum, 85
Eranthis hyemalis (winter

aconite), 262–3
erigeron. 163, 293
Erinus alpinus, 118, 206
eryngiums, 135, 157, 163–4, 186, 209, 289
Eryngium agavifolium, 158
  amethystinum, 157–8
  giganteum (silver thistle), 155, 157–8, 162, 190, 296
  oliverianum, 157–8, 186, 209, 226
  planum, 209
  proteiflorum, 158
  serra, 158
  tripartitum, 158, 209
  varifolium, 158
  x *zabellii*, 209
Erysimum alpinum, 109
  marshallii, 109
erythroniums, 181
Erythronium dens-canis (dog-toothed violet), 64, 67, 86–7
  giganteum, 86–7
  grandiflorum, 87
  oregonum, 87
  revolutum, 87
escallonias, 15, 206, 219
Escallonia 'Iveyi', 60, 188
  macrantha, 59
  revoluta, 60
  virgata (*E. philippiana*), 59
Eucryphia milliganii, 188
  x *nymansay*, 188
Eulalia zebrina (*E. japonica*) *see Miscanthus sinensis* 'Zebrinus'
euonymus, 217
Euonymus alatus, 216
  europaeus (spindle tree), 216, 242
  fortunei 'Coloratus', 253
  japonicus, 286
  radicans, 60
  sachalinensis, 216
  yedoensis, 216
euphorbia, 296
Euphorbia characias, 57
  epithymoides (*polychroma*), 280
  robbiae, 57
  wulfenii, 139
eurya, variegated *see Cleyera fortunei*
Evelyn, John, 241
evergreens, 49–51, 54, 241, 252–3, 264
everlasting flower *see Helichrysum bracteatum*

Fagus sylvatica (beech), 43, 238, 263, 319

sylvatica heterophylla (cut-leaved beech), 173
Felicia amelloides (*Agathea coelestis*; blue Cape daisy), 189, 290–1
ferns, 179–80, 204, 270
  broad buckler *see Dryopteris dilatata*
  dilated shield *see Dryopteris dilatata*
  hard *see Blechnum spicant*
  lady *see Athyrium filix-femina*
  male *see Dryopteris filix-mas*
  marsh *see Thelypteris palustris*
  mountain *see Thelypteris limbosperma*
  prickly shield *see Polystichum setiferum*
  royal *see Osmunda regalis*
fertilizers, 221
Ferula communis (giant fennel), 36
  cheliantha (giant fennel), 36
fescue, Chewing's *see Festuca rubra* spp *mutata*
Festuca ovina (sheep's fescue), 235
  rubra spp *mutata* (Chewing's fescue), 235
  rubra spp *rubra* (creeping red fescue), 235
feverfew, golden *see Chrysanthemum parthenium* 'Aureum'
filbert *see Corylus maxima*
Filipendula rubra 'Venusta' (*Spiraea venusta*), 302
  ulmaria (*Spiraea ulmaria*; meadow sweet), 302
fir, Scotch *see Pinus sylvestris*
fly agaric *see Amanita muscaria*
foam-flower *see Tiarella cordifolia*
Folly Farm, 15, 20
forget-me-not *see Myosotis dissitiflora*
  water *see Myosotis palustris*
  wood *see Myosotis sylvatica major*
Forsythia suspensa, 80, 91, 120, 319
  viridissima, 91
foxgloves, 41, 69, 139, 163, 274, 283
fox grape, northern *see Vitis labruscae*
Fragaria vesca (wild strawberry), 218

freesias, 38
Fritillaria imperialis (crown imperial), 86, 282
fuchsia, 166, 234, 321
Fuchsia riccartonii, 293
Fumaria bulbosa (*Corydalis bulbosa*), 64–5, 87
fungus, 191
funkia *see hosta*

gaillardia, 225
Galax aphylla, 44
gale, candleberry *see Myrica cerifera*
  sweet *see Myrica gale*
galega, 225
Galeobdolon luteum 'Variegatum' (*Lamium galeobdolon*), 177
Garden, The (journal), 87, 162, 196
'Garden of Eden' (Giudecca, Venice), 72
Gardening Illustrated (journal), 117, 165
Garrya elliptica, 59, 115, 251
gaultherias, 68, 100, 226, 250, 252
Gaultheria shallon, 31, 37, 56
gazanias, 295
Gazania rigens, 292
Genista aetnensis (Mount Etna broom), 294
gentian, willow *see Gentiana asclepiada*
Gentiana acaulis, 110
  asclepiada (willow gentian), 69
George, Sir Ernest, 16
geraniums, 18, 221, 259, 262, 281, 292
Geum montanum grandiflorum (*G. aureum*), 225
Geranium 'Johnson's blue', 280, 282
  x *magnificum* (*G. ibericum platyphyllum*), 139, 141, 163
gilliflower *see carnation*
gladiolus, 160, 181–3, 189, 207, 223, 292–3
Gladiolus brenchleyensis, 182
  callianthus, 182
  gandavensis, 182
Gledstone Hall (W. Yorks.), 15, 20
glory of the snow *see Chionodoxa*
Glyceria aquatica 'Variegata' (*G. maxima*), 289, 292
Glyphosate (herbicide),

196–7
Gnaphalium orientale (*Anaphalis nubigena*), 205
godetia, 296
Godetia 'Double Rose', 189, 210
golden rod (solidago), 207, 224
Goodyera repens (creeping lady's tresses), 180–1
gorse *see Ulex europaeus*
gourds, Orange, 320
Graff, Jan de and Hyams, Edward: *Lilies*, 71
grape, Oregon *see Mahonia aquifolium*
grape-vine *see Vitis vinifera*
grass, smooth-stalked meadow *see Poa pratensis*
grasses, 234–5
Guelder rose (cultivated) *see Viburnum opulus*
Gunnera manicata (giant gunnera), 304
gypsophila, 140, 163–4, 189, 296
Gypsophila paniculata, 145, 160, 210, 280, 293

Hacquetia epipactis, 100
Haplophyllum patavinum (*Ruta patavina*), 181
hartstongue *see Asplenium scolopendrium*
hawkweed, 80
hazel *see Corylus avellana*
heartsease *see Viola tricolor*
heather, bell, 242
hebes, 200
Hebe pinguifolia 'Pagei', 177
Hedera arborescens, 44
heleniums, 163, 166, 281
Helenium autumnale 'Pumilum', 224, 292
helianthemums, 295
helianthus, 166, 222, 224, 295
Helianthus annuus (annual sunflower), 165, 181–3
  atrorubens (perennial sunflower), 182, 207
  decapetalus (*H. multiflorus*; pale primrose sunflower), 182, 187, 222–3
  laetiflorus, 182, 223
  salicifolius (*H. orgyalis*), 165, 186, 222
  scaberrimus (*rigidus*), 182, 222
helichrysums, 57, 181, 221
Helichrysum bracteatum (everlasting flower), 39, 183

hellebores, 125
Corsican *see Helleborus corsicus*
Lent *see Helleborus orientalis*
Helleborus atrorubens, 264
bocconei, 32
colchicus, 87
corsicus (Corsican hellebore), 32
cyclophyllus, 32
foetidus, 32
niger (Christmas rose), 36, 38, 54, 225, 233, 262–3
niger macranthus (giant Christmas rose),
H. maximus, H. altifolius, 54, 233, 263
orientalis (Lent hellebore), abschasicus, olympicus, 31, 64, 87, 264; hybrids, 54; for house decoration, 100–1
viridis, 32
hemerocallis, 281
hemerocallis 'Citrinum', 294
'Marian Vaughan', 294
fulva 'Flore-Pleno' (day-lily), 65, 93, 163, 166, 280
Hepatica trans-silvanica (H. angulosa), 53
nobilis (Anemone hepatica), 53
Heracleum mantegazzianum (great cow parsnip), 304
Hermodactylus tuberosus (Iris tuberosa), 285
Hestercombe (Somerset), 15–16, 117, 120, 122, 144–50, 266, 274, 297, 305, 312, 314, 317
Heuchera americana (H. richardsonii; satin leaf), 97, 141, 182, 223–4, 271, 283
x brizoides, 44
Heucherella x tiarelloides, 44
Hidcote, 297
Hillier, Harold G.: Manual of Trees and Shrubs, 50
Hippophae rhamnoides (grey-leaved sea buckthorn), 190, 210
Hoheria glabrata, 166
lyalli, 166
hollies, 240–2, 287
holly, common see Ilex aquifolium
golden, 286
hollyhocks, 163–4, 178, 190, 209–10, 250, 289, 292–6

honeysuckle (lonicera), 79–80, 226
Japan see Lonicera japonica
hoops and hoop-making, 253–5
hop see Humulus lupulus
hornbeam, 311, 319–20
hostas, 289, 302
Hosta fortunei, 155
plantaginea grandiflora (Funkia grandiflora), 178 216
sieboldiana (Funkia sieboldiana), 32, 182, 216, 314
tardiana, 314
Humulus japonicum (Japanese hop), 320
lupulus (hop), 81
lupulus 'Aureus' (golden hop), 320
Hutchinsia alpina, 93, 200
hyacinth, grape see Muscari neglectum
Roman, 38
wild (bluebell) see Endymion non-scripta
hydrangea, 160, 234
Hydrangea quercifolia (oak-leaved hydrangea), 115, 265
villosa, 188
Hypericum calycinum (St John's wort), 119
frondosum (H. aureum), 175
moserianum, 175
patulum, 294
patulum uralum, 294
x odorum 'Elstead', 188
Hypolepsis millifolia (New Zealand dwarf bracken), 108
Hyssopus officinalis, 206

iberis, 270
Iberis amara (I. conoraria), 195
gibraltarica, 195
sempervirens, 139, 270
umbellata, 195
ilex, 219
Ilex aquifolium (common holly), 20, 22, 29, 31, 41, 46, 50, 54, 56, 142, 207, 218
x altaclarensis
.'Camelliifolia', 31
Incarvillea delavayii, 141
Indigofera gerardiana, 188
Ingwersen, Will, 93
Ipomaea purpurea (morning glory), 320–1

vericolor (Mina lobata), 321
Iresine herbstii, 292
iris, 164, 225, 257, 283
Algerian see Iris unguicularis
flag see Iris pseudocorus
wild see Iris foetidissima
Iris alata (scorpiodes)
(I. planifolia), 35–6
flavescens, 283
foetidissima (wild iris), 40, 58, 204, 218
florentina, 272
graminea, 40, 225
kaempferi, 301
laevigata, 301
ochroleuca, 302
pallida 'Queen of the May', 142, 182, 283
pallida dalmatica, 139, 276, 283
pseudacorus (flag iris), 93 141, 272, 304
reticulata, 40, 65
scorpiodes see alata
sibirica, 302
tuberosa (Hermodactylus tuberosus), 285
unguicularis (I. stylosa), 34–8, 40, 54, 67, 99, 251
Itea ilicifolia, 188
ivy, 44, 56, 320
Boston see Parthenocissus tricuspidata
ground see Nepeta glechoma

jasmine, 58
white see Jasminum officinale
yellow see Jasminum nudiflorum
Jasminum nudiflorum (yellow jasmine), 36, 54, 80, 250
officinale (white jasmine), 79, 203, 318, 321
Jekyll, Gertrude: WORKS
'Border plants that succeed best on light soils', 162
'Changing fashions of gardening in the nineteenth century', 18
Colour schemes for the flower garden, 18, 22, 61, 64, 69, 79–80, 86, 139, 184, 189, 223, 245, 263, 265, 277, 288, 293, 297
'Designing a rose garden', 146
'The early anemones', 53
'Evergreens on walls in winter', 58, 184
Gardens of England, 257
Gardener's testament, 52,

73, 79, 107, 209
'Green things of the winter garden', 54
'Grouping of hardy bulbs', 87
'The Guelder rose', 67
'The hardy flower border', 163
Home and garden, 16–17, 73, 83, 92, 93, 103, 153, 184
'The idea of a garden', 237
'Lent hellebores', 67
'A little August garden', 184
'Native ferns in the garden', 117
Old West Surrey, 21
'Spring planting for the summer garden', 165
'Streamside garden', 299
Wall and water gardens, 18, 92, 110, 118, 146, 303
'The water garden', 301
Wood and garden, 13, 15–16, 23, 45, 162, 168, 284, 309, 319
(with E. Mawley) Roses for English gardens, 77, 130, 136
(with L. Weaver) Gardens for small country houses, 20, 55, 151, 278, 312–13, 319
juniper, 50–2, 203, 241–2
Juniperus chinensis (Chinese juniper), 50
communis (common juniper), 49–50
communis 'Hibernica' (Irish juniper), 50
sabina (savin), 119, 220–1

kalmias, 302
Kalmia latifolia, 56
Kelway's (nurserymen), 123, 290
Kerria japonica 'Flore Pleno' (buttercup bush), 91, 173, 319
kniphofias, 181, 225, 234, 292, 295
Kniphofia 'Maid of Orleans', 280
'Royal Standard', 280
caulescens (Tritoma caulescens), 182
praecox, 295
rooperi, 295

Labrador tea see Ledum palustre

laburnum, 319–20
lady's smock see Cardamine
    pratensis
Lambay island (Ireland), 20
lamiums, 120
Lamium galeobdolon
    [Galeobdolon luteum
    'Variegatum'], 177
maculatum, 57, 177
larkspur see Delphinium
    consolida
Lastrea dilatata [Dryopteris
    dilatata; dilated shield
    fern; broad buckler fern],
    180
Lathyrus albo-roseus, 96
    aureus (Orobus aurantiacus),
    109
latifolius 'Albus' (white
    everlasting pea), 22, 72,
    160, 162, 164, 184, 186–7,
    189, 210, 226, 289, 293
vernus (Orobus vernus;
    bittervetch), 96, 109, 225
laurel, Alexandrian see
    Danae racemosa
victory see Danae racemosa
Laurus nobilis (bay), 20, 54,
    58, 139, 293
laurustinus see Viburnum
    tinus
Laurustinus lucidus
    (Viburnum tinus lucidum),
    293
lavender, 115, 121, 171,
    189–90, 203, 208, 314
dwarf, 135
Lavandula angustifolia, 178,
    290
Lavatera olbia, 190, 210, 296
lawns, 234–6
leaf-mould, 238–9
Ledum palustre (wild
    rosemary; Labrador tea),
    68
Leonardo da Vinci, 17
Lespedeza thunbergii
    (Desmodium
    penduliflorum), 80, 120
Leucojum vernum, 65
leucothoe, 45, 68.
Leucothoe catesbaei
    (L. axillaris), 56
catesbaei fontanesiana
    (Andromeda catesbaei), 31,
    56, 71, 253
Leycesteria formosa, 173
Ligularia dentata, 295
hodgsonii, 295
Ligustrum japonicum (Japan
    privet), 37, 293
ovalifolium (oval-leafed

privet), 47
ovalifolium 'Aureum'
    (golden privet), 141, 186,
    286, 292
lilacs see syringa
lilies, 69, 72, 250
Bermuda see Lilium harrisi
day see Hemerocallis fulva
    'Flore Pleno'
herring see Lilium
    bulbiferum croceum
Lent see Narcissus pseudo-
    narcissus
madonna see Lilium
    candidum
martagon see Lilium
    martagon
St Bernard's see
    Anthericum liliago
St Bruno's see Paradisea
    liliastrum
Lilium auratum, 71–2, 179
bulbiferum croceum (herring
    lily), 72, 140, 153, 163
candidum (madonna lily),
    72, 163, 210
croceum (L. bulbiferum
    croceum), 72, 140, 153, 163
giganteum (Cardiocrinum
    giganteum), 161, 229
harrisi (L. longiflorum;
    Bermuda lily), 163, 178–9,
    189, 210
henryi, 72
hollandicum, 278
longiflorum see harrisi
martagon, 72, 227
monadelphum szovitsianum,
    294
regale, 72, 163, 179, 280
szovitsianum, 72–3, 289
lily-of-the-valley, 41
large see Convallaria majalis
Limnanthes douglasii
    (poached-egg flower), 195
linarias, 200
Linaria alpina, 201
cymbalaria, 201
Lindisfarne, 20
ling see Calluna vulgaris
Linnaea borealis, 180–1
Lippia citriodora (lemon-
    scented verbena), 206
Liriope specatum (Ophiopogon
    spicatum), 37
Lithospernum prostratum, 289
Lloyd, Christopher, 318
lobelias, 158, 189, 259, 262
Lobelia erinus, 259, 290
London Pride see Saxifraga
    umbrosa
Lonicera fragrantissima, 39

japonica (Japan
    honeysuckle), 119, 318
periclymenum (woodbine),
    59, 318
pileata, 68
standishii, 39
loose-strife see Lysimachia
    vulgaris
loquat, 139, 294
Lorimer, Sir Robert, 16
love-in-the-mist see Nigella
    damascena
lupins, 141–2, 163, 283, 289
tree see Lupinus arboreus
Lupinus arboreus (tree lupin),
    163, 283
Lutyens, Sir Edwin L., 15,
    20, 92, 117, 142, 146, 237,
    312
Luzula sylvatica (wood rush),
    107, 252
lychnis, 224
Lychnis chalcedonica, 163, 280
lyme-grass see Elymus
    arenarius
Lysimachia vulgaris (loose-
    strife), 302
nummularifolia (creeping
    Jenny), 57, 287

magnolia, 173–4, 176, 227
Magnolia conspicua
    (M. denudata), 174, 187
delavayi (evergreen
    magnolia), 58
denudata see conspicua
grandiflora, 282
grandiflora 'Exmouth', 37,
    58, 282
liliflora 'Nigra'
    (M. purpurea), 174
stellata, 91, 174, 176
x loebneri 'Leonard Messel',
    176
x soulangiana, 174, 176
mahonias (berberis), 38–9,
    45–7, 217, 219
Mahonia aquifolium
    (Berberis aquifolium;
    Oregon grape), 37, 39,
    45–6, 57, 60, 203
japonica, 38
lomarifolia, 38
pinnata, 39
x 'Undulata', 91
Maianthemum bifolium
    (convallaria; Smilacina
    bifolia), 107–8
maize see Zea mays
Malcolmia maritima
    (Virginian stock), 105
Malus baccata (M. x robusta),

319
floribunda (Pyrus malus
    floribunda), 319
trilobata, 176
Manchester Guardian, 15
Maranta arundinacea
    'Variegata', 87
marigold, 207
African see Tagetes erecta
French see Tagetes petula
marsh see Caltha palustris
orange see Calendula
    arvensis
orange pot see Calendula
    officinalis
marjoram, golden-leaved see
    Origanum vulgare
    'Aureum'
Marsh Court, 15–16, 312
mastic bush see Caryopteris
    incana
Mawley, Edward and Jekyll,
    Gertrude: Roses for Engli...
    gardens, 77, 130, 136
meadow sweet see Filipendu...
    ulmaria
Meconopsis baileyi
    (M. betonicifolia), 252
cambrica (Welsh poppy),
    204
grandis, 252
nepaulensis (M. wallichi;
    blue Himalayan poppy),
    252
medlar see Mespilus
    germanica
megaseas see bergenias
Mentha rotundifolia, 292
Mertensia virginica
    (Virginian cowslip), 86,
    137
mespilus, snowy
    (amelanchier), 93, 319
Mespilus germanica (medlar
    68, 218, 320
Mexican orange see Choisya
    ternata
Michaelmas daisies, 215,
    223–5, 250, 297–8
Milium effusum 'Aureum'
    (Bowles' golden grass), 28
milkwort, 80
Millmead (near Bramley), 20
Mimulus guttatus, 302
Mina lobata [Ipomaea
    vericolor], 321
miscanthus, 289
Miscanthus sinensis
    'Zebrinus' (Eulalia zebrin...
    E. japonica; Japanese
    striped grass), 39, 184,
    186, 216

nocassin flower, N. America
  see Cypripedium spectabile
nonarda, 224, 281
Monarda didyma, 166, 295
'Croftway Pink', 280–1
nontbretia, 295
noon daisy *see*
  Chrysanthemum serotinum
norell (edible fungus), 105
norning glory *see Ipomaea*
  purpurea
norus nigra (black
  mulberry), 218
oss, sphagnum, 142
nottisfont Abbey, 130
nountstewart (N. Ireland),
  315
nutans *see* paeonies
nugwort, creamy-white *see*
  Artemisia lactiflora
nulberry, black *see Morus*
  nigra
nules, Dr, 270
nulleins, 221
nullein *see Verbascum*
  olympicum
nunstead Wood, 15, 17, 19,
  20, 22, 30, 70, 80, 92, 176,
  187, 257, 278, 297
nuscari botryoides, 88
nomeum, 88
neglectum (grape hyacinth),
  64, 88
nyosotis, 70–1
nyosotis dissitiflora (forget-
  me-not), 86, 137
nalustris (water forget-me-
  not), 302
nulvatica major (wood
  forget-me-not), 96
nyrtle, 58, 188, 321
nog *see Myrica gale*
Mediterranean (*Myrtus*
  communis), 59, 174, 189
nommunis 'Tarentina', 59
nyrica cerifera (candleberry
  gale), 56
nale (sweet gale; bog
  myrtle), 68, 100, 174, 252

nandina, 234
nandina domestica, 57, 176
narcissus, 225
heasant's eye *see Narcissus*
  poeticus
noet's *see Narcissus*
  poeticus
nrcissus bicolor, 65
nrnuus plenus, 34
nclamineus, 65
nsertus ornatus
  N. poeticus ornatus), 267

horsfieldii, 65, 88
incomparabilis, 266
majalis patellaris, 267
minor, 65
nanus (dwarf daffodil), 65,
  68
pallidiflorus (N. pallidus
  praecox; Pyrenean
  daffodil), 65, 68, 266
poeticus (poet's or
  pheasant's eye narcissus),
  267
princeps, 88
pseudo-narcissus (Lent lily),
  65
serotinus, 36
nasturtium, trailing *see*
  Tropaeolum majus
National Trust, 21, 130, 278,
  297
navelwort, Venus's *see*
  Omphalodes linifolia
Nelson, Rev. J. G., 63
nemophila (Californian
  bluebell), 196
Nemophila menziesii, 195
nepeta, 208, 225
Nepeta glechoma (ground
  ivy), 43
x faassenii (catmint), 135,
  141, 171, 189
Nigella damascena (love-in-
  the-mist), 195
nut-walks, 31–3
nymphaea *see* water lilies

oak, 43, 49, 143; felling and
  splitting, 105–6, 247–8,
  250; bark, 106; leaf-
  mould, 238–9
Kermes *see Quercus*
  coccifera
oenothera, 163
Oenothera biennis, 294
erythosepala
  (O. lamarckiana), 183
fruticosa, 292
fruticosa youngii
  (O. youngii), 225
tetragona 'Riparia'
  (O. riparia), 225
Olearia gunnii
  (O. phlogopappa), 60, 141,
  271, 283
hastii (O. x hastii), 60, 181,
  187–8, 203
macrodonta, 60
phlogopappa (O. gunnii;
  O. stellulata), 60, 141, 271,
  283
solandri, 188, 286
stellulata *see* phlogopappa

waikariensis, 188
x scilloniensis, 141, 271
Omphalodes linifolia (Venus's
  navelwort), 116, 195, 205
verna (blue-eyed Mary), 81
Ophiopogon spicatum
  (Liriope spicatum), 37
Opuntia ficus-indica (prickly
  pear), 36, 203
raffinesquii, 203
Orchis apifera (bee orchis), 36
Origanum vulgare 'Aureum'
  (golden-leaved marjoram),
  287
Ornithogalum nutans, 88
Orobus aurantiacus
  (Lathyrus aureus), 109
vernus (Lathyrus vernus;
  bittervetch), 96, 109, 225
osier, golden *see Salix alba*
  'Vitellina'
Osmanthus delavayi, 91
x burkwoodii, 91
Osmunda regalis (royal fern),
  180, 304
othonnopsis, 121, 296
Othonnopsis cheirifolia
  (Othonna cheirifolia), 57,
  109, 314

Pachysandra terminalis, 57,
  120
paeonies, 94, 114, 122–5,
  164, 202, 250, 274, 276;
  dividing, 225
  tree, 175
Paeonia arietina, 124
daurica [P. triternata], 124
decora [P. peregrina], 124
lactiflora [P. albiflora],
  123–5, 274
lobata [P. peregrina], 124
lutea 'Ludlowii', 123
mlokosewitschii, 124
officinalis, 123, 125, 271
peregrina [P. decora;
  P. lobata], 124
potaninii, 124
suffruticosa, 122–4
tenuifolia, 124
wittmanniana, 124
pansies, 101, 141, 272
Papaver orientale (oriental
  poppy), 93, 140, 164, 182,
  226, 283
Paradisea liliastrum
  [Anthericum liliago;
  St Bruno's lily], 204, 226,
  272
parahebes, 200
Parahebe catarractae, 201
perfoliata, 201

Paraquat/Dignat, 196
Parkinson, John, 53, 158
Parrotia persica, 217
parsnip, great cow *see*
  Heracleum mantegazzianum
Parthenocissus quinquefolia
  (Virginian creeper), 207,
  314–15
tricuspidata (Boston ivy),
  207, 314
Passiflora caerulea (blue
  passion-flower), 321
pear tree, 320
pear, prickly *see Opuntia*
  ficus-indica
pelargoniums, 221, 259
Pettaria alliacea, 283
Peltiphyllum peltatum
  (Saxifraga peltatum),
  301–2
pennywort *see Umbilicus*
  rupestris
penstemons, 163, 206, 209,
  292
Penstemon barbatus 'Carnea',
  189
campanulatus, 164, 189,
  209, 296
gentianoides, 164
gloxinioides, 164
hartwegii, 163, 296
isophyllus, 296
Penzance, Lord, 74
pergolas, 73–9, 81, 309–21
pernettya, 68, 120, 253
Perovskia atriplicifolia, 187
periwinkle *see Vinca*
phacelia, 289
Phacelia campanularia, 110
philadelphus, 46–7
Philadelphus 'Belle Etoile',
  265
'Innocence', 291
coronarius 'Aureus', 287
microphyllus, 175
phlomis, 121, 176, 314
Phlomis anatolica, 177
chrysophylla, 57, 176
fruticosa (Jerusalem sage),
  57, 60, 120, 175–6
italica, 57, 146
phloxes, 163–4, 209, 223–4,
  280–1, 292
Phlox paniculata, 295
phormium, 296
Phygelius aequalis, 296
capensis, 166, 296
Physocarpus opulifolius
  'Luteus', 287
pieris, 45, 68
Pieris floribunda (Andromeda
  floribunda), 56, 91, 302

japonica (*Andromeda japonica*), 90
pinks, 122, 159–60, 171
Cheddar *see Dianthus caesius*
rock *see Dianthus petraeus*
white, 224
Pinus sylvestris (Scotch fir), 29, 51, 70, 95, 97, 106, 142, 234, 241–2, 249
piptanthus, 234
Piptanthus laburnifolius (*P. nepalensis*), 260
plane tree, 319
golden, 286
Platanus x *hispanica* 'Suttneri', 286
platycodons, 291
Platycodon grandiflorus, 181
mariesi (*P. grandiflorus* 'Mariesii'), 181
Platystemon californicus, 195
plum trees, 320
Plumbago capense (*capensis*), 289
larpentae [*Ceratostigma plumbaginoides*], 35, 289
Poa pratensis (smooth-stalked meadow grass), 235
poached-egg flower *see Limnanthes douglasii*
polyanthus, 267–8
Polygala chamaebuxus, 251
Polygonatum multiflorum (Solomon's seal), 69, 86, 89, 106–7, 271
polygonum, 226
Polygonum aubertii, 319
baldschuanicum, 318–19
cuspidatum 'Compactum' (*P. compactum*), 224
Polypodium vulgare (common polypody), 57, 202, 204, 206, 252, 263
Polystichum setiferum (prickly shield-fern), 57, 108
pomegranate, 234, 321
poppy, blue Himalayan *see Meconopsis nepaulensis*
oriental *see Papaver orientale*
potentillas, 294
Potentilla fruticosa, 120, 166, 295
vilmoriana, 295
primrose, 19, 22, 81, 101, 226, 267–8
evening, 213; *see also*

Oenothera
wild *see Primula vulgaris*
Primrosa denticulata, 88
primula, 224
Primula auriculata, 224
denticulata, 88, 224, 303
florindae, 303
japonica, 303
officinalis (cowslip), 105, 268
rosea, 137, 224
sikkimensis, 303
veris, 105
vulgaris (wild primrose), 267
privet, golden *see Ligustrum ovalifolium* 'Aureum'
Prophet flower *see Arnebia echioides longifolium*
Prunus avium (wild cherry), 95
laurocerasus 'Otto Luyken', 176
pissardii, 292
subhirtella, 95
Pteris aquilina (bracken), 29, 41, 43, 142, 168–9, 179, 216, 241
Pterocephalus parnassi, 181, 200
pulmonaris, 57
Pulsatilla vulgaris (*Anemone pulsatilla*), 54
Puschkinia scilloides, 64
Pyracantha coccinea (*Crataegus pyracantha*), 318
Pyrethrum uligonosum (*Chrysanthemum serotinum*; moon daisy), 224, 298
Pyrford Court, 287, 297
Pyrus japonica [*Chaenomeles speciosa*], 120
malus floribunda [*Malus floribunda*], 319
mauleii [*Chaenomeles japonica*], 91

Quarterly Review, 236
Quercus coccifera (Kermes oak), 36
Quercus ilex, 46, 55
quinces *see Cydonia oblonga*
Japan *see Chaenomeles speciosa*

Ramscliffe, 153
Ranunculus montanus, 93
rhododendron, 39, 41, 56, 70–1, 110–14, 179

Alpine *see Rhododendron ferrugineum*
Rhododendron catawbiense, 70
ferrugineum (Alpine rhododendron), 31, 68, 100
hirsutum, 71
luteum (*Azalea pontica*), 113–14, 173, 217
minus, 71
myrtifolium (*R. kotschyi*), 68, 71
ponticum, 70, 112
praecox, 31, 87
Rhodotypos scandens (*R. kerrioides*), 318
ribes, 46
Ribes sanguineum, 91
Ricinus gibsonii, 292
Robinia hispida, 187, 293, 319, 321
Robinson, William, 18, 109, 278; *The English Rose Garden*, 107
rockeries and rock gardens, 198, 201; *see also* walls
rodgersia, 301
Rodgersia pinnata, 302
podophylla [*R. japonica*], 302
tabularis, 302
roots, 219–20, 225–6
roses, 73–8, 129–36, 142, 166–8, 173, 177–8, 190–1, 207, 282–3, 314, 316–18
rose, Christmas *see Helleborus niger*
dog (wild), 76, 81
Guelder *see Viburnum opulus*
Rosa alba, 130
alba maxima, 130
arvensis, 131, 218
brunonii (*brunosis*), 75, 131, 168, 316–17
centifolia (cabbage or Provence rose), 129
chinensis (China rose), 58, 272, 274, 283, 314
cinnamomea, 173
damascena (damask rose), 94, 129
filipes, 168, 318
gigantea, 77
helenae, 168
laevigata, 78
longicuspis (*R. mulliganii*), 168, 318
moyesii, 133
multiflora (*R. polyantha*), 131, 135, 317
pendulina (Alpine rose), 73
pimpinellifolia

(*R. spinosissima*; Burnet rose, Scotch briars), 80, 121, 132, 177, 203, 226
rubiginosa (sweetbriar), 68, 74, 94, 173, 178, 218, 26[?]
rubrotincta, 130
rugosa, 178, 191
sempervirens, 178
virginiana (*R. lucida*), 121, 132, 173, 178, 203
wichuriana, 121, 131, 317
x *damascena versicolor* 'York and Lancaster', 12[?]
'Max Graf', 121
'Paulii', 121
'Paulii Rosea', 121
rose bay willow herb *see Epilobium angustifolium*
rosemary, 20, 60, 121, 135, 314
wild *see Ledum palustre*
Royal Horticultural Society colour standards, 285; Dictionary, 124
Royal muscadine (grape vine), 78, 315
Rubus deliciosus, 44
fruticosus (blackberry), 11[?]
thibetanus, 44
tridel, 69
ulmifolius, 44, 319
rudbeckias, 281, 295
Rudbeckia fulgida [*R. newmannii*], 183
speciosa, 165
rue *see Ruta graveolens*
Rumex hydrolapathum (grea[?] water dock), 304
Ruscus aculeatus (butcher's broom), 240
racemosus [*Danae racemosa*; Alexandrian o[?] victory laurel], 37, 56, 24[?] 250
rush, flowering *see Butomus umbellatus*
wood *see Luzula sylvatica*
Ruta graveolens (rue), 140, 184
patavina [*Haplophyllum patavinum*], 181

sage, 271
Jerusalem *see Phlomis fruticosa*
St John's wort *see Hypericum calycinum*
Salix alba 'Chermesina' (*S. britzensis*), 264
alba 'Vitellina' (golden osier), 264
fargesii, 264

ragilis decipiens (cardinal willow), 264
lpiglossis, 209
lutation, The, 55
lvias, 189
lvia ambigens (*guaranitica*), 289
arinacea 'Victoria', 289
emorosa (*S. virgata*), 164
fficinalis 'Purpurescens', 271
atens, 289–91
liginosa, 289
mbucus nigra (elder), 137
nigra 'Aurea' (golden elder), 286
acemosa 'Plumosa aurea', 286
ndwort *see* Arenaria serpyllifolia
nguisorba canadensis, 291
ntolina, 20, 121, 135, 140, 171, 184, 257, 293, 296, 314
aponaria officinalis (double soapwort), 189, 210
rcococca hookerana, 38
humilis, 38
uscifolia, 38
asa tessellata [*Bambusa ragamowski*], 175
vin *see* Juniperus sabina
xifrage, 115, 118, 270
axifraga moschata (mossy saxifrage), 64
eltatum [*Peltiphyllum peltatum*], 301
tolonifera, 57
mbrosa (London Pride), 57, 204–5, 314
ent, 20
illa, 270
cilla amoena, 64
bifolia, 63–4
ampanulata [*Endymion hispanicus*], 63, 106
maritima [*Urginea maritima*], 36
sibirica, 63–4
cott, Sir Walter, 236
*a-holly *see* eryngiums
*a-kale *see* Crambe maritima
*edge, 242
*edums, 115, 118, 281
edum 'Autumn Joy', 280
spectabile, 298
nnecio 'Sunshine' (*S. greyii*), 57, 60, 296
bicolor (*Cineraria maritima*), 140, 176, 189, 211, 257, 290, 293, 296
monroi, 57

Sharp, Cecil, 21
Silene alpestris (Alpine catchfly), 198
Sissinghurst, 74, 115, 297
skimmias, 174, 176, 252–3
Skimmia japonica, 56
Smilacina bifolia (*Maianthemum bifolium*), 107–8
racemosa, 107
snapdragons (antirrhinums), 118, 189, 209, 287, 289–91, 296
snow, 50–1
soapwort, double, *see* Saponaria officinalis
Solanum crispum, 319, 321
jasminoides, 321
solidago (goldenrod), 207, 295
Solidaster hybridus, 295
Solomon's seal *see* Polygonatum multiflorum
Sophora macrocarpa (edwardsia), 234
Spartium junceum (Spanish broom), 287, 294
spiderwort, 291
spindle tree *see* Euonymus europaeus
spiraea (astilbe), 224
Spiraea aruncus [*Aruncus dioicus*], 184, 283, 289–90, 302
bumalda 'Goldflame', 287
prunifolia, 175
thunbergii, 91, 176
ulmaria [*Filipendula ulmaria*; meadowsweet], 302
venusto [*Filipendula rubra* 'Venusta'], 302
x *arguta* (bridal wreath), 91
squill, Spanish *see* Endymion hispanicus
stachys, 140, 184, 279, 293, 298
Stachys lanata, 135, 145, 171, 184, 189, 211, 296
Stellaria graminea (lesser stitchwort), 204
holostea (greater stitchwort), 204
Stephanandra incisa (*S. flexuosa*), 175
Sternbergia lutea, 227
Steuart, Sir Henry: *The Planter's Guide*, 236, 238
stitchwort *see* Stellaria
stock, night-scented, 213
Virginian *see* Malcolmia maritima

Stokesia laevis, 291
stonecrops *see* sedums
strawberry, wild *see* Fragaria vesca
stuartia, 206
Styrax japonica, 174, 176
sunflower, annual *see* Helianthus annuus
pale primrose *see* Helianthus decapetalus
sweetbriar *see* Rosa rubiginosa
sweet peas, 136, 195
Symphoricarpos orbiculatus, 68
syringa (lilacs), 47, 173
Syringa microphylla, 48
vulgaris, 47–8
x *persica*, 48

tagetes, 207, 295
Tagetes erecta (African marigold), 141, 182–3, 209, 221, 287, 292
patula (French marigold), 181, 209, 221
Tamus communis (black bryony), 81
Tanacetum densum, 57
Taxus baccata (yew), 54, 179, 220–1, 289, 293
Tellima grandiflora, 44, 57
terracing, 118–20
thatching (chip), 255
thalictrum, 163, 289
Thalictrum aquilegifolium, 165, 184
speciosissimum (*T. flavum*; *T. glaucum*), 158, 164, 292, 302
Thelycrania sanguinea (*Cornus sanguinea*; dogwood), 69, 264
Thelypteris limbosperma (mountain fern), 108
palustris (marsh fern), 108
thistle, globe *see* echinops
silver *see* Eryngium giganteum
Thomas, Graham Stuart, 21, 74, 108, 124–5, 130, 277–9, 281, 297
thorn trees, 241–2
thrift *see* Armeria maritima
Thunbergia alata, 321
gibsonia, 321
thyme, 20, 80
Thymus serpyllum (white thyme), 181
Tiarella cordifolia (foam-flower), 44, 57, 86, 97

Tinley, G. F., Humphreys, T. and Irving, W.: *Colour Planning of the Garden*, 259
Tintinhull, 99, 115, 117, 209, 227, 297, 317
tradescantia, 291
Tradescantia virginica, 158
trees: transplantation, 236, 238, 243; felling and splitting, 247–9
Trientalis europaea, 180–1
Trillium grandiflorum (N. American wood lily or wake robin), 106, 180–1
tritomas *see* kniphofias
tropaeolums, 292
Tropaeolum peregrinum (Canary creeper), 321
majus (trailing nasturtium), 321
speciosum, 178
tulips, 86, 98–9, 271
Tulipa acuminata, 98
clusiana, 99
fosteriana, 99
gesneriana, 98
greigii, 99
kaufmanniana, 99
retroflexa, 98, 270–1
saxatilis, 99
sylvestris, 99
tarda, 99
Tussilago farfara 'Variegata' (variegated coltsfoot), 289

Ulex europaeus (gorse), 97
Ulmus x *sarniensis* 'Dicksonii' (Dickson's golden elm), 287
Umbilicus rupestris (pennywort), 118
pendulinum, 204
Uvularia grandiflora, 69
Urginea maritima (*Scilla maritima*), 36

vacciniums, 217
Vaccinium myrtillum (whortleberry), 41, 95, 107, 142
Valeriana phu 'Aurea' (golden valerian), 65
Veitch, John Gould, 71
veratrums, 94, 225
Veratrum album, 95
nigrum, 95
verbascum, 281, 291
Verbascum chaixii (*vernale*), 138, 183
olympicum (mullein), 138, 163, 294
phlomoides, 138, 183

verbena, lemon-scented *see Lippia citriodora*
veronica, 200
Veronica prostrata, 109, 201
rupestris, 109
teucrium, 201
traversii (Hebe brachysiphon), 60
viburnum, 217
Viburnum betulifolium, 176
davidi, 57, 68, 120
dilatatum, 176
farreri, 251
hirtum (V. tinus hirtulum), 59
opulus 'Sterile' (Guelder rose; water elder), 66, 114, 139–40, 173, 207–8, 218, 319
plicatum, 47, 115
tinus (laurestinus), 37, 58, 59, 100, 115, 139, 319, 321
tinus lucidum (Laurustinus lucidum), 59, 293
x *bodnantense*, 251
vinca, 225
Vinca difformis (V. acutiflora; Mediterranean periwinkle), 57, 119, 227
major (periwinkle), 119, 227
minor (periwinkle), 119
vine, black Hamburg, 34
claret *see Vitis vinifera*

'Purpurea'
cut-leaved *see Vitis vinifera* 'Apiifolia'
parsley *see Vitis vinifera* 'Apiifolia'
trumpet *see Campsis radicans*
Viola cornuta (tufted viola), 274
gracilis, 274
tricolor (heartsease), 272
x *wittrockiana*, 272
violets, 82
czar, 37, 227
dog-toothed *see Erythronium dens-canis*
Virginian creeper *see Parthenocissus quinquefolia*
Vitis coignettii (coignetiae), 78–9, 207, 315
cordata [Ampelopsis cordata], 315
davidii, 79
labrusca (northern fox grape), 78
vinifera (grape vine), 78, 314
vinifera 'Apiifolia' (parsley or cut-leaved vine), 315
vinifera 'Purpurea' (claret vine), 183, 207, 315

wake robin, N. American

see Trillium grandiflorum
wall pennywort *see Cotyledon umbilicus*
wallflowers, 118, 271
alpine, 94
walls, 115, 117–19, 201–7; *see also* rockeries
Ware of Tottenham, 36
water-elder *see Viburnum opulus*
water gardening, 18, 301–7
water lilies (nymphaea), 133–4, 304–5
water plantain *see Alisma plantago*
weigela, 46
Wellington apple, 34
Welsh poppy *see Meconopsis cambrica*
West Dean (Sussex), 320
white thorn *see Crataegus monogyna*
whortleberry *see Vaccinium myrtillus*
willow, cardinal *see Salix fragilis decipiens*
weeping, 49; *see also Epilobium*
Wilmott, Ellen: *The Genus Rosa*, 133
Wilson, G. F., 72, 133
winter sweet *see*

Chimonanthus fragrans
wistaria, 314–15, 321
Wistaria sinensis (*Wistaria chinensis*), 79
woodbine *see Lonicera periclymenum*
wood lily, N. American *see Trillium grandiflorum*
woodruff *see Asperula odorata*
woundwort, woolly *see Stachys lanata*

Xanthoceras sorbifolium (*sorbifolia*), 175

yew *see Taxus baccata*
yuccas, 182, 184, 210, 257, 279, 289, 296
Yucca filamentosa, 156, 293
flaccida, 121, 156, 184
gloriosa, 121, 139, 156, 293
recurvifolia (Y. recurva), 121, 139, 256, 293

Zantedeschia aethiopica 'Crowborough', 101
Zea mays (maize; Indian corn), 155, 216
mays 'Variegatum', 289, 2
zinnias, 181, 183, 209, 221